Praise for *When Mayor Doug Wilder Ruled Richmond*

"I've always appreciated Doug Wilder's prioritization of 'necessities before niceties.' The stories in this fascinating book give greater understanding of the undaunted, spirited leadership of Mayor Wilder who skillfully instilled accountability and integrity to entrenched, stolid bureaucratic governmental agencies that were failing to effectively and efficiently serve the people."

— George F. Allen,
former governor of Virginia

"Provides a candid and informative look at the history-making, distinguished former governor who became mayor of his home city, Richmond, Virginia, a place he loved. He was unafraid to make tough decisions designed to lead to a more responsive and effective city government. This book captures Governor Wilder's laser focus on accountability and results. You knew where he stood and where the buck stopped."

— Robert F. McDonnell,
former governor of Virginia

"Linwood Norman's detailed new book provides a clear recounting of the discipline, clarity, and reform that Governor Wilder brought to Richmond following his term as governor. His achievements as mayor were yet another legacy to be remembered. This book recounts this legacy with candor and detail and is not to be missed."

— Eva Teig Hardy,
former Virginia secretary of health and human resources

"A must-read for those who consider themselves students of politics, generally, but Southern and urban politics, specifically. There are few books about African American mayors written by political insiders that are at once scholarly, entertaining, and accessible to the general public. *When Mayor Doug Wilder Ruled Richmond* is an attention grabber chock full of nuggets to which only an insider would have access. Linwood Norman paints a portrait of a complex man whose personality is an acquired taste, yet whose commitment to the city in which he was raised was on full display every single day he served as mayor of Richmond. Wilder entered the mayor's office as arguably the most accomplished African American politician in U.S. history. With this book, Norman situates Wilder as one of the 21st century's most important political figures."

— Judson L. Jeffries, PhD,
professor of African American and African studies
at Ohio State University and author of *Virginia's Native Son:
The Election and Administration of Governor L. Douglas Wilder*

"*When Mayor Doug Wilder Ruled Richmond* is a must-read for both students and practitioners of public administration. It highlights the gnarly effects of city charter reviews and changes that invariably lead to unintended consequences, particularly with respect to the distribution of executive authority. In this case, just enough fragments of executive authority remained with the city council. This led to confusion with respect to executive v. legislative authority, which made cooperation between the two branches of city government extremely difficult."

— Harry Black,
city manager, Stockton, California
(former deputy chief administrative officer, City of Richmond, Virginia)

"Former Governor Doug Wilder was one of the most consequential Virginians of the past half-century. While we know a good deal about his landmark term as governor, there has been relatively little attention paid to his equally significant time as mayor of Richmond. Linwood Norman, Wilder's former press secretary at City Hall, fills that gap

with this compelling, fast-paced and well-written study of those roller-coaster years."
— Stephen J. Farnsworth, PhD,
professor of political science and international affairs
and director of the Center for Leadership and
Media Studies at the University of Mary Washington

"Mr. Norman delivers an unapologetically realistic description of former Governor L. Douglas Wilder's career from his humble childhood to becoming Richmond's first dynamic and controversial strong mayor. Norman takes you behind the scenes, giving you a glimpse of the man who defied conventional politics and blazed his own path to establish himself as arguably the most influential politician in the Commonwealth. This is great history!"
— Chris Beschler,
director of energy resources, Rocky Mount, North Carolina
(former deputy chief administrative officer, City of Richmond, Virginia)

"Linwood Norman's engaging new book clearly depicts Doug Wilder's elements of leadership that were necessary to guide a 'new' Richmond. With vivid detail and behind-the-scenes context, *When Mayor Doug Wilder Ruled Richmond* shows how Wilder understood the politics of city government and could identify the real issues and solutions, even when his candor and practical approach many times flew in the face of the control biases held by council and the 'establishment.' Norman paints a highly entertaining portrait of a man who never quit in supporting the need for 'strong mayor' governance in Richmond."
— John C. Watkins,
former Virginia state senator

"A fascinating account of one of America's most remarkable political figures. Linwood Norman reminds us in these pages that while all politics may be local, certain politicians make an impact far beyond their constituencies—and Doug Wilder was certainly one of them."
— Jonathan Eig,
author of *King: A Life*

"It is entirely fitting that former Governor Wilder's actions as Richmond's first strong mayor are now memorialized. Linwood Norman's book offers numerous firsthand accounts of Wilder, serving as a reminder of how much he accomplished to move Richmond forward."
— Thomasina "Tommie" Binga,
Richmond, Virginia, public school system

"*When Mayor Doug Wilder Ruled Richmond* is a must-read study regarding the realities of local government management. It deftly describes the policy aspects and drama of resolving a difficult issue like the city's proposed performing arts project. Although many disagreed with his methods, Mayor Wilder dealt directly with this challenging issue. A time of action, not political messaging."
— John Gerner,
City of Richmond's liaison consultant for
Mayor L. Douglas Wilder's Performing Arts Committee

"Douglas Wilder is one of the most important—and fascinating—political figures Virginia has seen. This book, which focuses on his post-gubernatorial career as mayor of Richmond, is a worthy addition to the reportage on Wilder and covers ground that other authors have not."
— Dwayne Yancey,
author of *When Hell Froze Over, The Untold Story of Doug Wilder:*
A Black Politician's Rise to Power in the South

WHEN MAYOR DOUG WILDER RULED RICHMOND

STRONG-ARM POLITICS IN VIRGINIA'S CAPITAL CITY

LINWOOD NORMAN

FOREWORD BY JON BALILES

Brandylane Publishers, Inc.
Publishing books since 1985

Cover photo taken at the mayor's inauguration, January 2, 2005. Photo courtesy of *Richmond Times-Dispatch*

Copyright © 2024 by Linwood Norman

All rights reserved. No part of this book may be reproduced in any form or by any electronic or mechanical means, or the facilitation thereof, including information storage and retrieval systems, without permission in writing from the publisher, except in the case of brief quotations published in articles and reviews. Any educational institution wishing to photocopy part or all of the work for classroom use, or individual researchers who would like to obtain permission to reprint the work for educational purposes, should contact the publisher.

ISBN: 978-1-962416-21-4
Library of Congress Control Number: 2023918504

Designed by Sami Langston
Production management by Jenny DeBell and Ceci Hughes

Printed in the United States of America

Published by
Brandylane Publishers, Inc.
5 S. 1st Street
Richmond, Virginia 23219

brandylanepublishers.com

For my parents, Mae and Paul Norman, who made it all possible.

Contents

Foreword 1

Prologue 5

1. A National Figure Takes on Local Politics 13
Mastery Over City Council
Wilder's Public Relations Machine
The Day Bill Cosby Called
Behind the Scenes with the Mayor

2. Just Getting Started 26
Staking His Territory
Richmond's New Form of Government
Assembling the Team
Battles Over the Budget

3. In the Thick of It 48
Building New Schools
Watching the Money
Getting Sued
The Police Chief
Facing Protests from Teachers to Pimps & Hustlers
Goldman's Departure

4. Water, Water, Everywhere: Floods and Cesspools and Sinkholes 75
Historic Shockoe Bottom
Northside's Battery Park
Time for a Stormwater Utility

5. Performing Arts: What Price Will We Pay for Culture? 85
Carpenter Center in Moth Balls
"American Idol" Elliott Yamin Sings
"B.B. King Day"
Close Call: Mayor Almost Knocked Out

6. Jump-starting New Business and Owning a Home 97
Downtown's New Hilton Hotel & Federal Courthouse
Fortune 500s Coming Downtown
Cleaning Up Broad Street
The Need for Affordable Housing

7. Demise of the Maymont Bears 106
A City in Mourning and Anger
The Thalhimer's Gift
The Mayor's Investigation
Maymont's New Star Attractions

Photos 119

8. The Mayor Touched the Queen 131
Preparing for the Royal Arrival
The Mayor's Touch
Oliver Hill's Key to the City

9. Game Over for the Richmond Braves 138
Renovation Plans Upstaged
Mayor "Smokes Them Out"
Building a New Ballpark
The Braves Decide to Leave

10. Mayor Fights for a Public Marina 149
"The View That Named Richmond"
Richmond's 400th Birthday
Building Public Support
Influence of the Downtown Master Plan

11. On the Campaign Trail 159
Political Endorsements
Campaigning for Obama
Hillary's "Hissy Fits"
The Second Black Governor
Election Night

12. Mayor Boots School Board Out of City Hall (for about six hours) ... 174
The Move Begins
The Computer Porn Investigation
A Little Backstory
School Board Deadline Kept Slipping
The Mayor's Sinking Popularity

13. Arrivals and Departures 195
"Love Affair at City Hall"
School System Involved in Plans to Move
City Council Investigates
Employee Car Allowances
Three Surprise Resignations

14. Seeking Clarity Over Who Can Do What 209
Mayor Pushes to Revise City Charter
Council Is in No Rush
No More Olive Branches
Public Assessment of Wilder
Appeals to Virginia Supreme Court Dropped

Epilogue 220
Endnotes 222
Selected Bibliography.. 241
Acknowledgements 242
About the Author.. 243

Foreword

Back in the time not too distant, in the twilight of an era when news was consumed in print and over the air (and not on a tiny handheld screen), there were few press assignments more unscripted or unpredictable than covering L. Douglas Wilder when he served as mayor of Richmond between 2005-2008.

And there was only one person who stood between the marauding gaggle of media and the Mayor's Office, whose job was to either try and clarify what had been said or done, or to try to spin or un-spin the tangled yarn. I had known Linwood Norman years earlier from our days on the board of our local neighborhood association, and when he was appointed as Wilder's press secretary after several others had tried unsuccessfully, I knew the Mayor had found himself an unflappable spokesman who would not break under the pressure from either direction.

Little did I know that just a few years later I would join the staff in the Mayor's Office at Wilder's invitation and would work with both men on a daily basis. My relationship with Linwood was a good one that involved a lot of humor, debates about wordplay and sentence structure, and the occasional shouting and cursing match over content. But all good working relationships include a slice of all of those characteristics.

To provide the details and citations for this book makes Linwood Norman the quintessential historian—and a work of this kind is instructive now more than ever, even fifteen years after Wilder left the Mayor's Office. Doug Wilder always left a cloud of dust in his wake— wherever he stood. It began with his upbringing in Church Hill in the east end of Richmond, on to the hills of Korea fighting as an infantryman and earning the Bronze Star in the process, and into his days at

Howard Law School, and his election to the Virginia State Senate as the first Black state senator to be elected since Reconstruction.

Wilder then ran and won election as Lieutenant Governor in 1985 (when my father led the ticket and was elected Governor that same night), and then four years later, in 1989, he became the first elected Black Governor in the United States. He came out of "retirement" to be elected the Mayor of Richmond, Virginia, the former Capital of the Confederacy, in 2004, with a whopping 79 percent of the citywide vote in a four-person race.

So why is this book relevant today? And why is it worthwhile to look back at a brief window in time at Richmond's government when the media generally referred to City Hall and Wilder's term as "chaotic" and "disruptive," among other less-friendly adjectives? One thing that is too easily overlooked is that Wilder's "disruption" had the effect of producing the change needed to break City Hall from its cycle of what Wilder famously referred to as a "cesspool of corruption and inefficiency."

Wilder was elected in the fall of 2004, not long after several members of city council had gone to jail for a variety of crimes. But what happened over the next four years, while sometimes unpleasant, also offered clarity. No one walked into City Hall and had to wonder or ask, "Who is in charge of this place?" Protests and demonstrations were not met with press releases, but with the mayor himself walking into them and asking what was wrong and what needed to be done. Harry Truman's adage of where the buck stopped was clear whether they chose to accept it or not.

In Wilder's last year, the proof of the direction of the City was affirmed by Richmond residents themselves. In what was called a Service, Efforts, and Accomplishments (SEA) Report required by city council, the independent auditor asked a large sample of Richmond residents questions about the city in general. The auditor's office found that in the spring of 2008, 81 percent of the people said that the city was moving in the right direction, and 74 percent approved of the way the Richmond Police Department operated (by drastically reducing crime during the Wilder administration). Approval numbers like that were similar or higher for departments across the city.

In the years that have elapsed since Wilder's term, the back-to-back terms of two subsequent but inconsequential mayors have seen a decline in the confidence in the government's ability to get anything done, and a rise in graft and a predilection for insider deals that benefit only the connected few at the cost of a larger population who gain nothing. The most recent SEA report in 2022 found that only 46 percent of residents believed Richmond was moving in the right direction. Linwood's book is a timely reminder that sometimes chaos is needed to produce real change.

Machiavelli wrote in *The Prince*, "There is nothing more difficult to take in hand, more perilous to conduct, or more uncertain in its success, than to take the lead in the introduction of a new order of things." Changing Richmond after decades of inefficient government was indeed difficult but the people had begun to see the changes and they liked what they saw.

Linwood Norman's look back at Wilder's tenure is a reminder of what is possible and what we as a city started to accomplish by turning around a city with so much promise and potential. Richmond has long succeeded as a city *despite* our government, not because of it. Wilder proved that change is possible if we choose to accept it and embrace it and make the hard choices to enact it.

—Jon Baliles

After leaving the City of Richmond's Office of the Press Secretary, Jon Baliles worked as the Assistant to the Director of the Planning Department under Mayor Dwight C. Jones (2009-2012), served on city council from 2013-2016, and later served as a senior policy advisor for Mayor Levar Stoney (2017-2018). Jon Baliles is the founder and editor of the *RVA 5x5* newsletter.

Prologue

HUMBLE BEGINNINGS

The man who would become Virginia's first Black governor, indeed the first elected Black governor in the United States, grew up during America's Great Depression in the strictly segregated Church Hill neighborhood in Richmond, Virginia. Born in 1931, the seventh of eight children, L. Douglas Wilder has described growing up in a supportive home environment where the children were motivated to learn and excel. His father, who never left the house without a tie and Homburg hat, sold insurance.[1] His mother ran the household and did maid work.[2]

Wilder's parents, Robert Judson Wilder and Beulah Olive Richards, were married in 1913, and "Douglas," as he was always known within the family, had one brother and six sisters.[3]

"We were a large family and poor as Job's turkey, but it was gentle poverty," he told a *Washington Post* reporter years later. "By that I mean we had music. The vases would have flowers from the yard."[4] All of the Wilder children took music lessons; Douglas studied piano. He also "made a name for himself" as a youngster singing in church socials, and later in bars as a young man.[5]

Forced by a stern father to wear knickers until he turned fourteen—reflective of an earlier era—the young Douglas Wilder was always asking questions and couldn't keep still. A nurturing mother, to whom Douglas was deeply devoted, instilled a strong sense of intellectual curiosity and self-worth in her children. If a child today, Wilder readily admits his parents would have given him Ritalin to calm down.[6]

Wilder polished his oratory skills as a kid while shining shoes near his home at Dick Reid's Church Hill Barber Shop. Black barbershops provided a forum for open discussion of the topics of the day and Wilder prospered from the experience of debating with his elders.

"I commanded center stage in the barbershop and did everything I could to impress any and all with my learning," he wrote in his 2015 memoir, *Son of Virginia*. "I enjoyed sharing what I'd learned, and they got a kick out of it. I'd bring in my encyclopedia, and they'd test my knowledge, getting a little betting pool going. It was fun for them, and it was good for me to hone my skills that way." [7]

Wilder described himself as "precocious" at an early age and a "ball of fire" at the segregated school he attended as a child.[8] A classmate remembered him from those days. "He was always gifted with the ability to speak. He had a golden tongue . . ." said Dr. Jean Harris Ellis in a 1982 interview about her old friend, referring to when both were students at George Mason Elementary School, decades before. "He was the one who was always being chastised for talking out of turn in class, or if there was any mischief under way, he always seemed to be a part of it."[9]

Wilder later sailed through his high school education and attended Virginia Union University, where he obtained an undergraduate degree in chemistry. In a segregated society, however, he could not get a job based on his qualifications.[10] He was soon drafted into the Army during the Korean War, earning a Bronze Star for his role in capturing a platoon of Chinese soldiers on Pork Chop Hill while rescuing wounded troops. He was later promoted to the rank of sergeant. The Army had been integrated by President Truman, which Wilder said was his first experience of interacting in a meaningful way with white people. [11]

Out of the Army and inspired by the landmark 1954 Brown vs. Board of Education Supreme Court decision, which outlawed segregation in public schools, Wilder made use of the G.I. Bill to pursue a law degree from Howard University in Washington, DC. Virginia law schools remained segregated and were off-limits to Blacks at that time, so he had to go outside the state to get the degree.[12]

Wilder returned to Richmond to launch his law practice in Church Hill in 1959 and quickly established himself as an up-and-coming criminal lawyer. He gained a reputation for flamboyance: driving convertibles and wearing stylish clothes, while also building a reputation for his competence in handling difficult criminal defense cases.[13] Along the way, he married Eunice Montgomery and became the father of three children—Lynn, Larry, and Loren—each with initials that matched his own: LDW.

JUMP INTO POLITICS

It was Wilder's successful law practice that led him into politics, and to date, several books have been written about Douglas Wilder's historic rise in Virginia politics. He announced his first Democratic Party bid for a vacant state senate seat in 1969. When he won a three-way race (with less than fifty percent of the vote), he became the first Black elected to the Virginia State Senate since Reconstruction. During the next sixteen years, he ran unopposed for re-election.[14]

Wilder has spoken freely about his enslaved grandparents, who married in 1856 and were later sold separately. The wife and two young daughters were removed to Ashland, Virginia. Every Sunday, his grandfather was allowed a "pass" to walk the twenty-mile distance from Richmond to see them. The family later reunited at the close of the Civil War and settled in Richmond. Wilder's father, born in 1886, was the second youngest of the couple's thirteen children. [15]

As a state senator from 1970 to 1986, Wilder fought for racial equity and did not hesitate to scorn vestiges of prejudice. In his first speech from the floor of the state senate, he condemned the state's anthem, "Carry Me Back to Old Virginny," which glorified slavery and plantation life as a virtue, even in the afterlife. He lobbied for years to repeal the state song.[16] The Virginia General Assembly finally retired the state song in the late 1990s, several years after Wilder's term as governor had ended.

Wilder also sponsored legislation to establish a state holiday honoring Dr. Martin Luther King, Jr., whom he had met. "I was the only person of color in the Virginia State Senate when I was elected in 1969. I introduced a bill to have a holiday for Dr. Martin Luther King. It took me eight years to get it done," he explained decades later. "I'd get it passed in the Senate and the House would kill it. I'd get it passed in both the Senate and the House and the governor would veto it. I went through that whole process twice and two governors vetoed it. But eventually, I was able to get Virginia to become the first state that had a legislative holiday for Dr. King, even before the federal government."[17]

As a state senator, Wilder held sufficient political sway to disrupt the United States Senate race in 1982. He threatened to run as an independent if State Delegate Owen Pickett of Virginia Beach became the Democratic nominee to replace the retiring Senator Harry F. Byrd, Jr. Wilder was angered when Pickett announced his candidacy and praised the Byrd Organization, the "political machine" led by Byrd's father, who championed racial segregation. Knowing that an independent candidate would mean a three-way race and likely diminish Democratic Party support, Pickett dropped out. And Wilder, now satisfied, didn't run.[18]

When Wilder was elected Virginia's first Black lieutenant governor in 1985, he became the highest-ranking Black state official in the South. When he successfully ran for governor in 1989, winning by less than one-half of one percent—a mere 6,741 votes—Wilder became the first Black to be elected governor in the nation. That distinction, among others, fueled his trajectory into history as Virginia's 66th governor; he served from 1990 to 1994.[19]

Wilder was recognized for sound financial management. *Financial World* magazine named Virginia the best-managed state in the nation for two consecutive years during his term.[20] Though Wilder had inherited a budget deficit of more than $2 billion, Virginia became one of only two states that managed to balance their budget without raising taxes. Wilder also established a $200 million "rainy day" contingency reserve fund to address a worsening economy.[21] Wilder's fiscal policies were so admired and appreciated by Virginia's next governor, George Allen, that he retained Wilder's secretary of finance, Paul W. Timmreck, and many of his finance personnel to serve in his own administration.

During his second year as governor, Wilder announced his run for the presidency on the Democratic ticket but pulled out after only a few months. (To this day, Wilder presidential memorabilia pops up for sale on eBay.) Leaving office in 1994, he ran briefly as an independent candidate for the United States Senate but later withdrew from the race and supported incumbent Charles Robb.

Retired from politics, Wilder stayed busy dabbling in activities that provided ready-made platforms to express his views. For several years, he hosted a morning radio show on WRVA-AM (theme song: The Troggs version of "Wild Thing")[22] and wrote guest columns for the *Richmond Times-Dispatch*. He was also a sought-after paid speaker.

In 1998, Wilder accepted and later declined an offer to be president of Virginia Union University, his alma mater.[23] He was briefly considered for a federal judicial appointment to the 4th U.S. Circuit Court of Appeals but had no interest in the position.[24] Wilder's great, long-held dream was to establish the United States National Slavery Museum. He tried time and again to establish both the funds and location, but eventually, donations could not keep up with expenses and the grand project fell into bankruptcy.[25]

Douglas Wilder is nonetheless widely recognized for his achievements, with an array of public buildings bearing his name: the L. Douglas Wilder School of Government and Public Affairs at Virginia Commonwealth University, where he taught part-time when he was elected mayor; the L. Douglas Wilder Library at Virginia Union University; the L. Douglas Wilder Middle School, in suburban Richmond; the L. Douglas Wilder Performing Arts Center, at Norfolk State University; the L. Douglas Wilder Dormitory, at Hampton University; and the L. Douglas Wilder Cooperative Extension Building at Virginia State University, where as governor he made headlines by firing the school's entire board of visitors in one fell swoop.

A bounty of photographs and honors awarded to him over the years fills a large trophy room at Virginia Union University. Wilder holds more than three dozen honorary degrees, as well as the NAACP Spingarn Medal, the Anna Eleanor Roosevelt Medallion of Honor, the SCLC Drum Major for Justice Award, the B'nai B'rith's Great American Traditions Award, the Thurgood Marshall Award of Excellence, and the International Civil Rights Walk of Fame. Framed photographs show him with iconic world figures that include Nelson Mandela, Mikhail Gorbachev, Desmond Tutu, and several United States presidents.

CHANGING CITY GOVERNMENT

Wilder had long wanted to change Richmond's form of government to make the mayor's job a full-time position, to be elected directly by the people. That proposal, largely opposed by Black elected leaders, was killed in the General Assembly. Wilder often complained that there wasn't enough accountability in Richmond's government.

"The buck never stopped," he explained. Before the change to an at-large mayor, the local government was run by a city manager who served at the discretion of nine "bosses"—the nine members of Richmond City Council. Each was essentially the "mini mayor" within his or her council district. The mayor was chosen by a majority of votes among council colleagues. It was a part-time, largely ceremonial position that carried very little management authority.

By the early 2000s, Richmond suffered from a malaise: downtown decay; the loss of 3,500 jobs over three years; one of the highest murder rates in the country; an astonishing twenty-five percent poverty rate; high rates of illiteracy, sexually transmitted disease and teenage pregnancy, and haphazard city services.[26] The situation was bleak.

"You name the category—public health, education, employment, the economy—we were hurting, and the leadership had not addressed it," observed Councilman E. Martin Jewell. "No one was accountable. The mayor was saying, 'Well, under the statute I preside over meetings and cut ribbons'; the [city] manager was not required to respond to any citizen or citizen issue; and the council was in a situation where you couldn't get three council members to agree on what was for lunch, let alone set benchmarks and hold the manager to those benchmarks."[27]

Wilder's push for an elected mayor gained steam when a careful reading of Richmond's city charter—which outlines the guiding laws, rules, and responsibilities of local government—found that any proposal could be put to a citywide referendum if enough people signed a petition in support of it. A popular local newspaper, *Style Weekly*, called the obscure charter provision "a never-used loophole . . . to everyone's surprise."[28]

This loophole provided the opportunity of making an end-run around earlier opposition, so in 2002, Wilder teamed up with former Virginia Congressman Thomas J. Bliley, himself a former Richmond mayor, to lead a commission on having a full-time mayor who would be elected "at large." The next year, a citywide referendum overwhelmingly supported those changes to the city charter by a landslide eighty percent of voters.

Six months before the 2004 election, Wilder made a surprise announcement that he would run for mayor. On the campaign trail, he pledged to end the "cesspool of corruption and inefficiency" at City Hall. Recent history offered him plenty to criticize. One former mayor had pled guilty to fraud, obstruction of justice, and tax evasion. A council member was convicted of bribery and lying to federal officials, while another was convicted of tax evasion. Between 1999 and 2004, three council members were sent to prison. High-ranking city employees were convicted for influence peddling and high-dollar billing scams.[29]

Wilder claimed he didn't want the mayor's job but had relented to those who encouraged him to throw his hat in the ring. Wilder's populist-themed campaign drew broad support. The *Richmond Times-Dispatch* endorsed his candidacy. He raised a war chest of more than $440,000, dwarfing the meager financial support for his three opponents. [30]

Elected as Richmond's mayor ten years after leaving the governor's office, Wilder received nearly eighty percent of the vote—winning handsomely in all nine council districts—and he quickly began to turn Richmond's political machinery upside down.

Style Weekly summed up Wilder's persona this way:

"When Wilder speaks—be it at press conferences, in speeches, or in interviews—he shifts easily from backslapping, long-lost buddy to fire and brimstone. And just when it appears Wilder's ready to tear you apart verbally, he flips on the charm. One minute his voice rises to an angry staccato, his face tightens and bears down upon you, and then he's laughing again. The effect is dizzying."[31]

This, then, is the story of when Mayor Doug Wilder ruled Richmond: Strong-arm politics in Virginia's capital city.

Chapter One

A National Figure Takes on Local Politics

It's only a three-minute walk from the governor's office at the Virginia State Capitol to Richmond City Hall, but the stature of the traveler makes all the difference. Compared to previous mayors, former Virginia Governor Doug Wilder brought light years of power and prestige to his new role as mayor of Richmond.

Now he was making history again—as Richmond's first directly elected mayor in decades. His return to the spotlight produced a flurry of national media coverage, from the *New York Times* to *U.S. News & World Report*, to the *Wall Street Journal*, and beyond.

"Wilder is known worldwide as a historic figure—the nation's first and only elected Black governor," proclaimed the *Washington Post* in a celebrity profile of him after a few months in office.[32]

Ushered in as Richmond's "freshman" mayor in 2005, Wilder was certainly no novice to politics. He knew state government from the top down. His collective twenty-four years in state government—as a state senator, lieutenant governor, and governor—gave him an innate understanding of how to get things done. He knew the rules and could draw on an extensive list of former colleagues whenever necessary.

Wilder was the first directly elected Richmond mayor in nearly sixty years. By reputation alone, he brought immediate celebrity to the job. A list of notable achievements in state government preceded his arrival as mayor.

"We are fortunate to have someone of that stature and knowledge coming into that position initially," Councilman G. Manoli Loupassi told the *Richmond Times-Dispatch* a few weeks after Wilder's election.[33]

Wilder was almost seventy-four when he became mayor, remarkably healthy and spry, carrying himself as a much younger man. He maintained a trim frame from regular calisthenics, did not wear glasses or hearing aids, nor have any need for a cane. He was a stylish dresser, particularly known for his trademark cowboy boots. Occasionally he sported a goatee.

Wilder's swanky inauguration at the Greater Richmond Convention Center drew more than 2,000 guests and featured an exuberant gospel choir that imbued a sense of righteous glee as well-wishers surrounded Wilder for a handshake, hug, or autograph. The new mayor, sporting a tailored tuxedo and Lucchese boots, greeted well-wishers alongside his longtime friend, comedian Bill Cosby, dressed, unwittingly, like a dour Mister Rogers. Cosby was still considered "America's Favorite Dad" at the time.

At one point during the celebration, Wilder spotted local community activist Alicia Rasin, who was gamely dancing in place, her hair braids bobbing and her long Ming dynasty fingernails gently slicing the air. Wilder, seeing the local television cameras nearby, returned the gesture with a slow, arm-swaying twist.

Cosby, the evening's keynote speaker, borrowed from Wilder's campaign pledge to clean up the corruption and inefficiency at City Hall by making references to Satan, and joking that city employees were "devilish people."

"Don't be surprised when he fires the whole city," Cosby claimed about the new mayor.[34]

Wilder's inaugural speech, while prophetic, drew from his populist roots to emphasize the importance of the work ahead. "I am here today as the instrument chosen by the people of Richmond for a single overriding purpose: to give them a government that serves the people, not itself," Wilder announced. His primary tasks were to reduce crime, streamline city government, and bring accountability to the public school system.

"There are some few who do not see the need for immediate action. I am reminded of the words of William Lloyd Garrison, the famed abolitionist, who was urged to be more moderate in his approach," the new mayor cautioned. "'Tell a man whose house is on fire to give a moderate alarm. Tell him to moderately rescue his wife from the arms of a ravisher. Tell a woman to gradually extricate her babe from the fiery furnace into which it had fallen.'

"I use this metaphor to illustrate that action should be predicated upon need. The need for us to act is now. And when a thing is right, the time is always right. Our time is now.

"All this will not be easy. It won't be accomplished in ninety days, or maybe even four years. But we must begin. I did not leave the ease of retirement from public service to succumb to the fatigue of failure. I come to urge action, not studies; work, not dreaming; results, not promises."[35]

The next night, the Richmond community celebrated Wilder's election with a black-tie "Mayor's Ball" at a downtown hotel. The sold-out event drew 1,500 supporters who paid $125 a ticket to welcome their new mayor.

During the four years Wilder served as mayor, he kept his pledge to the people. He would take action—surprising many with his boldness.

MASTERY OVER CITY COUNCIL

Immediately recognizable, Wilder took command of City Hall with the smiling, at-ease confidence of someone who knew his way around. He was frequently stopped with hellos and handshakes as he walked to his office in the cavernous government building. People were then—and still are—drawn to him. Even many of his adversaries seemed to secretly admire him. Though they might disagree on certain issues, they still wanted to engage him.

Wilder's ability to scout out who was in a crowd—and how to evade those he didn't care for—became comically apparent at an evening reception that included several council members. As the mayor's press secretary, I had already spoken with this particular councilman, Bruce W. Tyler, who said he wanted to discuss something with the mayor that night.

The mayor, however, had already spotted the councilman and deftly worked the room, staying a good fifteen feet ahead of him. The mayor and the councilman were both moving in a counterclockwise manner, chatting hellos with clusters of people along the way. The two never did speak that evening.

As Richmond's new "strong" mayor, Wilder assumed many of the responsibilities and duties that under the old form of Richmond government had belonged to the city manager. Yet there was one big difference: as mayor, Wilder was his own boss. He didn't have to answer to the council members the way the city manager had in previous administrations. He answered only to the voters.

Still, the new mayor had to work with city council to get things done. The newly-revised city charter called for the mayor to select a chief administrative officer (CAO) who would manage city department operations—at the direction of the mayor. And the mayor's selection of the CAO had to be approved by council.

Wilder acknowledged that being mayor was far more demanding than serving as governor. "This is a tougher job, without any question," he told the *Richmond Times-Dispatch*. "And it's an everyday job, and it's an all-day job.[36]

"When a new governor comes in, the bureaucracy is already in place, so it's a matter of just putting the people in place . . . that fit the mold of the new administration," he told *Virginia Business* magazine. "This [job] is totally different. We're moving into recharting the course of government in Richmond as to how it operates and for whom it operates."[37]

As routine for any mayor, Wilder developed policy, oversaw City operations, made hiring decisions, met with community big guns, issued announcements on topics large and small, greeted foreign dignitaries, and smiled with babies. But for Wilder, there was something more. A grand master of public relations, Richmond's new mayor spun a web of attraction with the media that far exceeded the ordinary.

Constantly accepting interviews with local and national media, Wilder generated far more news coverage ("more ink," as they say in the newspaper business) than your average city mayor. He relished hosting press conferences, which some critics described as the mayor's favorite way to ambush city council, by announcing its shortcomings on this issue or that. Wilder's battles with council were chronicled by more than two dozen editorial cartoons by *Richmond Times-Dispatch*'s Gary Brookins. One showed a wrecking ball about to strike City Hall. Another depicted Wilder as a tornado sweeping past city council. Many of those cartoons were mounted on the wall outside the mayor's office.

Aside from Wilder's battles with city council and school officials, he participated in diverse occasions ranging from the mundane to the sublime. Welcoming Queen Elizabeth and Prince Philip to Richmond as part of celebrating the 400th birthday of Jamestown was notable. Hosting a Downtown celebration and presenting the key to the city to American Idol singing contestant, Elliott Yamin, who gave an outdoor performance, was also a high point. Delivering the eulogy for two black bears laid to rest at Richmond's Maymont Park and taking the time to give welcoming remarks to a "Sister City" delegation that arrived from Saitama, Japan were other examples of his diverse role as mayor.

The mayor was also drawn into dark, unexpected staging. He stood beside the police chief who announced the Harvey family murders on an unseasonably mild New Year's Day. He attended vigils for other crime victims, such as when seventy-year-old Susanne L. Thompson was stabbed to death as she walked her dog one morning on West Broad Street.

As promised at his inauguration, Wilder came prepared to shake things up. The mayor's office is located on the second floor of Richmond City Hall, just across from the city council chambers. It's a corner office with a spread of windows on two sides, the vertical blinds always drawn shut, presumably for security reasons.

Wilder governed from an executive-sized desk that faced a round table with four chairs and a television. Photos and plaques covered the wood-paneled walls. A bookshelf held even more photos, and gifts that ranged from baseball hats to coffee cups. A rear door led to a private bathroom.

This was ground zero of Richmond politics. And into this office came a panoply of politicians and wannabees, business executives, national celebrities, media types, old friends and supporters, council members, and elementary school students.

Understandably, many people wanted the mayor's ear. The gatekeeper granting access through the door marked "Office of The Mayor" was Ruth Jones, Wilder's trusted secretary for more than thirty years. She managed much of his day, scheduling appointments, fielding phone calls, arranging travel plans, picking up medicines, preparing checks from his business ledger, and through it all, holding an arsenal of Wilder's strictly personal secrets collected over the years.

For his full daily schedule, Wilder's natural stamina came in handy. He tackled it all with a level of energy unexpected for a man well past retirement age. Still, in between appointments, he sometimes could be found taking an impromptu power nap on the tufted leather sofa in his office. Ruth held his calls and rescheduled visitors so the mayor could recharge.

Wilder was chauffeured by a security detail consisting of two plainclothes police officers, who would pick him up in the morning, take him where he needed to go during the day and drop him off at home at night, providing physical protection along the way. This was the same set-up he had as governor, and it worked well.

Some things were different from those days as governor, however, such as the manner in which he timed his arrival to speak at city council meetings. He used the trappings of his office to determine precisely when he would appear. Discussions could drag on for hours. He was not required to attend or even sit through the entire meeting. "I couldn't imagine having to put up with all that drivel," he once joked.

With his office just across the hall, it was only a short distance to the council chambers. The question focused on "when." And as with so many things in life, timing is everything. That's where the television came into tactical use. He knew exactly when to take the walk into the council chambers.

Richmond aired its live council meetings on the city's public access cable channel. Watching the meeting in action, he knew the council's every step. When the time was right, Wilder—followed by an entourage typically consisting of his CAO, chief of staff, finance director, and me, his press secretary—would unassumingly stride down the aisle. He always took the end seat in the front row.

Sometimes those speaking would pause at the sight of us. Scoping out the audience, the mayor would occasionally wink or nod to familiar faces while waiting to be given the floor to speak. Every hair in place, he occasionally exhaled with his cheeks blown out like Louis Armstrong on the trumpet.[38] Of course, Wilder only showed up when he had something to say. Often, it was about the operation of the city's school system—and not often with a pleasant message to deliver. Yet when he did speak, everyone snapped to attention.

Richmond Magazine summed it up this way: "When most people walk into a City Council meeting, reporters glance at them and look away. When Doug Wilder makes one of his periodic strolls through Council chambers, the place murmurs to life: Doug's here! Previously slumping reporters get up from their seats and follow him, pen in hand. When Wilder's around, Council is forgotten."[39]

The press' reaction to seeing Wilder was not lost on the council members, either. It was not unusual for the council president to stop in the middle of discussion to acknowledge the arrival and welcome him.

Soon enough he would yield the floor to the mayor, who would take full advantage of the televised occasion.

"Do you have anything you'd like to engage us with? It's always good to see you, Mr. Mayor," began Council President Manoli Loupassi with a cordial welcome during Wilder's early days. At center stage now, Wilder began to question the operation of the city schools and how they compared with other school systems across the state. He focused at length on whether an actual financial audit existed regarding school system spending.

"Let me ask you," Wilder motioned. "Will one of you furnish me one copy of the audit review of the School Board spending? If you have it, will you let me have it? Which ones of you have it?" A cat-and-mouse exchange of collegial, protracted debate ensued between the mayor and several council members. Everyone knew that no audit existed, but that didn't stop the back-and-forth banter. For a council meeting, the exchange offered comic relief.

Finally, Wilder signaled he was done for the evening. As he began to depart up the aisle, he was repeatedly called back by one council member or another. "You gonna leave before we have a chance to talk?"[40] Councilman William J. Pantele asked at one point. With each exchange, Wilder would come forward to answer another question and then take a few steps back, at one point cupping his ear as if he was now too far away to hear what was being said. He stepped forward again, then backward again, until finally it was time to go. We staff members followed behind like baby ducks. An otherwise glum council meeting was infused with a sense of grand theatre, compliments of the playful antics of the mayor, who savored every moment of it.

"He's a rock star," Council President Loupassi later commented, freely admitting that city council was overmatched by the mayor. "He's a master. I learn something from him every day. He's someone who just automatically gets a lot of attention, and he's somebody who really likes getting that attention—and it shows."[41]

Following each council appearance, all of us would retreat to the mayor's office to debrief and reflect. We chuckled at what had been said and by whom. Then we bade our goodbyes and called it a night.

WILDER'S PUBLIC RELATIONS MACHINE

No mayor of Richmond utilized an arsenal of public relations tactics to match Wilder's. His oratory skill, charm factor, and national prominence helped make the difference. Many mayors find contentment with Rotary Club speeches, appearances before city council, the occasional press conference followed by a press release, and the city's annual report describing municipality progress.

Wilder had all of that, plus much more. He was regularly courted by the national media. He made numerous appearances before business and community groups. His press conferences were frequent and well-attended. His announcements were broadly carried by the local papers and television stations. The mayor's popularity transcended land and air. The magazines *Richmond TRAVELHOST* and *River City* carried his "welcome letter" and official photo in each issue. One of the city's larger hotel chains featured the mayor's video welcome to arriving guests. US Airways *Attaché* magazine presented him in a celebrity profile.

Only days after entering office, Wilder took questions during a live, hour-long TV show, "Call 12 Special: Ask the Mayor." It soon blossomed into an "Ask the Mayor" column that appeared weekly on Richmond.com and the city's website. Questions came pouring in on topics as diverse as neighborhood cleanup, utility rates, and court sentences. One mother asked if her son could be paroled from prison. "People think the mayor is omnipotent," I told a *Style Weekly* reporter.

During his second year of office, Wilder launched an online newsletter called *Visions* that was emailed to more than 25,000 subscribers. Available in English and Spanish, it included video segments of the mayor commenting on topics du jour. The local press followed *Visions* religiously. It often included a bombshell announcement, such as when the mayor suggested that council's budget cutbacks might lead to a reduction in city services.

Wilder's deftness in carrying his message to the public was praised by Richmond publisher and journalist, James A. Bacon, in his longtime political blog, *Bacon's Rebellion.*

"I continue to be fascinated by the e-mail missives sent out by Richmond Mayor L. Douglas Wilder as he bypasses the Mainstream Media to take his case to the public. His weekly *'Visions'* newsletter contains data that often gets filtered out in space-constrained news stories, as well as video sound bites that the televisions don't have time to run. The merits of his arguments aside, the newsletter is one of the more sophisticated uses of digital media that I've seen employed in Virginia government. More savvy, even, than the communications coming out of the Governor's office."[42]

Wilder also seized the moment by returning as a guest columnist for the *Richmond Times-Dispatch*, providing a bully pulpit to advance his views on national politics as well as local and state issues.

And beyond the printed word, came the airwaves. As an occasional guest anchor of the WRVA radio morning show, his deep voice rolled smoothly as he spoke about attracting new businesses and jobs to the city. He interviewed city department heads about improving roads and sidewalks. He took a few call-ins, and once off the air, chatted with newspaper reporters who covered his guest spot. On the way down the hallway, we passed the large glass window of another deejay who exclaimed to his listeners, "Look, there's Mayor Wilder who's walking by!" I recall the mayor popped into his studio to say a few words.

Another PR tactic, "A Minute with the Mayor," ran daily on WRIR-FM, an independent community radio station based in Richmond. His sixty-second, taped messages covered topics like community-sector policing, the city's summer youth program, and free smoke detectors. He held a monthly "Radio Town Hall Meeting," airing on Radio One's four affiliated stations with program host Clovia Lawrence, to discuss community concerns called in by listeners. Wilder was a favorite of local PBS commentator Barbara Berlin who would devote her entire program to him in an armchair Q&A format that suited them quite well.

The mayor also had the power of television automatically available to him, compliments of the city's public access cable channel, which replayed the city council meetings. This ensured that his appearances before council and his press conferences, as well as speeches he made elsewhere, would air twice a day for a week or longer. The city's website provided additional outreach to present his views, with video links to his council appearances and press conferences. This integration of media platforms greatly advanced the mayor's agenda.

During his last year in office, Wilder sought to promote transparency in local government by introducing a new website, RichmondsMayor.com. Its goal was to provide "clear communication of the issues of the day as well as serve as an archive where you (and even other elected officials) can access information about developments occurring in our City." The website, as described, "enables citizens to better track ongoing issues and obtain more detailed information on complex topics. It also provides access to papers, letters, documents and spreadsheets so citizens can gain a more in-depth understanding of the issues."[43] With the mayor having little time left in office, however, the website never gained sufficient traction to become well known.

Perhaps not surprisingly, Wilder's PR machine was largely dismantled with the election of Rev. Dwight C. Jones, who followed him as the next mayor.

The Day Bill Cosby Called

It was just another morning in the city's press office. No overnight calamity required an immediate response from the mayor. No controversial meetings to prepare for later in the day. Everyone simply performed their daily work routine. Things remained quiet.

Then the phone rang. Ruth, the mayor's secretary, announced that she was forwarding a call to me.

"Linwood, I have Mr. Cosby on the line for you."

I already knew who "Mr. Cosby" was; a personal friend of the mayor, he led fundraising events to raise money for the mayor's envisioned National Slavery Museum. They spoke frequently. He would visit the mayor's country home overlooking the James River in Charles City County. The mayor cooked the hamburgers. They were tight.

Somewhat startled but trying not to show it, I recall saying something obsequious along the lines of being honored to speak with him, which turned out to be a mistake. I addressed him as "Mr. Cosby" rather than "Bill." "Linwood, stay linear with me," he advised, with the same cadence he would use instructing his children on *The Cosby Show*. He went on to express his concerns about the mayor's lagging popularity following numerous newspaper headlines about his budget battles with city council and the school system. The solution, suggested Mr. Cosby, would be to recruit church pastors who could encourage their parishioners to write "letters to the editor" to the local newspapers to help sway public opinion in the mayor's favor.

I listened intently. I allowed several seconds to elapse before responding to every point that Mr. Cosby made. I wanted to make certain he had finished his thoughts without interrupting him. "That sounds like a promising idea," I replied. "I'll look into that, and we'll see what we can do." He gave me his cell phone number so we could stay in touch.

When I met with the mayor later that morning, he asked me about speaking with Mr. Cosby before I even had a chance to bring it up. Ruth must have let him know about the call. "What was it that he wanted to speak with you about?" the mayor asked, curiously. When I told him about what Mr. Cosby had suggested, the mayor simply scoffed at the idea and said not to bother with that. So, I didn't.

I never followed up with Mr. Cosby and he never called me again. I may have had his cellphone number but did not need it.

Behind the Scenes with the Mayor

During the time I served as the mayor's press secretary and communications director, friends would privately ask what it was like to work for him. It was an easy question to ask, but not always an easy one to answer.

It may be safe to say that some staff members were awestruck or intimidated—or some combination of both. I fell somewhere in that space, yet I recall many instances of how thoughtful the mayor could be and how much fun it was to be around him.

I met with him almost every morning to discuss upcoming issues of the day. One morning in April 2007, I received an emergency call that my father was dying, and I had to rush to the hospital. Unfortunately, I didn't get there in time but spent the next three days orchestrating his funeral and reception. Though the mayor didn't attend, he sent a letter of condolence that was read during the service. Having words of sympathy coming from the mayor added a nice touch to my father's eulogy, and I could tell the preacher enjoyed reading it to everyone.

Dear Linwood,

It is with deep regret and sorrow that I learned of the loss of Linwood Paul Norman Sr. On behalf of the City of Richmond, I extend our deepest sympathy. May it be of some comfort to know that our prayers are with your family.

May you also realize that our loved ones never really leave us. It is said they simply move deeper into our hearts. The kindness and compassion shown by Linwood Sr. will never be forgotten. May there be comfort, as you reflect back, to remember his life, his love, and his wisdom.

May God grant you strength, faith, and courage during your bereavement.

Sincerely,

L. Douglas Wilder

What I found to be equally thoughtful came later when I returned to the office. The mayor asked that I add a note that his *Visions* newsletter had been delayed due to my father's passing. This was shown at the top of the newsletter:

4/19/2007
Dear Citizens,

With the City of Richmond's tremendous potential, today's challenges can become tomorrow's opportunities as we work toward creating a better future for all citizens. Please share this information with your friends or they can register to automatically receive future issues of *Visions* by visiting the City's website at www.RichmondGov.com.

This edition of *Visions* is delayed by the death of the father of *Visions* editor Linwood Norman, to whom we extend our condolences. Our regular schedule returns on April 30.

Mayor L. Douglas Wilder

As the mayor's spokesman, I spent considerable time with him to develop messaging on this issue or that. He was kind-hearted, instructive, patient, jovial, and loyal. We fell into a standard routine, such as going across the street to the Library of Virginia to wait out whenever City Hall had a fire drill. On one occasion we scurried over in the rain, the mayor and I huddled under a severely broken umbrella he was holding. It must have been a comical sight, I thought to myself at the time. During another fire drill, everyone was sitting outside in the sunshine, and the mayor shook hands methodically with three older women as we passed by. One of them beamed up at him with the sweetest smile. I already knew that she was his ex-wife, Eunice, who was the city treasurer.

I remember one day the mayor kicked off a press conference on some long-forgotten topic and within the first minute, the fire alarm blared. The mayor continued his remarks as if nothing had happened. I sat there on the side of the room, feeling somewhat helpless, but everyone carried on undeterred and finally the alarm was shut off.

Another time the mayor and police chief were scheduled to attend an evening vigil for the elderly lady stabbed to death on Broad Street. I suggested he might want to swap his turtleneck for a coat and tie, but the mayor grumbled. I said nothing more about it. That night, I noticed on the late news that he had changed into a suit for the occasion.

I always sat in on Wilder's phone interviews and learned more about him through those conversations. He enjoyed chatty exchanges with PBS' Gwen Ifill and NPR's Juan Williams, who were both writing books on race relations. He spoke with Chicago author Jonathan Eig about his recollections of seeing Jackie Robinson on opening day with the Brooklyn Dodgers. On another occasion, Virginia Historical Society's Charles Bryan interviewed the mayor about his motivation to become an attorney and enter politics.

I joined Wilder to tape the videos for his newsletter. I would pose the question, he would give his response looking at me off camera, and the videographer captured it all. Children often wrote to the mayor, and in return, would receive a letter and photograph. Other times they came to City Hall to meet him. Coincidentally, in a single week three children wanted an interview with him. I casually mentioned that one of those kids lived next door to me. "Well, if he's your neighbor, then I know I will have to let him interview me," he replied.

Wilder had a quick sense of humor, often walking around the office joking with the three secretaries. He also liked to pull a prank. I was coming down the steps at City Hall one day at lunchtime when the police chief and mayor rode by, suddenly pulling over when they saw me. The mayor, with a serious face, asked about a meeting scheduled that afternoon and waited for me to answer. As I stood there looking perplexed, the mayor pointed his finger at me with a burst of laughter and off they went. There was no meeting. The joke was on me, but a harmless one.

As a close associate to the mayor, I remember the many places where one gets to go—and the new faces one gets to see: meeting Barack Obama on three occasions, for example; using the mayor's skybox at the Coliseum for a concert; dinner at the Commonwealth Club with corporate titans; tickets to see Dave Matthews, Margaret Cho, B.B. King, and others who came through town; VIP treatment wherever we went that included front door drop-offs and not having to wait in a line.

Working for Wilder became a fun-filled roller coaster ride. You quickly learned to fasten your seatbelt because you had no time to spare.

CHAPTER TWO

Just Getting Started

Staking His Territory

Wilder's landslide election in 2004 carried a sense of jubilation that better times were coming. The business community seemed almost giddy with excitement for Wilder's star quality and no-nonsense manner. Others, though, harbored a sense of dread in having to face someone so powerfully equipped to get his own way.

Wilder acted like he was already on the job, though his official duties would not begin until January 2005. He informed both the city manager and the police chief to begin looking for a position elsewhere. Within a week of being elected, he announced a blue-ribbon transition committee representing a cross-section of Richmond's citizenry who would recommend key personnel appointments for the new administration. Other committees would address issues including education, efficiency and effectiveness, finance, human services, affordable housing, and regional cooperation.[44] They had their work cut out for them.

Wilder cast warnings and gave orders about what would happen on his watch.

He publicly released the letter he had sent to the city manager and council members to refrain from acting on any non-personnel matters that could be resolved by the new mayor and/or council.

"As relates to personnel decisions, other than critical public safety needs, I would further request that the current city administration and/or the current City Council impose a freeze on new hiring and likewise refrain from taking any action relative to changing the pay, benefits, or similar matters affecting either the current or future compensation of any current or former employee."[45]

He sent a separate letter to the outgoing mayor, Rudolph C. Mc-Collum, about the need to investigate the Richmond Hospital Authority, which he said received a $250,000 annual city contract without a formal bidding process.

Wilder met informally with council to discuss the future of the city. For more than an hour, he led a frank discussion of issues he saw as the incoming mayor. At one point he railed against the city's hospital authority, which he had wanted the city attorney to investigate for alleged financial mismanagement that included making political contributions. "It's amazing that you have a hospital authority, authorized by the city, making [political] contributions," he said. Councilwoman Delores L. McQuinn then interrupted to remind him of the purpose of the meeting. "We wanted to really have an opportunity to have some discussions on the agenda line items," she said before Wilder shot back at her: "If for any reason you feel that you're in a position to tell me what to say here, you're mistaken."

He later told an NBC12 reporter about the meeting, "I was expecting a road that wasn't smooth. But I didn't know that it would have mountain-sized, upside-down holes in it to the extent that if you take one false step, you might never be seen again!"[46]

Wilder had complained for weeks about council's approval of a $174,000 severance package for the outgoing city manager, Calvin D. Jamison. Such packages are considered standard fare, but it angered Wilder. He pledged to call a special council session to consider what he called "an Anti-Cronyism and Corruption Act."[47]

"This is not [council's] money. Not a dime of it. It's the taxpayers' money," he scolded. "I just cannot believe that the City Manager could justifiably say to anyone that he is entitled to something."[48] Wilder took the matter to court to recoup Jamison's payout, but the court rejected it.

He wanted to base severance payments on one's performance instead of the length of service; strengthen rules for out-of-state travel; crack down on lobbying at City Hall; and do away with the free buffet meals routinely provided before council and agency meetings.

Denouncing other examples of City Hall cronyism, Wilder wanted to eliminate the "pay-go" accounts that each council member could spend on discretionary activities in their district, such as children's books for library branches and neighborhood tree plantings.

Only three weeks after being elected, Wilder met with the Richmond School Board to discuss his involvement in selecting the school superintendent and expanding the school board to include at-large members. One proposal would allow the mayor to appoint the superintendent. "The mayor should seek authority to appoint, with the advice and consent of the School Board, the superintendent of schools," Wilder explained.

"If the School Board does not agree, nothing happens. There's no appointment," Wilder reassured the board. But he cautioned that as mayor he intended to do more than simply "to whisper in your ears."

"I don't want to be in a confrontational stance," Wilder told school officials. At the same time, he said he agreed with proposals to alter the superintendent selection process and reformat the school board structure by adding three at-large members to the nine-member board.[49] Some school officials seemed supportive of the recommendation while others were skeptical. Two months later, however, the school board voted to extend the superintendent's contract. Wilder objected and declared the action illegal under state law, while still pushing for the authority to appoint a new superintendent.

The battle lines were forming for the turf disputes that would soon follow.

Richmond's New Form of Government

First came the city charter change enabling Richmond citizens to directly elect their mayor. Richmond hadn't had that option since Truman was in the White House. The mayor would be elected "at large" by a majority of voters, for the first time since 1948. To win, a candidate now needed a majority of the vote in at least five of the city's nine council districts. Winning in a four-man race, Wilder had carried all of the districts with nearly 80 percent of the vote.

While about half of Virginia's thirty-eight independent cities already had mayors elected at large, none came close to wielding the breadth of authority held by Richmond's mayor.

Richmond became the first city in Virginia to have a "strong mayor." Some viewed the city's transition to this model of local government as a "political experiment in progress." Richmond's experience could become a potential blueprint for other cities to follow, they thought.

With the new "mayor-council" form of government—and Wilder in office— numerous changes emerged that clearly contrasted with Richmond's bygone days of having a city manager appointed by council.

Richmond's new government drew a clear separation of power between the legislative and executive branches, similar to that at the state or federal level. Like the governor or president, the mayor held chief executive officer (CEO) authority to oversee the city's administration and was directly accountable to the voters. Meanwhile city council, like the General Assembly or Congress, took a legislative role in setting policies.

Richmond's strong mayor system was outlined in revisions made to the city charter. Within weeks of his landslide election, Wilder pushed for additional powers.

Like the strong mayors of cities like Chicago, New York, and Houston, Wilder's duties included submitting the annual budget to the city council, advising council on the city's financial condition, and introducing tax rate proposals and other budget ordinances.

Yet unlike anywhere else in Virginia, Richmond's mayor selected a chief administrative officer (CAO) who was directly responsible for the city's day-to-day operations among city departments. The mayor's selection of a CAO required the approval of council, and that individual would be answerable solely to—and could be dismissed by—the mayor. With the CAO directly accountable to him, the mayor held broad leverage in shaping city policy, even though he could not vote on matters before council.

Richmond's new form of government left city council members without the considerable power they once held when the city manager reported directly to them. Now they had a mayor to contend with—and he did not report to them.

Changes to the city charter strengthened the mayor's position in overseeing the operation of local government. He received line-item veto authority for the city's annual budget (subject to a two-thirds override by city council), the ability to hire and fire top city officials, and authority to allocate funding to the school system within specific budget categories—such as instruction, administration, and facilities—for greater emphasis on academic performance and operational efficiency.

Wilder's push for expanded control of the city budget and school funding signaled that he would operate with the same financial belt-tightening fervor that he had as governor. "It is really important for [council] to understand that we're moving in a different direction as relates to fiscal responsibility and accountability."

Wilder had sought the expanded mayoral powers, city council agreed, and the General Assembly granted approval for the charter changes to take effect. "The only thing I want to do is to be in a position to have some say-so," he told council. "Even that say-so is limited because you have the power to override."[50]

A charter change in 2006 required the mayor to carry out any ordinance adopted by council. The mayor, in turn, could veto the ordinance and the council could then override it with a two-thirds (six member) vote.

The line-item veto authority strengthened the mayor's hand in getting what he wanted. Before that change took place, he needed the support of five out of nine council members to gain approval. With the line-item veto, however, six council members were needed to vote to override the mayor's actions. That meant the mayor only needed the support of four council members to prevent an override.

Council initially wanted to require the mayor to carry out all ordinances it passed, but Wilder objected. That's when State Senator John C. Watkins, R-Powhatan, negotiated a compromise for alternative language about the veto, before sponsoring the bill in the General Assembly. Though Wilder said he wasn't pleased with the new provision, he accepted it without a fight. "Everybody's got to hate it a little bit," Watkins said, explaining that the veto served as a check on the council's power while the override was a check on the mayor's authority.[51] Noting that "this is a new way of setting up city government in this state," Watkins said it was important to have an equitable balance of power between the executive and legislative branches.[52]

"We've tried to work out whatever difference there was and reach some kind of compromise that people feel comfortable with," Council President Loupassi told the *Richmond Times-Dispatch*. "I think both sides had to give and take a little bit, and I think it will ultimately prove to be a good system."[53]

On the day the measure was being considered by the assembly's Senate Committee on Local Government, Wilder walked across the street to the General Assembly Building to attend the meeting. Watching Wilder make an arrival and work a room was always a source of entertainment. He knew many of the legislators from his old days at the state capital. Handshakes and backslaps were abundant.

Then I noticed the mayor do something odd.

Just before he started around the room, he pulled something from his mouth and calmly slipped it in his jacket pocket. I found out later that his bridge had come loose, so he took it out. It didn't seem to bother him at all or slow him down. It wasn't too long before the committee unanimously approved sending the measure to the full Virginia State Senate for a formal vote. A similar proposal worked its way through the House of Delegates. After both houses agreed, the governor signed the measure into law.

Wilder was privately delighted that he would only need the support of four council members to prevent a veto override. Another charter change granted him the ability to hire outside legal help if the city attorney was unable to provide assistance. "Mayor Wilder does not take objection with the proposal that was worked out," I told reporters after the committee hearing.

From his early days in office, Wilder wasted no time in reconfiguring his cabinet of nearly two dozen department heads. He vowed on the campaign trail to shrink the number of agencies and departments. He was not shy about keeping his promises.

In his first month, he required the heads of city departments and agencies to reapply for their jobs and compete with outside applicants. In March, in a single day, he had wiped out three small agencies: intergovernmental relations; management services; transportation, and a hiring freeze was put in place due to an expected $6 million budget shortfall.

It sent tremors throughout the city's workforce.

Reported the *Richmond Free Press*: "The 15 employees who reported to the ousted [agency] directors felt the shockwaves, with all being sent home worrying about their futures at City Hall." The newspaper predicted that most of them would be laid off due to the hiring freeze.[54] Each city department also was asked to show what a 15 percent cut in their budget would look like as a "benchmark guide" for the new mayor.

This was just the beginning.

By mid-July, nine more department heads were fired—or "separated" from city government—as described in the press release announcing each departure.

In September, Wilder made an unexpected appearance at the CAO's weekly staff meeting with the department heads. That morning, as they sat around the massive boardroom table in the second-floor conference room, Wilder delivered words of caution that produced pin-drop silence, wide eyes, and stunned faces. "Some of you aren't on my team," he calmly declared. "I am numero uno," he said, holding his index finger in the air for emphasis. He could feel some nervousness among the group but reminded everyone that "operating in your own little fiefdoms . . . that's over with." He opened the floor for questions, of which there were few, and said he expected to hear from each department head individually—or else. Everyone was now put "on notice." Over time, all of them would be replaced with fresh faces.

Style Weekly named Wilder "Richmonder of the Year" in 2005, noting he was perhaps more powerful as mayor than when he was governor.

"For the last 12 months, Richmond's first popularly elected mayor in half a century hasn't only shaken things up, he's jackhammered the foundation," *Style Weekly* observed. "Single-handedly, Wilder's taken on Richmond's ruling business class, challenged City Council at every turn, and asserted his influence in a tight gubernatorial race."[55]

Assembling the Team

As Wilder sculpted city operations for greater efficiency, he made three significant hires soon after entering office. These individuals played critical roles: public safety, government administration, and grand policy idea-maker.

Wilder's first big hire, made during his first month, was a new police chief named Rodney D. Monroe. The two men developed a strong and enduring friendship, regularly having lunch together to catch up on the heartbeat of the city. Monroe had the mayor's immediate attention; when the chief dropped by, other staffers were asked to leave and come back later. A self-effacing man at five foot seven, Monroe once joked he became a good street fighter as a kid to overcome being "vertically challenged." In photos together, he and Wilder stood virtually eye-to-eye.

Monroe came to Richmond after four years as the police chief in Macon, Georgia. He previously served twenty-two years with the Washington, DC, Metropolitan Police Department, with a focus on reducing gang-related activity. He helped steer DC's young people away from a path of crime and brokered truces with rival gangs. Monroe's criminal investigations involved working with federal agencies such as the FBI, DEA, U.S. Secret Service, and ATF. He managed major events such as the 1995 Million-Man March and the 1997 Presidential Inauguration.

In Richmond, he quickly made an impact on the community through in-depth neighborhood involvement. Monroe was revered for his success in establishing "sector policing," and he had work to do. Richmond already suffered from its reputation of having one of the highest murder rates (per capita), according to an annual survey among similarly sized cities.

He reinvigorated Richmond Police, placed an additional 110 officers on the job, and reorganized the force into twelve geographic sectors where police officers patrolled the same territory to become familiar with the people and unique situations in their neighborhoods. In addition to vehicle patrols, officers spent more time walking their beat. Soon, citizens were getting to know their officers. This interaction was far different from before, when police officers rotated patrols across the city.

"The most valuable partners have been the citizens themselves," the mayor said. "They are coming forward like never before to help the police department in its ongoing effort to make Richmond a safe place to live and work." [56]

By the end of 2006, Richmond experienced its lowest crime rate in twenty-five years. Crime was cut across the board by 22 percent, and the city's conviction rate soared.[57] Monroe later created a police cadet academy to prepare young recruits for a career in law enforcement. He also led the mayor's Commission on City Jail Issues which issued a report on replacing the aging, overcrowded facility.

After just eighteen months on the job, Monroe was honored at a citywide reception—the theme was "Hail to the Chief"—where he received a plaque of appreciation inscribed by more than one hundred civic and community organizations. Virginia Governor Tim Kaine, himself a former mayor of Richmond, and other dignitaries sent letters of congratulations to Monroe. "By strengthening the relationship between your officers and people throughout the city, you are encouraging the communication, cooperation, and trust that is necessary to thwart criminals and hold them accountable for their actions," Kaine wrote.

Chief Monroe was named *Style Weekly*'s "Richmonder of the Year" in 2007. People loved him.

With public safety addressed, Wilder turned next to administration. During his third month, he chose William E. Harrell as the city's CAO. Wilder recommended him as required by the city charter, and council unanimously approved. Harrell was no stranger to City Hall, having served as a deputy city manager for five years. He and Wilder developed a cordial relationship based on a mutual respect for their boundaries. It grew tortured over time.

Eager to follow Wilder's wishes on matters large and small, Harrell was initially able to deftly manage the expectations of a city council that already knew and worked with him. He did his best to maintain morale among long-time employees who felt their careers threatened, though it must have been agony to have to terminate so many colleagues.

Wilder's third major appointment was a longtime advisor who monumentally helped shape his political career. A scruffy political consultant and lawyer from New York, Paul Goldman was hired as the mayor's senior policy advisor. Dubbed as "the man behind the curtain" by *Style Weekly*, Goldman was widely credited with originating the mayor's "City of the Future" program that promised up to $300 million for new or renovated schools, extensive street and sidewalk upgrades, and major improvements in the city's cultural arts centers, libraries, and neighborhood recreation centers.[58] Much lesser known is that the "City of the Future" title was coined by Harry Black, the city's chief financial officer who was the actual architect of the intricate funding plan.

Goldman had been with Wilder since the 1980s, guiding his successful run for lieutenant governor and governor. In turn, Wilder propelled Goldman to get elected as chairman of the state Democratic Party. They were close. Wilder served as best man at Goldman's wedding, held at the Governor's Mansion in 1992.[59] Over the years he worked tirelessly for Wilder. He spent hours standing outside Ukrop's Market in Richmond's Carytown and elsewhere collecting signatures for the referendum for an "at large" mayor and later, obtaining signatures to place Wilder's name on the ballot. Disheveled in demeanor yet sharp in strategy, Goldman kept a low-key, "off the record" profile at City Hall. He was considered undisciplined in matters of protocol and generally did what he wanted, coming and going as he pleased.

Though somewhat peculiar, the Wilder-Goldman duo proved to be highly effective. Dwayne Yancey described their relationship in *When Hell Froze Over*, his biography of Wilder's successful run for lieutenant governor in Virginia.

"At first glance, Doug Wilder and Paul Goldman are a most unlikely political odd couple—the polished, immaculate Southern black with the soaring cadence of a Baptist preacher, whose hopes of winning depended on how well he courted the state's conservative establishment, and the ill-kempt New York Jew who mumbled vague nonsense and had made a political career out of attacking the establishment.

"But, no matter how much he fretted about Goldman's appearance, Wilder was eventually able to overlook these transgressions. Wilder didn't hire Goldman for looks. He hired him for his mind. Goldman was just the sort of scheming character Wilder needed to make his long-shot, high-risk campaign work. ("I'm not crazy," Goldman once laughed, "but I am devious.") And scheme Goldman did."[60]

By the time Wilder left office, his three most prominent appointments would already be gone.

Battles Over the Budget

If the pace of employee turnover at City Hall wasn't enough to unsettle the city's genteel citizenry, Wilder's interaction with council in preparing the city's annual budget created shockwaves one could hardly imagine. A budget battle erupted in each of the mayor's four years, frequently with council's threat of a lawsuit.

"We need to review our past performance," the mayor said. "Just because it's been done in the past, doesn't mean we have to continue to do it." He said he learned a great deal about the "true costs" of decisions made by previous administrations.

"Change is here, change is on the move and it's going to continue at a rapid pace," he told council when presenting his inaugural budget in April.

Wilder's proposed budget reflected his top three priorities: reducing crime, promoting education, and improving city streets. He pledged to put more police officers on the job and upgrade the department's computer-aided dispatch system. He proposed new or renovated schools, an increase in classroom spending, additional full-time math and reading specialists, and an expanded foreign language program. He launched an aggressive street repair program that initiated action within forty-eight hours of problems reported.

As a former governor known for fiscal prudence, Wilder knew how to sweeten the pot. Few could dispute the virtues of public safety, education, and smooth roads. He knew that. He recommended a four-cent decrease in the city's real estate tax rate. He called for more funding for the city bus system to prevent hikes in bus fares so people could afford to go to work.

What caused a community uproar, however, was his proposal to eliminate $12 million in discretionary funding for business booster organizations such as the Greater Richmond Partnership and Richmond Renaissance, as well as cultural and community groups like the Richmond Symphony, Children's Museum of Richmond, Meals on Wheels, and many smaller local non-profits. He also railed against the City's longstanding business agreements such as funding for the Greater Richmond Convention Center.

"We just don't have it," Wilder explained. "But I want to be equal about it and treat everyone the same."[61] As one columnist put it, Wilder proposed a city operating budget that took the city's "sacred cows" and "carved [them] up into hamburger."[62]

Council's public hearing on the budget drew more than 400 people, with nearly 100 signing up to speak in protest of the cutbacks. Many children came, some with violins. A dancer appeared in a red flamenco skirt and black corset. Some musicians played Mozart beside the elevators. With all of the seats taken, clusters of people choked the council chamber doorways. Hand-held signs read, "Richmond's Children Deserve More." One after another, for three hours, representatives of groups whose funding was on the chopping block spoke about the services they provided. Wilder did not attend the hearing, but on nearly everyone's mind was his proposal to give the school system $5 million less than the school board had requested.

Yet council had ideas of its own: taking an ax to the mayor's office, for one. Council's amended budget included eliminating five Wilder staff positions—including those of Senior Policy Advisor Paul Goldman, and Policy Analyst Isaac Graves—who happened to be Wilder's nephew—and stripping out nearly $550,000 to eliminate the mayor's nine-person security detail. Council's budget largely returned funding for most of the business and cultural groups as well as the $5 million to the school system that Wilder had removed.

The battle lines were drawn.

Time was running out for council to adopt a budget. The city charter required that council pass a balanced budget no later than May 31. Otherwise, the mayor's original budget would automatically take effect. Negotiations later occurred during one council meeting where some members awkwardly ducked in and out several times with Wilder's staff to discuss where cuts could be made.

Council passed its version of the budget but did so during a "special session." Wilder argued that the city charter called for budget adoption to take place during a "regular meeting." He said the charter plainly stated, "A proposed ordinance . . .shall be finally passed at a regular meeting."

Council's budget, the mayor declared, was "illegal."

"It is as clear as the nose on your face," Wilder said. "I for one want to follow the law." Soon a "constitutional crisis" loomed over Richmond's strong mayoral government that continued for weeks. Determining the balance of power depended on who you asked.

Council tried to smooth over budget differences, with Council President Loupassi extending an olive branch. Despite good intentions, his efforts did not end well. "We had a pleasant conversation and he agreed we ought to work together and then the last thing he brought up was, 'I think you can't do it.' [referring to a vote on the budget]," Loupassi told a *Richmond Times-Dispatch* reporter. Wilder then handed him a copy of the law and a press release he was planning to issue later that day explaining his legal argument. "They had already written up a press release. It's completely shocking," Loupassi said.[63]

The CAO—who reported to the mayor—planned to certify the mayor's version of the budget. The city clerk—who reported to the city council—intended to certify council's budget. Council retained an outside attorney for guidance. Several council members and City Hall observers expected the dispute to go to court.

The outdated wording of the city charter itself only confused the matter. A section of the charter stated that a copy of the budget "as finally adopted shall be certified by the City Manager and City Clerk." However, with the change in government, the city manager position no longer existed. The newly revised city charter was not, by any means, crafted with the most careful scrutiny. Wilder complained that for the most part, the term "city manager" had been replaced with "mayor" using the standard computer find-and-replace function.

Wilder lamented that the city attorney did not take the lead to correct the charter language. "The City Attorney should be leading the charge to the General Assembly to have these changes made, because of all City officials, the City Attorney should be charged with knowing the substantive effect of changes necessitated by the change to a strong-mayor form of government," the mayor wrote in his newsletter.[64] Wilder declared that council's version of the budget was illegally adopted and therefore invalid. The mayor, himself a lawyer, stood ready to defend his first budget.

He relished a good fight.

"Let me say definitively that there is no legal action that is required of me in order to implement my budget," Wilder announced. "Further, it would be a waste of time and tax dollars for anyone else to attempt to use the courts to block what the charter so plainly authorizes this administration to do."[65]

In the end, the standoff ended with a compromise with each side essentially getting most of what it wanted. Wilder went along with most of council's budget revisions such as funding for the community groups and the city's longstanding business agreements. In return, funding was restored for the mayor's staff and his security detail. Wilder also agreed to close an approximate $13 million budget shortfall. He said his administration could make up the difference through job cuts and by streamlining city operations.[66]

Wilder, commenting on the shakeup of city government during his first year in office, agreed he was ready to take bold action. "I guess they thought I was going to just sit around and cut ribbons, that I wouldn't have the energy to do what I've been doing," he told the *Washington Post*. "I know a lot of people are wondering . . .what's the old bastard going to do next?"[67]

Wilder's drive for greater efficiency extended beyond the city's workforce, however. He insisted that four booster groups—Richmond Renaissance Inc., Richmond Riverfront Corp., River District Alliance, and City Celebrations—consolidate their activities into one organization. "This consolidation will save the city several hundred thousand dollars each year," he noted. "It only makes sense for the city to have one organization promoting its Downtown area to get the job done, instead of four organizations with four executive directors, four offices, and four budgets."[68]

The mayor's style of budget management was summed up in a glass-enclosed display titled "Cut the Fat," given to him by local business leader, Booty Armstrong. It featured a meat cleaver, a butter knife, and a nail file, with this quote from Wilder: "I recall once when I was asked to trim the fat out of a budget, I joked that it wouldn't require too heavy a cleaver, that it would take a butter knife. I'll tell you what I think in this instance: I can do it with a nail file."

Chess-game skirmishes about the budget would continue each year as Wilder submitted his proposals. And it wouldn't be the last time that Wilder accused council of missing a deadline in completing its work. At least the two sides were becoming more familiar with each other.

When proposing his next city budget, in early 2006, the mayor again prepared for battle. He warned council not to tamper with it. While he now had the power to veto any changes that council made to his budget, he said he was reluctant to use it. "I've always thought that vetoes should be sparingly used," Wilder said, reflecting on his days as governor.[69] Yet, as politicians do, he made exceptions to that rule. He vetoed so many items in council's revised budget that a front-page headline of the *Richmond Free Press* declared in bold lettering: "Wilder Goes Veto Happy."[70] The mayor already knew one council member was lobbying to build a $850,000 teen center in her Church Hill district while another member wanted a nearly $2 million community center in Southside's Broad Rock Road area.

Mindful that each council member kept a wish list of projects to please their constituents, Wilder announced a new administrative regulation that future proposals before council would require a fiscal impact analysis. "Understanding the financial impact of a proposal is one of the surest ways to measure the true value of that proposal and whether to proceed," he said, recalling the same practice as governor. [71]

He vetoed both the proposed teen center and community center, saying no funds had been budgeted to operate them. He removed nearly all funding for the Richmond Slave Trail Commission, saying he wasn't sure how the money would be spent. Wilder vetoed a council proposal that the city administration must spend what the budget called for, saying it could interfere with the city's day-to-day financial management. He vetoed another proposal that would guarantee the school system receive a share of any year-end budget surpluses. He also vetoed council's proposal to increase school funding by $9 million to allow for a 5 percent raise for teachers.[72]

The mayor's discussion with council about school funding became so heated that School Board Chairman David L. Ballard, who attended the budget meeting, commented to a reporter afterward, "If I met the mayor now, I'd have to kill him." The mayor did not hear the remark, but the city police later questioned Ballard, who promptly apologized and later chose not to run again for his school board seat.[73]

Wilder warned council not to attempt to restore the teen center or the community center by tampering with the city's capital improvement budget. In veiled terms, the mayor's press release suggested that any such attempt could jeopardize City of the Future funding for other projects in their district.

> The override of any portion of the FY 2007 capital improvement plan will have serious consequences, as it was presented as a package of one thing depending upon another.
>
> To the extent that monies are siphoned off for individual projects that offer neither concrete, sufficient design planning nor any measure of sustainable long-term operation, there should be no illusion for anyone to believe that this will not detract and take away from examining the City's needs overall as compared to district by district. The public has already spoken on that, in terms of what is best for the city.
>
> In the wake of these highly questionable undertakings, there will be significant impact, delay and possible defeat in those areas relating to City of the Future funding for new schools, recreational centers, and similar community improvements.[74]

Council did override many of the mayor's vetoes, however, including the two centers, but Wilder said it did not matter since construction could not begin until they were fully funded.

Council also imposed a one percent across-the-board cut in department budgets. That amounted to almost $600,000 sliced from the city's department of public works, which is in charge of street repairs and trash collection. The new budget had been in effect only a month before Wilder reminded council of the impact that funding cuts could have on city services. He was ready to "talk trash."

Wilder understood that a sure-fire way to stir up people would be to hint about disrupting their trash pickup. And he knew of no better way to announce that possibility than in the inaugural issue of his online newsletter, *Visions*.

This headline caught the eye of more than one reporter:

Cutbacks Mean Cutting Back

It's too early to know whether the FY 2007 cutbacks made in the City departments' operating budgets will lead to future interruptions in municipal services. At my insistence, funding was not reduced for the vital services provided by Police and Fire.

A nearly $600,000 reduction made in the City's Department of Public Works could impact trash collection. A $140,000 reduction in the Department of Parks and Recreation might lead to early-hour closings of neighborhood recreational centers. With the fiscal year just underway, we are in the process of assessing the impact of Council's reductions. Please be assured that the Administration is committed to lessening the impact, to the extent we can.[75]

For the next two days, the *Richmond Times-Dispatch* carried news articles about the future of trash collection. One headline blared: "Mayor Warns of Cutback in Trash Collection – Wilder Says City Council's Budget Reductions May Necessitate Move." Another read: "Wilder's Trash Threat Draws Fire From Council."

City council, getting an earful from constituents, cried foul over the situation. Council President Loupassi's anger was obvious. "We can come up with $600,000. All [Wilder] has to do is get rid of those guards he's got," Loupassi said, referring to the mayor's nine-person security detail.[76] In the end, however, Wilder found other ways to manage the one percent across-the-board cut in city departments without reducing citizen services. The city's trash got picked up on time. Constituents were relieved.

As the year rolled on, Wilder continued to combat the use of public dollars for council members' pet projects. He refused to support a "Back to School" parade in Church Hill that had been a longtime annual event hosted by Councilwoman Delores McQuinn. It almost didn't happen. A city permit was issued to hold the event, but the organizers learned at the eleventh hour that $6,000 would be required to pay the city police officers who set up barricades and provided security along the parade route. The city covered that cost in years past, but not the Wilder administration. Instead, expenses were paid by councilmembers' pay-go funds and private donations.

In 2007, budget negotiations between the mayor and council again proved to be bumpy. Nearly two months before council approved its own version of the budget, Wilder held a press conference to announce that approximately 2,800 elderly and disabled city homeowners would get "100% tax relief"—while also blaming council for not fully funding the program. Excerpts of the press release read as follows:

> The subject of the $1.4 million shortfall for the City's Real Estate Tax Relief for the Elderly and Disabled Program is the result of the City Council not putting in enough money to support that program. Council created this unfortunate situation. As a result, many of our citizens have been put through needless worry and concern over how they would be able to pay their tax bill this year.
>
> There are too many people who have placed their faith and confidence in me through the years who know that I would never desert them during their time of need, and I won't desert them now. It is more important for these people to have this relief now when it is needed.[77]

Budget negotiations extended well past the July 1 start of the new fiscal year. Both the mayor and council agreed to fully fund the tax relief program, expand transit service for the disabled between the city and Henrico County, and support Wilder's proposal to establish a new police cadet program that council had initially cut.

The mayor and council also agreed on a cost-of-living increase for city retirees but disagreed over how to pay for it. Wilder's plan would provide funding upfront, while council wanted to amortize some of the expense over several years. Council's version of the budget also restored about $500,000 for projects that Wilder had cut, such as reimbursing $250,000 to a private redevelopment organization formerly led by Councilwoman Ellen F. Robertson; $30,000 for an annual back-to-school parade hosted by Councilwoman Delores L. McQuinn; and $220,000 for new council staff positions and management studies.

The day after council's vote, Wilder held a press conference to announce he was using his "executive authority" to implement his version of the budget. He said council by law could only vote on his proposal up or down as it was presented, rather than tinker with it. He directed the city's finance director to operate under his version of the budget.

The mayor emphasized that his budget identified both the projects to be funded and the source of the funding. "I am legally authorized to do that under the Charter at any time during the fiscal year," he said in a press release. "Council, under the Charter or any other provision of law, <u>does not have</u> that authority. They can reduce the amount of the funding, but not change the projects. They have no authority to amortize *any* budget items without direction and certification from the executive branch wherein the sole responsibility resides."[78]

Wilder carried out his budget plan without delay. By the time council approved its version of the budget in August, the city had already sent refunds to elderly and disabled homeowners who had paid their real estate taxes in full.

When questioned by the *Richmond Times-Dispatch*, Council President William Pantele said it would be premature to conclude who had the legal authority during the budget dispute. "I think that there's so much smoke and mirrors on the second floor of City Hall that it's very difficult to sort out fact from fiction," he mused. "Trying to sort out the facts from the fistfuls of rhetoric is often difficult."[79]

In 2008, Wilder's final year in office, the council's approval of the budget was plagued by issues as serious as in 2005, and as before, council threatened a lawsuit.

Council had not met the May 31 statutory deadline for adopting a balanced budget, the mayor said. He relied on the plain words shown in the city charter to justify that his budget—not council's—would dominate. The rules were spelled out in Section 6.11, which read:

> Not later than the thirty-first day of May in each year the council shall adopt the budget, the appropriation ordinances and such ordinances providing for additional revenue as may be necessary to put the budget in balance.
>
> If for any reason the council fails to adopt the budget on or before such day, the budget as submitted by the mayor shall be the budget for the ensuing year and the appropriation ordinance and the ordinances providing additional revenue, if any, as recommended by the mayor shall have full force and effect to the same extent as if the same had been adopted by the council, notwithstanding anything to the contrary in this charter.

A mighty tug-of-war between Wilder and council reflected the balance-of-power conflict between the executive and legislative branches. Searching for ways to cut costs, council put the mayor's press office squarely on the chopping block with an eye to slash its funding by more than half. No other department budget was hit that hard. Some council members called the mayor's *Visions* newsletter a "propaganda" tool that was used to bash council. They seemed especially upset with a new forty-two-minute DVD titled "Mayor L. Douglas Wilder: A Review of Accomplishments" that featured clips of the mayor's State of the City address, and interviews with community leaders about crime reduction and downtown revitalization. "I just thank God for our mayor, Doug Wilder," gushed community activist Alicia Rasin at the beginning of the video. Soundbites also came from MeadWestvaco's CEO John A. Luke Jr., RRHA executive director Anthony Scott, local real estate developer Robin Miller, and members of Wilder's executive staff.

Council was not pleased. The DVD was part of "a PR eruption by the city administration" that "underscores why council will be making some moves in significant reductions in the public-relations machine . . ." said Council President Pantele.[80]

Council proposed reducing the press office's annual budget from $555,000 to $243,000, which would effectively gut our six-member staff. The press office, already operating under a 25 percent cut since 2005, produced newsletters, brochures, and annual reports as well as handling press events, video programming, and website maintenance.

Though worried about the severity of the proposed cut, I privately took satisfaction in knowing that the press office must be doing a good job in getting our message out, or council would not have been so intent to clip our wings. Questioned by the media, I was quick to defend our work. "The responsibilities far outweigh the resources," I told a *Richmond Times-Dispatch* reporter. "When you look at the magnitude of work we do, it speaks well to have a six-man office."

Some council members, though, didn't see it that way. "As we looked at the budget, we had a lot of question marks beside the amount spent for public relations," Councilman Tyler said. "My big concern is how you have six people pumping out information for the city."[81]

Aggravating the situation was that some *Richmond Times-Dispatch* reporters often noted my salary in their news stories, almost as if to try to embarrass me for not giving them the information they were seeking. A typical example would be: "The mayor has no further comment on that matter," said city spokesperson Linwood Norman, who makes $96,000 per year. Still, the salaries of the city's press office staff were considerably lower than what was paid to their counterparts in Henrico and Chesterfield counties, according to a *Richmond Times-Dispatch* analysis of comparable incomes.

All told, more than a dozen press releases were issued as the mayor and council continued to battle over the budget.

Council adopted its budget on May 27, but Wilder pointed to the city charter language requiring that it must be balanced by showing all funding sources. Council did not balance its budget until June 9, when it approved the carryover of more than $2.1 million in unspent funds, he said. While the shortage represented only a mere fraction of the city's $650+ million general fund budget, it still did not meet the charter requirement of adopting a balanced budget by the May 31 deadline.

Since February, early in the budget discussions, the mayor had warned that the nation's worsening economy would result in significant revenue shortfalls for the city. He scolded council for proposing a cut in the real estate tax rate by three cents, further reducing revenues by $6 million. With state funding projected to be cut by $8 million, the city faced a $14 million deficit at the very start of budget preparations, he cautioned.

"It's unfathomable to suggest altering the tax rate as the City is facing challenges to keep services continuing at the current level for our citizens," Wilder warned in a press release. "It's not necessary to start the new budget year $14 million in the hole and be forced to cut back on public safety, human services, refuse collection and other essential services. I have a record of fiscal accountability and responsibility, and nothing will swerve me from that commitment. While the temptation may be ripe for some to offer promises to voters during an election year, I will continue to put principle over politics."[82]

Dour economic forecasts and potential service cutbacks were noted in additional press releases issued in early April. "I am aware of no other localities in the Commonwealth of Virginia—or any I can find in the entire country—that are talking about slashing their tax rate, which is their main source of revenue, in these economic times," he chided council in another release.[83] He warned that the $6 million reduction due to a lowered real estate rate could lead to reducing summer park programs, library hours, leaf collection, emergency responses, and street repairs.

The day after council approved the $2.1 million carry-over to balance its budget, Wilder held a press conference to announce that his own budget—not council's—would take effect. The mayor scolded council in this press release:

> Unfortunately, some of the lessons from 2005 have already been forgotten by Council just three years later. City Council has again delivered a budget that is out of balance, this time by more than $2.1 million.
>
> Council's failure to complete its work by the required deadline forced them to amend these ordinances and continue them until its June 9 meeting. It saddens me that Council's most important task—indeed, their *paramount* responsibility to balance the budget on time—once again failed not only to meet its required obligations, but also failed the people they represent.[84]

The next day council retaliated with its own press release. Titled "Council Passed A Legal, Valid and Balanced City Budget on May 27, 2008," it stated the carryover ordinances in question applied to the current fiscal year and not the upcoming one. It read in part:

> The bottom line is that these are entirely different fiscal years, with the budget that was adopted on May 27, 2008, using available carried forward balance from the sizable surpluses of prior years that had never been appropriated. I am sure that once the Administration realizes that the Ordinances, on which it basis (sic) its arguments, apply to the current fiscal year, not the next, that this matter will be resolved, and that we can go on with providing services to our citizens and not engaging in further conflict.[85]

Council's press release concluded with this: "A written opinion from the City Attorney has been requested." When I read that final sentence, I knew it would ignite the mayor's extreme dissatisfaction with the designated role of the city attorney. Wilder had often criticized the city attorney who, as stated in the city charter, served a dual role in representing both the council and the mayor.

The day after council's press release, we followed up with our own. By this point, it represented the mayor's seventh press release about the budget battle. This time, the mayor's press release criticized the city attorney as well as council.

"It is not surprising that the City Attorney, who is hired by and reports to the Council, would be called upon to rescue them from their dilemma," it read. "What is more surprising is the ethical dilemma of the City Attorney who, while also required to represent the City Administration, now is taking a stand against the Administration. This is all the more reason for the need for City Charter reform, as we have said for the past several years."[86]

Our press release included embedded links to videotaped council meetings to show that council's $2.1 million in carryover funds were related to the upcoming fiscal year, as the mayor had noted.

When July 1—the start of the new budget year—rolled around, Wilder wasted no time in announcing via another press release that the City of Richmond would be operating under his version of the budget. He noted, however, that he would be making $6 million in cuts to his budget to accommodate council's three-cent cut in the real estate tax rate.

Wilder also referred to council's threat of a lawsuit. "I have never filed a lawsuit against Council. Threats of another lawsuit filed by Council demonstrate they would rather govern through the courts than follow their mandated responsibilities. I think the taxpayers are sick and tired of their tax dollars being wasted by all the lawsuits initiated by Council. Only in Richmond would the City Council sue the Mayor because *they* forgot to do their homework."[87]

To resolve the stalemate, both sides quietly began a series of closed-door meetings to hash out their differences. Neither side backed off from its position on the budget, but despite that, no one wanted to have to go to court. "The taxpayers are looking for the best efforts that we have because with as tight as money is today, we don't want to waste money," Wilder told the *Richmond Times-Dispatch*. Added Council President Pantele, "All lawsuits deserve efforts to be avoided."[88]

By mid-September, well beyond the start of the new budget year, most funding issues had been worked out. The mayor's final budget battle was now behind him. A lawsuit was avoided. It was time to move on to other issues.

CHAPTER THREE

In the Thick of It

Building New Schools

One of Wilder's greatest frustrations as mayor involved his dealings with the Richmond school system. The city's public schools were among the most dilapidated in Virginia. Student academic performance and graduation rates were among the lowest in the state, with the drop-out rate six times higher than the statewide average. Richmond's schools also were among the most expensive to operate in Virginia. Wilder fought to have a complete audit of school system spending to understand why. He sought to influence school system officials using a carrot and stick strategy. It revolved around money and the promise of building new schools.

Wilder had long extolled the value of education, linking it with economic development and affordable housing. In his view, school facilities and housing issues were inseparable entities to spur economic growth in the Richmond area.

Education became a central element of Wilder's sweeping $300 million "City of the Future" plan, an ambitious five-year plan to build or renovate fifteen city schools—without any increase in taxes.

"I have waited all of my lifetime in politics to have the opportunity to make all this happen in my native city," Wilder confided, when unveiling the plan during his State of the City address in January 2006 before a packed City Hall audience.[89] A new high school had not been built in the city in nearly forty years, he noted.

His plan also would include a new "high school for the arts" and a "science and math high school" that students from across the city could attend. In addition, the city's vocational technology center and the city library would be equipped with the latest technology.

Rather than raise taxes, funding for Wilder's plan came from three sources: revenue from the city's expiring fifteen-year tax abatement program for renovated real estate; a percentage of the city's meals tax; and savings from conservative budgeting, he said.[90] The unique funding plan, developed by Harry Black, the city's chief financial officer, incorporated a "just in time" loan financing mechanism that enabled the borrowing of funds only as needed within specified points in time, thereby precluding unnecessary payments of interest. The city's financial advisor, Davenport & Company, reviewed and approved the plan.

Richmond's business community, a key Wilder ally, greatly supported the plan and promised to chip in as much as $50 million to improve education for new generations of workforce talent. Wilder promoted the plan before an enthusiastic audience of 200 community supporters at a Richmond Renaissance meeting that summer. He held Town Hall meetings across the city. He commended Richmond Public Schools for developing a list of proposed school closings and student population rezonings. Things were looking up.

Once the school board validated the closures, the city administration and city council could move ahead with new construction. Wilder said he wanted "shovels in the ground" beginning in spring 2007. Wilder envisioned the adaptive re-use of the empty school buildings to invigorate old neighborhoods. Schools that were permanently closed could be transferred to the city and redeveloped into mixed-income, affordable housing neighborhoods where teachers, police officers, and other city workers would want to live. To attract and keep jobs and families in the city, however, he stressed that improvements had to be made in the quality of services provided by the city's school system.

Wilder closely watched the efforts of mayors in other cities who engineered reform of their own school system. Washington, DC, Mayor Adrian Fenty was one of more than a dozen mayors beginning to take charge of their school district. In 2007, the DC Council passed the DC Public Education Reform Amendment Act which consolidated control over public education in the mayor's office. Fenty soon appointed a school chancellor who would report to him.

Wilder paid close attention.

The similarities between DC and Richmond schools—dilapidated buildings, small student enrollments, low academic achievement—were evident. Yet in Richmond, it was the school board—not the mayor—that selected the superintendent and made funding and construction decisions.

In DC, the new education reform law abolished the decision-making power of an elected board of education (the equivalent of the Richmond School Board). The new law also created a new office, the chancellor, who was appointed by the mayor and served as CEO of the school system.

Fenty appointed Michelle Rhee as the chancellor. She gained national stature by turning DC's failing school system into a national laboratory for education reform. Rhee closed twenty-three schools in one year alone, primarily those with low enrollments and outdated buildings, and relocated several thousand students. She fired more than 200 under-performing teachers and more than thirty principals considered ineffective, and instituted a pay-for-performance system based on student test scores.

DC's reforms represented a painful but fiscally prudent remedy since DC had lost more than 100,000 students since the 1960s. Many DC parents worried that successful neighborhood programs benefiting their children would disappear as schools were closed and consolidated. Richmond parents had the same types of concerns about school closings in their own neighborhoods.

Yet Wilder wasn't the only one wanting to see change come to the Richmond Public Schools. While he sought to have input on the selection of the school superintendent, Richmond's corporate community in 2007 pressed for even more fundamental changes.

A letter signed by twenty-six titans of Richmond's business community was hand-delivered to the mayor and each council member. It carried a dire warning. "Richmond's schools are not producing the type of employees we need for the future in sufficient numbers. We believe that extraordinary efforts are required to bring the Richmond Public Schools and the City of Richmond to the world-class level of which it is capable. Too many generations of children have already been lost."

The proposal called for abolishing Richmond's elected school board. In its place would be a formula where the mayor and council would appoint school board members. Other cities like Norfolk, Cleveland, Boston, and Hartford already had put similar systems in place. The business leaders cited educational statistics that were "alarming and constitute, in our view, an emergency situation that must be dealt with immediately and with bold action," lamenting that less than 57 percent of funds actually went toward instruction rather than administration.

They also recognized the efforts of school board members who wanted to improve education for the city's children. "We have no quarrel with the members of the School Board who have done their best—rather we believe a fundamental flaw exists in the governance structure which cannot be solved without a new approach to leadership and accountability for the success of the schools," read the five-page letter.

Their plan called for a school board nominating committee, consisting of five people recommended by the mayor, and appointed by the council. They would screen candidates much like a panel that recommends the names of potential members for the governor to appoint to a university's board of visitors. Under the proposal, the nominating committee would then give each council member a list of three individuals, one of which would be chosen to represent that council district for a three-year period. The three-year terms would be staggered so that three members would be appointed each year.

The corporate leaders explained their rationale in this excerpt of their letter:

> We believe this method of selection will result in a School Board composed of individuals who have good judgment and the required expertise to drastically reform the City Schools. It will also place responsibility for the proper functioning of the schools with the elected representatives who control the purse strings – the Mayor and the City Council. All of us would know who should be held accountable for the schools.

The letter urged the mayor and city council to support the new process, which would require the General Assembly's approval of new amendments to the city charter. The corporate leaders later sent the city council president a brief background paper highlighting the details of their proposal. Its recommendations included goals for improving graduation rates, SAT and SOL scores, finance, truancy, and building new schools.

The background paper included ominous observations by the Virginia Secretary of Finance about the operation of the Richmond school system. "One of the key factors preventing the division from moving forward with facility changes is resistance at the neighborhood level to changes related to the local school. School closures/mergers are always a case of 'great in theory, just don't close mine' ideas. As one School Board member told an area newspaper regarding the facilities plan, 'I think that the way that this is going to be seen is as a . . . hit list [for my district].'"

While Richmond's form of government had changed, the selection process for the city's school board remained the same. In many ways, elected school board members were viewed as "little school superintendents" in their districts. City council had long known about Wilder's desire to alter the selection process for the school superintendent. The business community's proposal, however, failed to change the mind of city council, which showed no appetite for revising the selection process. Unable to gain traction, the proposal went nowhere.

Wilder viewed the business leaders' concerns as confirmation of his own thoughts about the school system. He pointed out, however, that he had no personal agenda in seeking a greater role in school affairs. "I don't have that type of ego, that I need any more feathers in my crown. I've got enough," he told the *Richmond Times-Dispatch*. "Particularly at this stage in my political career. I'm looking to go nowhere."[91]

As DC moved ahead with its reforms, Wilder continued to rail about the high cost of Richmond's school system. Though recent statistics suggested that academic achievement was on the rise, the cost to operate the public school system was about $71 million more per year than the statewide average. When Wilder entered office, Richmond was spending $12,385 per pupil per year, which far exceeded $7,467 in Chesterfield; $7,637 in Henrico; or $7,496 in Hanover.

Richmond had too many schools for the number of children in the system. Enrollment in many schools was far under capacity, and the cost of keeping the buildings open—both in personnel and facility maintenance—contributed to the problem. The city operated 60 schools for about 23,000 children. Chesterfield County had 59 schools for 56,000 kids and Henrico County had 66 schools for 46,000. Meanwhile Norfolk, another aging Virginia city like Richmond, provided 53 facilities for its 34,000 students. "It simply is not logical," Wilder said in his 2008 State of the City address, "that we still have the same number of facilities . . . now, as we had back in the 1950s and early 1960s when we had a student population of some 50,000 children in our system.

"Today, it is costly to maintain all of these buildings for the current student enrollment that we have, and many of these schools are half-empty and within close distance of other schools that are also half-empty," he noted.[92]

Wilder insisted that some schools would need to be closed before he would authorize City of the Future money to build new ones. However, deciding which ones to close would be up to the school board. "Before the first school is built or renovated under the 'City of the Future' Plan, the Richmond School Board needs to realign the student population within a lesser number of facilities," the mayor told *Richmond Magazine*. "The Mayor's Office is not authorized to undertake this. We have not, nor will we, suggest which schools will be closed."

It never happened.

Though critical of the school system's operation, Wilder also wanted to be clear that taking control of the schools was not his intent. "I don't want to take over the schools. I've never suggested I want to take them over," he told the *Richmond Times-Dispatch*.[93] Sensing little cooperation by school officials, he pulled his original school construction plan off the table little more than a year after announcing it. An increasingly icy relationship developed between the mayor and the school board, standing in the way of building new schools.

Watching the Money

Throughout his long political career, Wilder often commented that "the one-word definition of politics is money."[94] Even as Wilder held out the carrot of building new schools, he repeatedly exercised his use of the stick to try to streamline the school system's operation. And he meant business.

The city charter had already been revised to give the mayor the authority to provide school system funding within eight specific budget categories—such as instruction, administration, and facilities—to place greater emphasis on student academic performance. Wilder took full advantage of that new authority.

Early on, Wilder appointed a string of advisory committees to obtain expert opinions about critical issues facing the city. Professionals examined diverse topics such as efficiency and effectiveness, human services, housing and infrastructure, performing arts, city jail issues, and regional cooperation.

An Education Advisory Committee examined the operation of

the city school system. It recommended an independent audit of expenses, a comprehensive capital improvement plan that included closing schools with low enrollment, and consolidating services such as accounting, procurement, and maintenance with those same departments within the city government. The committee, composed of prominent attorneys, businesspeople, and academic officials, also suggested the mayor should be involved in selecting school board members, rather than them being elected. It recommended taking the issue to citizens in an advisory referendum. A change in governance has proven to be effective in cities such as New York City, Boston, Chicago, Hartford and Norfolk, the report said.

Wilder also appointed a Schools Oversight Committee that would be "aggressively looking over the shoulders of this school system's decision-makers" to advise him and the public of problems that needed to be addressed.[95]

"Today as your mayor I am taking steps to end the complacency and dysfunctionality that plagues Richmond Public Schools," he declared, describing the city schools as "one of the best-funded yet poorest-performing systems in the Commonwealth of Virginia."

The mayor later told the media, "The bottom line is that Richmond's public education system remains at a point of crisis and if the School Board and administration are unable or unwilling to address it, then my administration as the system's single largest fund provider has a duty to step in and hold them accountable."[96]

At Wilder's insistence, council passed an ordinance authorizing the city auditor to review the books of the school system. The mayor viewed an audit of the school operations as an urgent necessity. When his meeting with the school superintendent to discuss a protocol for an audit was cancelled, he claimed she was directed to do so by the school board, to whom she reported. The city auditor delivered his report in early 2007; however, he explained, it was not an actual audit because school officials did not cooperate by providing information on school system central administration, procurement, or facilities management. Those categories typically represent significant sums of money in any municipal budget, but particularly in school budgets.

The city auditor explained in his report: "RPS managing staff was reluctant in providing needed information in a timely manner and was not very forthcoming during the interviews. The city auditor had to complete the audit only with the available information; therefore, does not have assurance of the completeness of information provided.

"In the future, the City must contractually or otherwise bind the School Division in order for the City Auditor's Office to have full access to the records and information to hold RPS accountable for managing resources."

Yet even the incomplete audit report cited nearly $20 million in potential savings in areas such as non-teaching positions, bus transportation improvements, and vehicle replacements. "Is it unreasonable to ask what other efficiencies could be identified and how many more millions of taxpayer dollars could be saved if the school system would cooperate fully?" Wilder asked in his *Richmond Times-Dispatch* commentary.[97] He also criticized the incomplete audit before business and community leaders at a Venture Richmond meeting, saying, "Have you ever heard of such a thing where the City is supporting an entity and then learns that the entity will not supply complete and total information necessary in order to conduct an audit of its operation?"

Wilder then announced a new approach to get the school system's cooperation: he tightened the city's financial control by issuing monthly—instead of quarterly—funding payments for schools to operate.

Deputy CAO Harry Black wrote to the school superintendent that, "This new process will improve the City Administration's ability to determine that Richmond Public Schools is effectively spending local funds and should document progress towards accomplishing operational efficiencies as recommended by the City Auditor and requested by City Council."[98]

The mayor said that practice would continue until the school system produced more complete information about how it would implement cost-saving recommendations made by the city auditor. The city began withholding half of non-payroll expenses until the school board agreed to an external audit by a Washington, DC, firm. An external audit was needed because the city auditor had not been aggressive enough in investigating school spending, the mayor said. He later backed off the plan after the city auditor and school system agreed to a second, more comprehensive audit that focused on central administration, facilities, and instructional programs.

The next month, the Richmond school system filed a lawsuit against Wilder, Black, and oddly enough, the city treasurer, Eunice Wilder, the mayor's ex-wife. The city had withheld more than $1.8 million in funding and the school system said it couldn't pay its bills.

The court upheld the mayor's position. The school board tried to appeal the decision to the Virginia Supreme Court, but it was denied. The tight release of funding would continue just as the mayor wanted.

Wilder was gleeful with the outcome. "Once again, the courts ruled that the lawsuits brought against the Mayor and the City Administration are fruitless and pointless. Rather than open their books for public inspection, the School Board chose to waste additional tax dollars by suing the Mayor and the Chief Financial Officer, at a time when the School Board had complained about a lack of funds to move out of City Hall, as had been requested for several years that it so to do."[99]

Meanwhile, Wilder said he was still waiting for information from the superintendent about which schools should be closed—and when. "If there's no answer, it will further postpone the time I can recommend that schools can be built," he told council members during an informal retreat aimed at finding ways to collaborate and iron out issues between the executive and legislative branches of the city's new form of government.[100]

Yet Wilder wasn't the only one complaining about the schools. Yes, he did lead the chorus. But he was joined by two school board members. School board member Carol A.O. Wolf, a colorful advocate long known for promoting adequate access for the disabled, often made critical statements that distinguished her from most of her colleagues. When Wilder first announced the need for an external audit, she quickly supported him. "There is no excuse good enough to justify not cooperating with an audit of the public's money," Wolf said.[101]

School Board member Keith West also sounded the alarm for more openness and spoke candidly about the school board's unwillingness to collaborate with the mayor. He lowered the boom when asked whether the mayor should withhold funding for new schools until some old ones were closed. His comments lifted the curtain—from the inside out. And they were broadcast on Jimmy Barrett's WRVA morning show for all to hear.

> The public spends lavishly on the Richmond school system, and I think they have a right to know how well that money is being spent. To me, it's a non-controversial idea that you would have somebody to come in and take a look at that, especially when you have so much evidence year after year, report after report, saying that a lot of money is not being

spent as well as it can.

But year after year, we've maintained a system of way too many schools for the number of students we have. That means we're spending money on partially empty buildings rather than better places where it would benefit the kids more.

If you look a couple of years ago . . . when the mayor came out with the City of the Future plan he gave the school system, the school board, the public, a wonderful gift saying that we're going to build you new schools and the only thing he asked was a plan for which schools you are going to close, so that we can free up the money to build these new schools. The school board came back with this very provocative document saying we're not going to close anything until you actually build us something else. How is that going about biting the hand that feeds you?

The school board has brought a lot of these problems on itself. I really do wish we would get away from that type of attitude and start trying to work together to benefit the kids rather than trying to take this stand about who's in charge of what.[102]

The mayor criticized the city auditor's delay in preparing his second report on school system spending. He took issue with the auditor's claim that staff turnover was a contributing factor, as reflected in this press release:

The City will continue to lose money until the City Auditor completes the financial audit of the school system operation, and other audits, to help identify areas of wasteful spending. We are concerned that recent statements would lead the public to believe that inadequate staff is the reason the requested audits have not been completed.

The City Auditor reports to the council, and as such, the council should hold him accountable for getting the job done. It's not a question of money because within the past five years, the auditor's staff has almost doubled, and his annual budget has more than doubled.[103]

The second audit report, issued in April 2008, revealed numerous discrepancies described as "gross noncompliance" with procurement law. The school system paid out $18 million in unauthorized purchase orders while more than $38 million was paid for invoices that were generated by school employees themselves rather than by the vendors, which is the standard practice. The school system received services from a construction company owned by a relative of a purchasing officer in charge of construction; another contract was held by an immediate family member of a plant-services department employee. Close to $7 million could be saved annually with stronger financial controls and streamlined purchasing procedures, the report said.[104]

A scathing editorial titled "Obscene" in the *Richmond Times–Dispatch* described the situation:

> It has been almost two years since Richmond auditor Umesh Dalal began examining the finances of the city's public schools. More than a year ago he released the scathing results of his initial review. His findings were limited, however, by the school system's reluctance to open all of its books. Mayor Doug Wilder eventually had to pry them open by withholding nonpayroll funds until school officials agreed to comply.
>
> Now we know why the school system was so reluctant to let the sun shine in. Dalal's new, more thorough report exposes a tapestry of inexcusable waste, inefficiency, and nepotism.
>
> City residents have long known that the per-pupil expenditure in Richmond is one of the highest in the state; last year it rose by nearly $800 per student, to $13,168. Dalal has provided evidence that far too much of that money might as well be tossed into an incinerator, for all the good it does. The school system evidently fails to abide by even rudimentary purchasing and accounting standards, and the result is a level of waste that cannot be considered anything but obscene. [105]

Within days of the report's release, School Superintendent Deborah Jewell-Sherman announced her resignation. Wilder issued this statement to the media, "Suffice it to say that Dr. Jewell-Sherman has brought improvement to the academics of the school system since taking the job, and she has received ample credit for that."[106]

School board member West said he had planned to call for the superintendent's resignation at the next school board meeting, but in view of her announcement to leave, ultimately did not need to. "Somebody has to be held responsible," West said. "We've known about some of these things [identified by the auditor] for a long time."[107]

Aside from the auditor's report, another aggravating factor was an Americans with Disabilities Act (ADA) lawsuit brought against the mayor, city council and school board for limited access for the disabled. Most of the city's schools were built well before the ADA came along. Wilder often noted that the ADA had been in effect nearly fifteen years before he became mayor. He did not believe the city was responsible for what he described as the school system's neglect of the issue.

In a federal court decision coming shortly after Wilder unveiled his City of the Future plan, the judge ruled that while finding no fault on the part of the city government in the ADA case, the city must cover the cost to retrofit schools for the disabled. Wilder then appealed the court's decision that the city had to pay for ADA improvements. The 4th U.S. Circuit Court of Appeals reversed the lower court's ruling and agreed with Wilder that the school system was responsible for its own actions.

The court recognized that the school board had the duty to use capital funds to make the necessary improvements to its schools, and that the city had done what it was required to do. The city funds the school system; it's then up to the school system to fix its buildings, the mayor noted.

"Even the lower court's ruling pointed out that the City had done nothing wrong and, for that reason, we thought it should be appealed so as not to give the impression that the City had done anything wrong. Even at that time, the lower court said the City had not engaged in any conscious or purposeful discrimination."[108]

When the court later ruled that the city did not have to pay the school board's legal fees, Wilder stated in another press release: "Today's decision further confirms our position because the judge has found no fault with the City Administration in this ADA (Americans with Disabilities Act) case while also indicating that the Richmond Public School System had breached its duty with regard to ADA compliance."[109]

In numerous speeches since that ruling, Wilder pointed out that the city had provided $134 million solely for capital projects since the ADA law took effect in 1992. However, by 2007, only four of the city's sixty school buildings were considered accessible. An article in his *Visions* newsletter titled "Where has the school money gone?" showed an image of a toilet stopped up with dollar bills. The school system's inaction on consolidating low-enrollment schools only led to digging a deeper hole for itself, the mayor noted, because new or renovated schools would have been ADA compliant.

In his annual State of the City address in January 2007, Wilder continued to criticize the pace of academic improvement in the city schools.

> Yes, it is true that a majority of the schools in the City system now, finally, meet minimum accreditation requirements. So the system passes that test.
>
> But when it comes to keeping our kids in school, providing them with a quality education, and preparing them for higher education or good paying jobs, the school system as a whole is failing miserably; and isn't that standard—our children's future—the only standard that should really matter?

The mayor proposed spending $169 million to create two charter school complexes—one for technology and vocational education and the other focused on math and science—to equip students with workforce skills to support the city's diverse economy. As charter schools, they would require school system approval but would then operate independently.

"By establishing these centers of academic excellence as charter schools, we can ensure that they will be free of the bureaucratic encumbrances that have held far too many of our schools back for far too long," Wilder said.

"These charter schools will be significant steps in the right direction, but they are but one example of the fundamental shift in philosophy, approach, and commitment that must be made in order to ensure the best for our children in the future."

Council rejected the mayor's charter school proposals, as Wilder lamented that no schools were being closed. "I had offered to build fifteen new schools as part of a $300 million dollar 'City of the Future' program to advance our children's opportunities for academic success, without requiring any increase in taxes. Yet Schools' continuing resistance put an end to this tremendous opportunity to replace our antiquated school facilities," he wrote in his newsletter.[110]

He soon shifted course, telling several officials at the city teachers' annual back-to-school convocation that he wanted his original fifteen-school plan to return as the centerpiece of his City of the Future program. Many were hopeful that his conciliatory remarks might encourage school officials to jump-start plans to close old schools and plan for new ones.

It did not happen.

Getting Sued

Wilder tested the limits of his "strong mayor" position by taking bold steps, unimagined by most, that led to lawsuits brought against him. Aside from legal tangles with the school system, Wilder battled over who had authority for the support staff working for city council and the city assessor. The mayor claimed he held the authority to hire and fire those employees.

Council only had authority over the offices of the city clerk, city auditor and city attorney, Wilder told council. "The simple math is this: when it comes to positions, council has three appointments," he advised. "I have one, that being the chief administrative officer, and the CAO . . . has all the others."[111]

Wilder relied on the wording of the city charter to challenge council's authority to hire anyone else. By this time, though, council had already spent $700,000 for new staff positions including a public relations professional. Without assistance from the city administration, council realized it needed to increase its own support staff to try to keep Wilder in check.

Council had been hiring employees to fill new positions that the city charter had not authorized, Wilder claimed. Those positions would have been hired by the city manager under Richmond's old structure of government. However, now the executive branch (mayor) held the authority instead of the legislative branch (city council).

The mayor later returned to remind council that the employees had not been hired in accordance with the city charter. In an open letter to council, Wilder fired the first broadside that smacked council right between the eyes.

> Almost one month has passed since I last appeared before you to advise the Council of its practice of appointing to positions when it has no authority to do so. This letter continues that discussion, as I have heard nothing from any of you regarding the issue since that occasion.

This Administration has performed a review of the positions which are affected: those positions are the City Assessor, Council Liaisons, Council Chief of Staff, Council Policy Analyst, Council Public Relations Specialist, and the Director of Legislative Services. Council's appointment to each of these positions is void. Further, the appointments made by the individuals who hold these positions are likewise void.

In a bold but not uncharacteristic move, Wilder announced that the fifty-four employees who made up the council and city assessor staffs would need to reapply for their jobs within five days. "Should none have applied by [the deadline], their failure to do so will be construed as a lack of interest in continuing employment in these positions . . . [and] my Administration will move forward to advertise the vacancies for permanent employment ..." Council's director of legislative services did not re-apply for her position and Deputy CAO Harry Black fired her a few days later.

Again, it was time for dueling press releases, with the war of words reaching full throttle. "Mayor Speaks on Council Staffing Situation" headlined the mayor's press release, indicating the positions were being advertised in area newspapers and that interviews would soon begin. Council followed with its own release, with a headline that blared, "Mayor's Action's Illegal," saying the mayor had no authority over city council employees.

In his *Visions* newsletter, Wilder offered his rationale for bringing up the hiring issue.

In calling for employees to reapply for their positions, it was not my desire to strip Council of any needed staff. Rather, it is to be assured that the employees who fill those positions have been hired in a manner consistent with the authority delegated by the Charter, i.e., through the proper reporting chain.

However, rather than sit down with me to discuss my understanding or misunderstanding of the Charter, as I publicly offered several times, City Council chose instead to sue me, my chief administrative officer and my director of human resources.

This dispute not only highlights Council's refusal to accept that it no longer controls the executive/administrative branch of City government, but it also reflects Council's unwillingness to accept that its authority is defined by the Charter.[112]

After a circuit court judge ruled that Wilder had no authority over the employees, he appealed the case to the Virginia Supreme Court. Until it could be resolved, he backed off requiring that employees submit to interviews to keep their jobs.

Black's adherence in carrying out the mayor's wishes, however, did not sit well with several council members. On the night the mayor first informed council about the hiring issue, the council rejected the mayor's request to confirm Black as the city's acting CAO. A majority of council members again refused to consider Black during a formal council hearing demanded by the mayor. The mayor defended Black, saying council should blame him instead. "I'm the bad guy, not Mr. Black," Wilder told a reporter afterward.[113]

Disputes over power were further complicated by the ambiguous language in the city charter defining the role of the city attorney, a position held by Norman B. Sales. The language seemed all-encompassing.

> The city attorney shall be the chief legal advisor of the council, the mayor, the chief administrative officer and all departments, boards, commissions and agencies of the city in all matters affecting the interests of the city.

With the charter's broad language, however, the question soon became: who did the city attorney represent if the mayor and city council disagreed? Wilder repeatedly brought up the subject with council, such as in this letter to Council President Loupassi in July 2006.

> Though I have previously spoken and written to you on several occasions regarding the City Attorney, to date, the concerns I have expressed have gone unaddressed.
>
> When disputes between the executive and legislative branches arise, as have already been the case, the City Attorney will be called upon to render advice. As a lawyer, *you* know that he is ethically unable to advise both parties, so which party do you believe he will continue to assist? The City Attorney has publicly stated his obligation is to serve the city council.

And he has proven his loyalty, in this regard, time and again.

Wilder framed the predicament: the City Attorney is appointed by city council.

After the school board sued him over the city's monthly funding of the school system, Wilder scolded the city attorney in a March 2007 letter that he cc'd to council.

> The School Board's case against Chief Financial Officer Harry Black and me is, to date, the best evidence that you are confused as to your legal responsibility to the City. This lawsuit is not against the City Council . . . it is, in essence, against the City itself: your professed client.
>
> Nonetheless, you determined that you could not represent the City because the City Council (who is not a party to the litigation at all) might take a position that is adverse to that of the City's. How does this make sense? (Please realize that I do not really expect you to answer that question; you cannot, in light of your previous protestations or the tortured logic you have in the past applied to your situation.)
>
> Face it: you will never be able to provide representation to the Mayor without having such representation first cleared with (and, tacitly, approved by) the City Council. This case cements your quandary as well as your tentativeness – neither quality is of value in a lawyer.

Wilder pointed out the irony that in another lawsuit, he was sued by the city attorney who, by charter definition, was supposed to represent him. That lawsuit, Commonwealth of Virginia v. Members of the City Council of the City of Richmond, existed long before Wilder was elected. However, Wilder claimed he was dragged into the litigation as a defendant after city council asked the city attorney to include him. Commonly known as the Public Safety lawsuit, the case was brought by the Richmond judges against the city for the alleged unsafe conditions of downtown's Public Safety Building, which provided space for some of their courtrooms.

Due to differing opinions between council and the mayor, each side had to hire outside legal counsel. The city attorney couldn't represent either of them.

"Without offering one word in its own defense, the council entered into a consent decree with the judges, which immediately exposed the City to a liability of $73 million to comply because the Council had put far more things in the consent decree than the lawsuit ever contemplated," Wilder wrote in his *Visions* newsletter. The mayor was able to replace council's costly agreement with an alternate plan that expanded the Manchester Courthouse to provide additional courtroom space. He said his alternative plan saved the city $34 million.[114]

The Public Safety lawsuit was one of a handful against the mayor. Each case required outside counsel due to the conflict of the city attorney's role in representing both sides. Meanwhile, outside legal costs climbed to more than a million dollars. The litigation "is bleeding the city," he told council. "Every time something happens, you have to go get a lawyer and I have to get a lawyer. The public doesn't want to see that."[115]

In his four years as mayor, Wilder never filed a lawsuit against anyone. He always smiled with satisfaction in being able to say that.

The Police Chief

Wilder and Police Chief Rodney Monroe shared a strong professional and personal bond, regularly meeting for lunch to trade notes. The chief proved his mettle early on by significantly reducing the city's crime rate. His experience in dealing with youth gangs equipped him for the significant problems facing the city. Monroe also played a significant role in keeping kids in the classroom. During his first year as chief, he led an initiative for the city to manage the truancy program instead of the school system.

"Richmond's tolerance of truancy will cease. We're gonna stop it," Wilder announced at a press conference held outside a local elementary school.

While some school officials seemed to resent Wilder's involvement, School Board Chairman Stephen Johnson welcomed the police department's involvement and commended Wilder's ability to obtain nearly $700,000 in state funding.

The new truancy program introduced the standard benchmark of three unexcused absences as the trigger point for intervention services, such as scheduling a conference with a child's parents. By that measure, nearly 8,800 of the school system's 23,000 public school students—or 38 percent—were considered truant. Under the old way, the school system did not designate a student as truant until there were ten unexcused absences.[116]

The city launched a public information campaign featuring televised announcements for citizens to report truant children through a confidential hotline at 646-ABCD. The mayor also released a report outlining ten issues for which the school system provided truancy data to the city administration. Broad issues. Kids were being counted as absent when school buses arrived late. Tardy students were marked as absent for the entire day. Some schools recorded daily attendance at 9:15 a.m. while others took a count as late as 2:30 p.m.

"The attendance list has been a nightmare," noted the 8th item in the report. "Citywide, we are experiencing that after the schools' attendance issues have been updated and resolved they are not being removed in a timely manner. . . This presents problems for the staff that have to call parents and inquire as to why their children are being truant and to find out that the students are attending other schools. Needless to say, parents are very angry that it appears our staff does not have the correct information and have to ask them what school the child attends."

Responding to School Superintendent Deborah Jewell-Sherman's letter in February 2006 about the school system's improved collaboration with the police staff, Wilder shot back with his own letter immediately disagreeing. He reminded Jewell-Sherman that the city had to go to court to get the school system to cooperate.

> You know that your office strongly and strenuously objected to our administration's involvement at all. Contrary to assertions in your letter, you were not providing the cooperation that you now claim you have provided.
>
> I also want to point out to you that we have had a very difficult time getting information and had to go to court and have the records of students subpoenaed before we could begin to do anything.
>
> Your office resisted turning any of this information over to us, claiming some sort of privacy concerns. I find it very difficult to see how that could be the case, when we paid for our schools to operate and paid for the operation to be successful and should be entitled to know just what is going on if anything. Shouldn't the Richmond Police Department be entitled

to that as a matter of enforcement?

Wilder also emphasized the responsibility parents should have for their child's education and welfare. He proposed the school system issue "parent report cards" that would grade them on parental involvement such as helping their kids with homework and making sure their kids showed up for school.

"I think it is a great idea," agreed school board chairman Johnson, who was approached on the idea by Wilder's senior policy advisor, Paul Goldman. "We will probably get some flak from some parents, but we need to start somewhere. We need to start holding the parents responsible for the actions of their children and for how their children are progressing in school. You know, on the school side, we can only do so much."[117] Wilder also planned to meet with the school superintendent about the idea, but in the end, the report cards were never produced.

Aside from contentious issues like truancy, Police Chief Monroe participated in lighter moments involving local students. He joined Wilder in hosting several "Youth Forums" where students asked questions ranging from summer jobs and cafeteria food to sexually transmitted diseases.

I recall one Youth Forum, held in the John Marshall High School auditorium, that triumphantly began with the police chief and mayor marching down the opposite aisles toward the stage, holding shiny brass cymbals that they clapped in unison. As they made their way, a string of tuba players followed behind, somewhat resembling a New Orleans second line.

It got the students' attention, for sure.

Wilder and Monroe continued their cymbal bashing on stage, swaying back and forth in unison, before settling down to take questions. All eyes were on the two most powerful figures of city government. It was fun to see the mayor laughing riotously and having so much fun that he excitedly uttered "God D---" under his breath. Perhaps no one else noticed at the time except our videographer, but the program was discreetly edited before airing on the city's public access cable channel. We made sure of that.

Another thing I especially remember about Monroe was his genuine affection and admiration for Wilder. In 2006, the mayor was grand marshal at an annual Hull Street Christmas Parade in Southside. It was his second Christmas as mayor. Wearing a tan jacket and jodhpurs, Canadian Mountie hat and dark shades, he led the parade atop a handsome chestnut horse, its mane flapping in the breeze, yet seeming a bit skittish.

Monroe, sensing the horse was nervous, took hold of its halter and led the horse along the parade route as the mayor smiled and waved from the saddle. He wanted to make sure the horse wouldn't bolt and topple the mayor. Monroe told me later that the horse seemed unnerved by the clank of the vendor carts along the parade route.

Monroe's success in reducing crime was noticed by other cities. Not yet a year on the job in Richmond, the chief was mentioned as a replacement for the retiring DC police chief, with whom he once worked. Monroe had spent twenty-two years there, rising to the position of assistant chief. He knew the DC terrain well.

As the job rumors picked up, Monroe informed Wilder, who then replied to him, "You're not going anywhere." Monroe smiled when he recalled having that conversation with the mayor.

FACING PROTESTS FROM TEACHERS TO PIMPS & HUSTLERS

The mayor seldom shied away from confrontation. He loved a good protest; it reflected "the will of the people."

One day across the street from City Hall, historic preservationist Jennie Dotts and two dozen Alliance to Conserve Old Richmond Neighborhoods (ACORN) supporters held a protest against the state's plans to demolish the Murphy Hotel, a grand lady in her heyday that had been converted to offices a decade before.

Wilder cut over to meet with them, his security detail following behind. He immediately charmed everyone by his appearance there. Just two months earlier, when he unveiled his City of the Future plan, he had proposed that the stately twelve-story building should be saved and converted into an urban law center and dormitory.

He was ready to speak up.

> We have an issue here in the downtown area: a bill is working its way through the General Assembly that includes funds to demolish and replace the Murphy Hotel, this beautiful hotel that was built in 1913.
>
> WRONG!!! Do you agree with me?
>
> Our City of the Future plan would like to see this beau-

tiful building renovated to become an urban law center as a joint venture between the University of Richmond, VCU and possibly William and Mary.

Architectural consultants say the best choice for the property is to refurbish the building, and that the least desirable course is to demolish the building and build anew on the site.

At one time, the old City Hall was being considered for demolition. How wrong was that? We look back now and question it.

Floating the idea for the urban law center gained little traction. Still, the protestors knew that the mayor supported their mission to preserve the building. However, the fate of the Murphy Hotel met a sad ending. The state tore down the hotel in 2007, eventually replacing it with a block-long parking garage facing Broad Street. Preservationists decried the replacement as a disgrace.

As often as not, Wilder's unexpected appearances faced hostile audiences. He pointedly confronted a group of Richmond PTA presidents and parents who urged him to "stop playing games with our children's education," according to their press release. About twenty-five people assembled outside Linwood Holton Elementary School to protest the city's funding of the school system on a monthly rather than quarterly basis. Organizers of the well-publicized rally even created a new website—TellWilderNO.org—to promote their cause.

It was time to face the protesters. A local news broadcast showed the mayor stepping from his Grand Marquis and striding directly toward the crowd, with Harry Black and me trailing slightly behind. We spent about thirty minutes there, with the mayor working the crowd, ready to discuss the need to eliminate school system waste with anyone willing to debate him. With the cameras rolling, Wilder began his courtroom defense.

"Now I ask you as a parent and you as a parent," the mayor summoned to the people gathered around him, "do you have any idea where the money is being spent? Yes, or no." For emphasis, he elongated the word "idea" in a robust, lawyerly manner.

Some parents claimed that the power struggle between the city and school system "would hurt" their children, while another called Wilder "a bully." The mayor, though, dismissed any notion that the new funding plan would harm the children, as his comments were captured by a local television crew for the evening news:

> All this hocus pocus about somebody going without food, that's not going to happen, not on my watch, nor will they be going without anything that they should have. The whole name of the game is education for kids' sake, and I'm going to be there, as I always have been.
>
> I don't mind people being upset with me. It's the story of my life.[118]

In his office later that afternoon, Wilder commented on his confrontation with the parents. "That will show them that I'm not afraid to face them and venture into the belly of the God-damned beast!" He spoke with an air of exaggerated indignation, and we both chuckled about his fearless foray into the unsuspecting crowd.

On another occasion, the mayor took particular offense when a group of citizens—including a former Richmond commonwealth's attorney—met at a downtown restaurant to discuss claims of local police brutality. Wilder labeled them "pimps and hustlers." The term "pimp" generally describes those who exploit others for their own gain. However, he observed that the term "pimp" had gradually transformed from its negative connotation to have an admirable meaning within hip-hop culture. Wilder's comment was timely, coming just days before the song, "It's Hard Out Here for a Pimp" from the movie "Hustle & Flow" won an Academy Award for best song.

His remark, made to a local broadcast reporter, drew fury from the restaurant patrons. David Hicks, the former commonwealth's attorney, was representing the family of a man shot dead by Richmond police in front of his home after running from an officer. Activists also noted another incident where a city schoolteacher was manhandled by police at a traffic stop on her way home from a dialysis treatment. "Had this been a white mayor who called anyone hustlers and pimps, we would have run this mayor out of town," exclaimed Daryl Holland, executive director of Youth for Social Change.[119]

Wilder, in one of his *Richmond Times-Dispatch* commentaries, decried that the "pimp" term was being glorified in a way that lessened "that sense of common decency and values instilled in us in African-American communities since the days of slavery."

"Those who continue to pimp the race issue for their selfish advancement by lowering moral standards may make money, but they rise to another level of pimping," Wilder wrote.[120] Days later when Phil Wilayto of the *Richmond Defender* newspaper asked what was meant by "pimp" and "hustler," the mayor simply replied to me: "The public knows. And I would be disappointed if it didn't generate some comment from those like Phil Wilayto."

A few months later the mayor encountered another protest rally, led by Holland, about allegations of police brutality and the mayor's cutbacks in school funding. Wilder, on his way to lunch, noticed the cluster of people on the corner at City Hall and came over to speak and playfully challenge what they claimed to be a "Day of Solidarity" protest. Waving his finger in the air, as reporters held their mikes toward him, the mayor said to the protesters, "Let me ask you a question. If you or anyone else has any evidence at all that you think should be brought before any investigators looking at police brutality, please bring it!"

Holland and his handful of followers grinned at each other and seemed thrilled the mayor had made an appearance. Their animated exchange lasted all of two minutes and then the mayor walked over to his waiting car, waving to other bystanders along the way. He ignored a reporter's question yelled to him about pimps and hustlers. Wilder later mocked the gathering. "There was no group. There was no expression," he told a *Style Weekly* reporter, noting that eight or so participants did not constitute a protest. "How many does it take to make a protest demonstration? That is the question. Next witness."[121]

Goldman's Departure

It didn't take too long for Paul Goldman, the mayor's senior policy advisor, to stir controversy. Shortly after the mayor's first year in office, he would be gone.

"I could have strangled him," Wilder privately said about the circumstances that led to Goldman's resignation in February 2006.

Christmas approached and the mayor was busy with tasks as diverse as school system funding, a new downtown Hilton Hotel in the works, and the annual holiday toy drive. Then along came a campaign funding disclosure report that dropped like a bombshell. The phones began to ring. A report surfaced that National Consulting Group, run by Goldman, received a $15,000 consulting fee for Get-Out-The-Vote services provided to Tim Kaine. The payment came only three days after Wilder endorsed Kaine for governor.

The optics of the situation posed a major dilemma for Wilder. Press inquiries intensified. Both Wilder and Kaine denied any connection between the payment and the endorsement. Shortly before his work for Kaine became known, Goldman privately acknowledged he had been paid for political consulting work for Virginia Delegate Donald McEachin the year before. It was the only outside consulting work he had recently done, he told the mayor. Then the Kaine connection surfaced. Goldman had not sought permission from the city to do any outside consulting work.

Goldman's evasion of being truthful bore a profound impact on Wilder after learning about the consulting work for Kaine. Wilder was angry and needed to publicly impose a just reprimand to address Goldman's conduct.

For a candidate who had promised to drain the "cesspool of corruption and inefficiency" at City Hall, Wilder knew he had a stench of a mess to mop up. And it was highly embarrassing to have come from a key member of his team.

Wilder's predicament was the topic of an editorial in the *Richmond Free Press*: "If taxpayers are paying Mr. Goldman a salary of $145,000 as a city employee to help deal with Richmond's myriad of challenges and opportunities, how does he have time to pull in side-money working for someone else? The City of Richmond has had far too much shady activity in the last few years, with some city officials going to jail, for the mayor and the city to wink at this latest episode of bad behavior by Mr. Goldman."[122]

Goldman's free-wheeling habits often stretched the boundaries. He was not shy in speaking with reporters. He also maintained a separate GoldmanUSA@aol.com email account on his work computer, which some presumed functioned as a way to thwart Freedom of Information Act (FOIA) requests. The issue festered for weeks. Wilder needed to announce a solution. "I'm running out of patience on this," he stewed about the situation.

Editorials in the *Richmond Times-Dispatch* suggested that Goldman would need to either return the money to Kaine or donate it to charity, but Wilder found an alternative remedy.

Just a few days before Christmas, Goldman was suspended without pay for six weeks. That equaled six weeks of his salary, or $15,000, the same amount as the consulting fee. From that point on, press inquiries about Goldman went unanswered as it became a "personnel issue." Not long afterward, the city's human resources department issued a new policy requiring advance written approval before an employee could take on a second job. During the time that Goldman was away from City Hall, he asked permission to perform consulting work to make ends meet. The request was denied. By the time his suspension ended, he chose to resign rather than return.

His poignant February 15, 2006, resignation letter to Wilder reflected the close bond between the two men. He reminisced about their days together on the campaign trail.

Dear Doug,

In the very near future, it will be four years since finding the little-noticed provision in the city charter which set in motion the 2003 referendum drive and then the 2004 passage of the law to create a popularly elected Mayor. I remember first telling you about discovering this provision and your reaction.

The other day my son happened to see the actual petition to the Richmond Circuit Court, with his father as the petitioner. Actually, there are two petitions, as I didn't get it right the first time.

So it has been a very historical 4 years for the City and the State, which now has a new model for local government.

I truly enjoyed being allowed to play a leadership role in all the facets of this change, especially creating a bipartisan coalition to give Richmond the opportunity to be all it can be.

Richmond has made great progress in this period and the best is yet to come. In my future writings and other involvements, I will continue to be an advocate for all these necessary changes.

With things moving so well on the right track, it is now the right time for me to focus my energies on other projects.

Accordingly, I am submitting my resignation effective today.

I wish you continued great success. It is a long way from Cujo's Cave, that's for sure.

Sincerely,

Paul

At City Hall that day, a one-sentence press release about his resignation was prepared but never issued. From my vantage point, the two men had no further contact. Goldman, the mayor's longtime ally and idea-maker who had been with Wilder since the 1980s, was no longer welcomed at City Hall.

Yet soon after, the Richmond School Board wanted to hear what Goldman had to say about building new schools with City of the Future money. A month after Goldman resigned, the school board's facilities committee invited him to speak on the theme of "Can I help bridge the gap?" Plans for his speech were announced in the local press. Goldman issued an advance statement as well.

"I have been asked to speak about my work/ideas that laid the foundation for the new/modernized school construction part of Mayor Wilder's 'City of the Future' initiative. SO MY GOAL FOR TOMORROW: Just what I told Channel 12 tonight when they interviewed me about what I'm going to say: TRY AND BRING PEOPLE TOGETHER on this so we can get all the oars pulling in the same direction. It is a 'we' thing, not a 'me' thing."

The next morning, I prepared a press statement for the mayor, which was instead issued under my name. It was a blunt reminder to Goldman on where things stood.

> For some time now, Mr. Goldman has been separated from the City Administration. As such, he has no further involvement one way or the other with regard to any of Mayor Wilder's initiatives to advance the city. This includes the Mayor's "City of the Future" plan. While Mr. Goldman is free to promote himself as best suits his causes, it should be evident that any efforts by Mr. Goldman for self-involvement regarding any of the Mayor's initiatives could prove to be counterproductive and non-beneficial.[123]

The next day, an article in the *Richmond Times-Dispatch* covered Goldman's speech and included my statement almost in its entirety. When a reporter asked about it, Goldman replied, "I'm not going to take anything Linwood has to say seriously."[124] Actually, I didn't take any insult with that. I heard nothing more from Goldman for the remainder of Wilder's term. And for that, I was thankful.

CHAPTER FOUR

Water, Water, Everywhere:
Floods and Cesspools and Sinkholes

Historic Shockoe Bottom

Wilder already knew he had a problem in Shockoe Bottom. It wasn't so much the weekend nightclub activities that might result in early morning shootings. Although that was a problem, too. It wasn't even a man-made problem. Instead, it fell from the heavens: in the form of severe thunderstorms.

Major flooding occurred when the rainfall run-off from the upper Downtown, Church Hill, and Highland Park areas gravitated to the "bottom" with no place to go. It was an age-old problem, characteristic of very old cities like Richmond. And it hit Wilder twice without any warning. Shockoe Bottom's ancient sewer system simply could not contain the flow. The Bottom's inability to adequately handle torrential rains—and the high probability of flooding—were well known. People there suffered time and again. Property owners had long been encouraged to carry flood insurance due to their location.

Memories were still fresh of the widespread flooding and destruction caused by the remnants of Hurricane Gaston in late August 2004. Within an eight-hour period, as much as fourteen inches of rain fell on an already waterlogged Richmond—and much of that water eventually funneled its way down to Shockoe Bottom. The damage was enormous. Twenty blocks of the Bottom were under water, while more than 100 roads across the city were closed. A massive sinkhole almost swallowed a house at 31st and Grace Street. A brick retaining wall at nearby St. John's Church collapsed. Portions of highway crumbled away in many flood-prone areas across the city.

Rushing waves of water as high as ten feet floated vehicles like toy boxcars. Shops and restaurants were swallowed up, ruined by mud and debris. Residents were trapped in their apartments above storefronts. Boats had to be brought in to rescue people. Police cordoned off the entire area for the long process of towing out dozens of destroyed, stacked-up cars. In the Richmond area, the flooding killed nine people and caused an estimated $60 million in damage to 42 businesses in Shockoe Bottom. City water engineers described it as a once-in-a-5,900-year rainfall.[125]

Recovery measures in Shockoe Bottom continued at a slow pace, with complaints the city wasn't doing enough to help bring the area back to its feet. Some businesses never returned; the lifetime investment losses were too great to carry on. Insurance companies wouldn't cover losses due to what they termed "an act of God."

In May 2005, Wilder appointed a fifteen-person Shockoe Advisory Committee for input on ways to improve the larger Shockoe area extending from Shockoe Slip to the eastern city line along the James River. The committee later recommended infrastructure upgrades to improve drainage, stepped-up code enforcement on blighted properties, and showcasing the 17th Street Farmers' Market to spur economic development in the area.

Then in mid-August 2006, almost two years after Gaston, it happened again. A thunderstorm dumped three inches of rain in about ninety minutes. Recurrent horrors of PTSD swept over those who worked and lived in Shockoe Bottom. The flash flooding, reaching up to five feet in some places, wiped out the interiors of many Shockoe Bottom businesses. Merchants felt the pain and frustration of having to clean up, take losses, and start over. The rainwater rose so quickly that many residents found themselves once again trapped in their second and third-floor apartments. The heavy rains created a mudslide that caused widespread property damage, submerged vehicles, and closed roads to traffic.

Wilder immediately issued a Declaration of Local Emergency. It would enable Shockoe Bottom merchants and others to appeal to the Commonwealth of Virginia for financial assistance. "It's very regrettable that the Shockoe Bottom merchants and others were impacted by the thunderstorm," the mayor lamented in a press release. He had seen the damage up close, as he lived in a Shockoe Bottom apartment at the time. "I am asking the City Council to ratify this Declaration of Local Emergency so as to expedite the assistance that can be provided to our citizens."[126]

A week later, Wilder held a Town Hall meeting in Shockoe Bottom to inform the public on what the city would do to address the flooding. The mayor and a panel of city officials unveiled a $20 million plan to upgrade Shockoe Bottom's sewer system with dozens of new and replacement drains that would lessen the impact of future downpours. The meeting drew more than one-hundred people who were desperate for financial help, and ready to tell their stories. Wilder's plan involved eight phases of construction to solve a variety of drainage issues. More storm drains would be added at the 17th Street Farmers' Market. Drainage in the adjacent higher-level neighborhoods would be redirected to reduce the gravitational flow.

Still, city officials acknowledged that those improvements alone would not solve a rapid flash flooding like the one that had just occurred. "This will really get the area up to being able to address a twenty-five-year event and that would be something that we could build on even further," explained CAO William Harrell. "It is important to note that if we had a similar event that occurred the other day, we would continue to have problems. What this will do will be able to address the issues of nuisance flooding."[127]

Some city council members questioned what Wilder had done with a $1.9 million appropriation in 2005 to conduct drainage infrastructure studies following the devastation caused by Gaston. Feeling it was not getting sufficient answers to questions, council withheld approval of the emergency declaration. Wilder explained he wanted to transfer the $1.9 million from one budget category to another, to become part of the $20 million package for drainage improvements. The stalemate with council became a topic in the next issue of his *Visions* newsletter.

With a headline that read "Many Ask Questions About Delay," the mayor wrote:

> Why City Council delayed money for flood control relief in Shockoe Bottom is a question many organizations and citizens are now asking. Heavy rains, inadequate sewer line capacity and the resulting flood damage have long plagued Shockoe Bottom, one of the City's increasingly vibrant com-

mercial and residential areas. We cannot believe that holding up money to help the residents and merchants in Shockoe Bottom serves any good purpose.[128]

Two weeks later, council finally approved the emergency measure that allowed state funding to be released to people with flood damage. By then, however, the city was facing a new problem. It, too, was unexpected, and caused by torrential rains, yet it was far different in scope than what had just happened in Shockoe Bottom.

NORTHSIDE'S BATTERY PARK

Only two weeks after the most recent flooding in Shockoe Bottom, another catastrophe hit Richmond. Another Declaration of Local Emergency became necessary. In Northside, the low-lying tennis and basketball courts at Battery Park transformed into a large and fetid lake. It became surreal to residents of that tranquil, tree-lined neighborhood. Wilder knew the area well. The brick colonial where he had raised his family was within sight, just a block up the hill.

On September 1, remnants of Tropical Storm Ernesto poured down more than two inches of rain over two days. The damage to Battery Park's aging infrastructure quickly became apparent. As the rain came down and the floodwaters began to rise in the tennis courts, the mayor authorized an emergency evacuation. In only two hours, some 420 households had been moved out safely. While most would eventually return to their homes, other dwellings were condemned. The city arranged temporary housing for more than 120 families, also providing financial assistance for mortgage and rent, vouchers for food, and moving and storage expenses.

Wilder, who as governor understood the levers of power, became the numero uno cheerleader in pulling the community together and spearheading relief efforts. "The men and women of the City's workforce as well as the families of Battery Park deserve tremendous praise for their collective efforts to ensure everyone's well-being," he wrote in his newsletter.[129]

After the rain ended, neighbors and city officials walked along the outer perimeter of the wide mass of dark water, assessing what to do next. Local camera crews on the scene suddenly had a strangely unusual topic to report on for that day, and many more to follow. For Wilder, Battery Park became the second of a one-two gut punch, following so close on the heels of Shockoe Bottom's recurrent flooding.

City inspectors discovered the flooding was due to a collapsed sewer line, buried more than ninety feet deep in the city's old landfill of compressed garbage and fill-dirt. With the sewer line partially blocked with debris, there was no place for millions of gallons of rainwater and sewage to go. City officials had already spotted a fifty-foot-wide sinkhole at the landfill as the rains still poured. They later found that an eight-foot by fourteen-foot tunnel section had also collapsed, some 400 feet from the sinkhole.

Wilder was quick to own the problem. "Help is on the way. This happened on my watch, and I'll fix it, bottom line," he told the *Richmond Free Press*. Federal Emergency Management Agency (FEMA) officials arrived a week later to assess the situation to determine eligibility for federal aid.[130]

During our morning meeting with the mayor, Harrell showed us an old newspaper clipping about landfills. Locating municipal landfills in Black communities had led to controversy for many decades, sometimes striking close to home. The city's landfill opened in 1946, just east of the newly built Brookfield Gardens complex of nearly 200 apartments that quickly became a magnet for professional Black people. The city then expanded the landfill in 1953, despite appeals by residents to stop it. The clipping noted that in neighboring Chesterfield County in 1965, a group of Black residents had asked the county to close a landfill located across from Hickory Hill Elementary School. They were represented by a young attorney named L. Douglas Wilder. It was a step back in time for him.

Harrell quickly summarized the root cause as "institutional racism." The mayor agreed, even using that term in his newsletter. "Unfortunately, the damage seen in Battery Park is the result of what is commonly termed 'institutional racism' by our City's forefathers, who should have never located a landfill there that could eventually bring damage to a major sewer line."[131]

The situation in Battery Park was bleak. The contaminated area was posted with signs warning of health hazards. City inspectors had to wait for floodwaters to recede enough to check the hardest-hit homes. Returning residents were given informational kits on proper cleanup procedures. The entire park was fenced off, leaving a foot of caked fecal muck on the ground after the floodwaters subsided.

City officials estimated more than $40 million in damages. Wilder said he would seek to have Battery Park declared a federal disaster area, which would trigger the release of housing vouchers and additional money for repairs. The city was already lining up contractors in hopes that FEMA funding would soon be available. "I've talked with the governor (Tim Kaine) about it. He says he's going to press it as hard as he can," Wilder assured.[132]

Weeks later, FEMA announced that funding would be granted to twenty-one Virginia localities impacted by Ernesto, including Richmond, and help cover the cost of replacing the collapsed sewer line. However, FEMA twice rejected the city's request for funding to individuals with damage to their home or personal property. Dozens of residents had lost everything.

Wilder later blasted FEMA at a City Hall news conference where he raised doubts about the agency's role and effectiveness. "When taxpayers, as close to Washington, D.C. as we are, cannot look to the government to bail them out when they have these losses, then why should government be called upon to spend money around the world?" he asked. "We're spending billions of dollars in Iraq, for problems that we created in Iraq. And people here in Richmond, or Virginia, who've done nothing other than pay taxes, can't get a return on their taxes," he said, criticizing FEMA's decision.[133]

Wilder then encouraged residents to file claims directly with the city for their losses. However, the discouraging news from FEMA was only compounded by the arrival of additional rains. Only five weeks after Ernesto hit, a second—and even larger—storm struck that poured down five more inches of rain, making the situation even worse than before. A second evacuation was required, affecting residents in almost a hundred separate apartments.

More than twenty feet of water stood in the Battery Park tennis and basketball courts. City pumps running around the clock—draining 40 million gallons a day—could not keep up. Work crews had to relocate some pumps that were almost swallowed up by the rising water. After the additional rains, the city stationed additional pumps throughout the park that could take out more than 200 million gallons daily.

Battery Park area residents were beside themselves, struggling to deal with the recurrent unsanitary mess. Contaminated foul-smelling water. Flooded basements. Rats. Snakes. Dozens of homes remained evacuated and posed public health risks. A young couple holding their four-week-old baby were among numerous people who came before city council to plead for help.

"Battery Park Exodus? Angry Residents Demand Action," roared a *Richmond Free Press* headline. People were desperate following the second evacuation. "I'm going to get the heck out of Dodge," Lucille Green, president of the Battery Park Civic Association, told the newspaper about leaving her Edgewood Avenue home of forty years. "My husband says we can't take it anymore. And my children say it's time to go. It's awful."[134]

Wilder launched extensive measures to help restore the Northside neighborhoods of Battery Park, Brookfield Gardens, and Southern Barton Heights.

He brought the services of Richmond City Hall to them.

A "mini" City Hall was set up at an elementary school so that residents did not have to travel downtown for assistance. Staff were on hand from the departments of community development, public utilities, public works, health, social services, and parks and recreation. The U.S. Small Business Administration also opened a satellite office, making it easier for people to seek low-interest loans to pay for damages not covered by insurance. The mayor appointed Mrs. Green, who remained in her home, as the city administration's citizen liaison to assist residents.

Wilder later toured the newly opened center after returning from a long-planned, ten-day trip to India with VCU President Eugene P. Trani designed to foster cultural exchange ties with several medical research and technology institutes. He spoke with Mrs. Green about a new phone citizens' assistance phone line—646-HELP—as well as a reverse 911 system that allowed police and fire departments to contact citizens. A monthly newsletter was started to keep residents informed about recovery efforts. The City collected clothes and household items for those in need. A Christmas toy drive was held specifically for neighborhood children.

Wilder announced a $1,000 personal contribution when he joined Radio One personality Clovia Lawrence to kick off a twelve-hour "Radio-thon" fundraising campaign to help displaced families. Altogether, the event raised more than $100,000.

The City held neighborhood meetings to explain the next steps. Displaced families were allowed to return to their homes after flooded roadways reopened. However, roads needed to be disinfected beforehand, requiring more time than initially expected. Approximately eighty-five homes in the lower-level areas were either condemned or limited to restricted occupancy. Nearly a dozen residential properties were beyond repair, which the City purchased at "pre-flood" prices and demolished. The vacant land became additional park space.

Some property owners threatened litigation, which prompted the mayor's swift rebuke. Titled "Legal Threats on Property Acquisitions in Battery Park Area Not to Be Tolerated," the press release read:

> What the City is doing for the residents of the Battery Park area is being done through a sense of concern for our citizens. The City has no liability for the unfortunate situation that has occurred there regarding the collapse of the sewer line, and the subsequent flooding.
>
> The City administration is coming forward with drainage improvement plans for the Shockoe and Battery Park, due to problems there which have existed for years. We have no fear of threats being made as to lawsuits that may be brought forward, and we will not be involved in acquiring properties where there are threats of a lawsuit. Those who feel they need to settle their claims through litigation should proceed to do so. We are not, nor will we be coerced in any way by the threat of a lawsuit.[135]

Solutions to prevent future flooding took time. The City hired engineers to assess the situation. Initial plans to patch and reline the collapsed sewer line were discarded; doing so could disturb hazardous wastes buried deep in the decades-old landfill. As an interim measure, a 1,700-foot emergency overflow relief tunnel was built along a new path that bypassed the landfill entirely. The six-foot diameter pipe provided temporary relief from flooding caused by heavy rains.

A long-term solution proved to be more complex. Engineers agreed on a nine-foot-diameter sewer line extending 3,300 feet, that also bypassed the collapsed line. It was completed about fifteen months later, in December 2007. The cost totaled $46 million with federal, state, and local funding. FEMA's $30 million payment to help Richmond represented its largest grant to any single locality since Hurricane Katrina devastated the Gulf Coast region in 2005, city officials noted.[136]

Wilder led an inspection of the work, with residents, city officials and reporters taking an elevator shaft deep into the ground to see the new sewer line before it was sealed and put into operation. He also hosted a Battery Park "rededication ceremony" to celebrate. "Construction of the permanent sewer line was finished ahead of schedule and under budget," he proudly announced about the project managed by Chris Beschler, the city's utilities director.

In his newsletter, the mayor again addressed the "institutional racism" that had led to the sewer collapse. However, this time, his conclusion was optimistic: "FEMA agreed with the City's position to build a new sewer line that bypasses an existing landfill. . . . With the bypass, we are correcting the mistakes of our forefathers."[137]

TIME FOR A STORMWATER UTILITY

Even with the drainage improvements in Shockoe Bottom and Battery Park, Wilder realized a solution was needed for future flooding across the city.

He proposed a stormwater utility program that would provide a dedicated funding source to improve the city's infrastructure to reduce flooding. It would charge a monthly stormwater fee while also bringing greater equity in monthly water rates. Residential customers were already paying an inordinate share of the cost as compared with commercial and industrial users. Wilder hosted a series of Town Hall meetings in late 2007 to introduce the stormwater utility program to the public. He had already presented the idea to city council, noting that many cities the size of Richmond already had a stormwater utility program in place.

Under his plan, proposed rate cuts would apply to about 70 percent of residential utility customers for five years. In turn, those customers would pay a monthly fee based on the size of their land and the amount of "runoff" involved. Rainfall runs off driveways, parking lots, sidewalks, rooftops, and similar hard areas where it cannot be absorbed into the ground. The mayor's plan also applied to government buildings, colleges and universities, and non-profit organizations including churches. The proposed rate schedules represented the City's first comprehensive review of its water and wastewater fees since 1997, he said. His proposal also would reduce pollution runoff where water with traces of fertilizer, pesticides, and other pollutants eventually make their way into the James River and Chesapeake Bay.[138]

Months later, however, the mayor withdrew his stormwater utility proposal, noting that residents were already facing higher utility costs in other areas. "The drainage needs of the city are well known, and we have made considerable progress in the last three years," he said.

"We consider it prudent to postpone this program as citizens who have already felt the impact of gas price increases are now likely to see increases in monthly electricity bills this summer."[139] The concept of a stormwater utility program did not fade away, however. City council adopted a stormwater management program in 2009, five months after Wilder left office.

CHAPTER FIVE

PERFORMING ARTS:
WHAT PRICE WILL WE PAY FOR CULTURE?

CARPENTER CENTER IN MOTH BALLS

It started out like a friendly game of poker, cordial in nature, yet guarded. The players, seated on each side of the table, held their cards close. The issue at hand involved the future of cultural arts in Richmond: what to do with the aging and shuttered Carpenter Center in downtown Richmond.

After eighty years, the historic theater was plagued with space limitations and condemned by the City due to electrical and other safety issues. But one thing stood in the way: there wasn't nearly enough money to renovate it.

Modernizing the Carpenter Center was but one element of a grand cultural venue envisioned by the city's moneyed arts patrons and the Virginia Performing Arts Foundation (VPAF), which led the fundraising and design work. The original plan also included a new symphony hall, community playhouse, jazz venue, and offices.

Now it was up to Dominion Energy CEO Thomas F. Farrell, who came to City Hall one afternoon to meet with the mayor. He told Wilder enough money had been raised to proceed with the Carpenter Center project, but he mostly spoke in broad generalities. This much money would come from here and that much money would come from there, he informed the mayor. He didn't spell out too much in the way of specifics.

At that point, after doing the math in his head, the mayor replied, "That still leaves about four to five hundred thousand to go, doesn't it?"

or something to that effect. Suddenly, Farrell's upright demeanor seemed to recoil as if he'd just been caught in a game of gotcha. He hesitated for a moment and acknowledged that the remaining money had been pledged and would be coming from this and that person. He then named some names, putting all of his cards on the table. I sat there listening and taking it all in, though I didn't recognize many of the names of those who were making large contributions.

Wilder was now satisfied with what he heard. The arts project dubbed "Richmond CenterStage" could proceed. Aside from city budget deliberations, the arts project represented the mayor's first major scuffle with council, centering on how the project would be financed. He inherited the situation, which was first proposed in 2001.

The mayor had long questioned VPAF's fundraising ability to build an arts complex on a vacant block of land on Broad Street where the bankrupt Thalhimers department store had been torn down to make room for the new arts center. Wilder nicknamed the open space as the "hole in the ground."

In March 2005, his third month in office, Wilder offered a benign assessment of VPAF's fundraising efforts. "I'm like the old elephant going across a bridge," he mused to a *Richmond Times-Dispatch* reporter. "I put one foot on it and shake it to see if it will take a second. I don't want to commit the city until I see a way across."[140]

He later railed against council's pledge to contribute more than $27 million as the city's share of the cost by increasing the local meals tax. He questioned the amount of private funds being raised. By 2005, preliminary construction bids for the grand original plan had steadily climbed to $112 million.

By May, Wilder called on VPAF to abandon its plans and return ownership of the Thalhimers block to the city. The mayor's press release reflected his displeasure with several aspects of the deal.

> Two years ago (in 2003), in an unprecedented move without adequate input from the public or adequate due diligence on the part of those heading city government, the Council and the Performing Arts Foundation passed a new tax dedicated to a private entity, and furthermore, gave that entity control over one of the most valuable pieces of land in Richmond.
>
> This unprecedented move was justified by City Council

and the Foundation on this basis: that the people were protected because the ordinance passed by the City contained a July 1, 2005 deadline for the keeping of the promises made to the public and the reversion of the property to the City upon default.

This deadline was put into law to ensure the public that those running the City were not making an open-ended commitment of tens of millions in tax dollars and other city resources to a private entity.

The Foundation has repeatedly lobbied for more and more public dollars—more taxes, even a new ticket tax under a different name—while falling short on the promised private dollars. Accordingly, at this point, I believe it is time for the Foundation to give the land back to the City. This will allow for the development of a new proposal to ensure the future of the Carpenter Center, the National Theatre, and the future of the downtown.[141]

He had already sent council a letter criticizing its funding plan as "a gross failure in judgment" and stating that he didn't want the deadline extended. The next week, however, council ignored his request by voting unanimously to give the VPAF an additional eighteen months to raise money.

The day after council's vote, Wilder called a press conference to lambast council and VPAF.

"They tell you they have raised $67 million," he growled. "I would ask how many of you in this room would believe that? When over forty-some-million dollars of that amount is from the public sector and when you consider that the tax credits they speak about isn't money that has been raised. So you have a shell game that is taking place.

"And now you come to the city. And you say, 'I want some more money now.' The real question is for what? Drive over to Broad Street and tell me what you see going on at the Performing Arts Center. Where is the work taking place? Do you see it today? I wonder why not? Well, it might be some past-due bills. Whose bills? Is it to fund the salaries of the [foundation employees]?

"My question is: If you excuse this deadline with no more evidence given to you than you heard, what is to stop the next one from coming up and saying, 'Hey, all we need is another six months this time, or maybe four months,'" Wilder cautioned. "Who have you heard really speak for the people?"

Questioning the level of overall public support for the arts center, Wilder at one point even considered holding a referendum on the project but did not follow through.

Clearly agitated by council's vote, the mayor could see how shaky the fundraising prospects were looking. At times, the mayor's tone would become combative, and then he would chuckle as if he were enjoying himself. He stood resolute in his position and dismissed any notion otherwise. "Nothing bothers me," Wilder declared. "I am not cotton candy that will disappear as soon as the weather gets hot. I am going to be around. I have been around. And I know my job."

Wilder also reacted to an earlier comment that local grocer magnate James E. Ukrop had made to a reporter: "I supported the mayor, and I still support the concept of a mayor-at-large. I don't know about the personality."

The mayor immediately shot back, "He might own some other people. He might bully some other people. But I owe my election, I owe my strength – and always have owed it – to the people. And he doesn't own, nor will he own or buy me."[142]

Wilder's response suggested "that he was one politician who was not under the thumb of wealthy business types like Mr. Ukrop," observed the *Richmond Free Press*.[143] Ukrop had contributed $5,500 to Wilder's election campaign, making him the mayor's third largest supporter.[144]

Angered by council's vote to extend the fundraising deadline for VPAF, Wilder later said council's time extension for the arts center was no longer in effect[145] and that he did not plan to give any more funding to VPAF. He pointed to a city auditor's report that questioned whether what the foundation claimed to have raised could be rightly considered available. VPAF also had sought reimbursement for items that didn't qualify as "pre-construction expenses," the report said.[146]

Wilder later recalled how the foundation had bypassed him by going straight to council for the time extension. "Yes, to hell with him. That's what they said," the mayor fumed. "To hell with him. Didn't ask me for the waiver, didn't discuss it with me. Council never discussed it with me. So then they do it."

Going around the mayor brought consequences. *Style Weekly* observed, "The performing arts center was probably doomed at precisely that point." Longtime friend and political analyst, Larry J. Sabato, described the situation. "You need to listen carefully, and you need to work with him and find out exactly what he wants and try to meet as many of the requests as possible," he said about Wilder. "To ignore him or to work around him is to guarantee his enmity. He's the mayor. You have to come to him. If you try to do big things without him, you're in trouble."[147]

At one point, the dispute between mayor and foundation appeared headed to court. VPAF retained an attorney by October 2005, and Wilder was unperturbed by the prospect. "As Marvin Gaye would say, 'Let's get it on!'" he told reporters.[148]

Unhappy with the VPAF's fundraising efforts, Wilder established his own Committee on the Performing Arts in November, with Farrell as finance chair. Despite the mayor's harsh words toward Ukrop, who was VPAF chairman, Ukrop was among the first members appointed to the mayor's committee, which was given a twelve-month deadline to develop a game plan.

Both sides settled into a truce as everyone agreed to move ahead with renovating the Carpenter Center. Wilder initially pushed to quickly reopen the building after repairs to accommodate arts groups' upcoming 2006-07 season. But the groups overwhelmingly agreed that major changes would be required to meet their long-term needs. While the compromise forged a path to restore a major downtown venue, the butting of heads rankled some VPAF members who resigned or withdrew their pledges—or both.

Needing to locate money to move the project forward, Farrell managed to tap into deep pockets within the community that the performing arts foundation could not shake open. Wilder backed off his demand that the Thalhimers block be given back to the city. However, he made clear that any agreement based on his committee's recommendations would take "precedence over any and all understandings between the City and the Foundation." Meanwhile, the Broad Street "hole in the ground" was eventually filled in and landscaped.

Wilder was alarmed to learn that VPAF's president and chief fundraiser, Brad Armstrong, was being paid more than $300,000 a year in salary and benefits, yet was unable to bring home the bacon. "A third of a million dollars!" Wilder shrieked during an interview with the *Virginian-Pilot*. "To do what? The job was to be raising money. If that was your job, then why haven't you raised any money?"[149] Now in Wilder's crosshairs, that arrangement soon came to an end when Armstrong resigned after five years on the job.

As Wilder formed his own Committee on the Performing Arts, the city's building inspector cited the Carpenter Center with thirty-two code violations, labeling it a fire hazard. The building had not been inspected for five years. Concerned about the safety of other city venues, Wilder also launched annual inspections for other aging facilities like the Richmond Coliseum and the Landmark Theater.

Old buildings need continual maintenance, which can be costly. Privately, the mayor once offered for the City to give the Landmark Theater to Virginia Commonwealth University, as the building was located in the heart of the university's academic campus. However, VCU President Trani declined the offer, citing the cost of upkeep. "Can you believe it? We can't even give that building away!" The mayor joked about the Moorish Revival-styled facility featuring a 3,600-seat theater and upper floors of office space.

For the Carpenter Center's inspection issues, the city gave VPAF a deadline to fix those problems, which made headlines in the local papers. The long list of inspection violations rattled some foundation members who sulked about the findings, labeling them "harassment" imposed by Wilder. An article in the *Richmond Times-Dispatch* summed it up: "The inspection seems likely to raise the temperature still more in the downtown arts-center scrap, which has pitted Wilder against powerful business leaders who have backed the project."

Meanwhile, senior policy advisor Paul Goldman, still several weeks away from the public disclosure of his outside political consulting work, chimed in with his own characteristic style. "You've got a fire trap at one end of the block and a hole at the other," he said about the Carpenter Center and the vacant Thalhimers block on Broad Street. "Obviously the Carpenter Center has been allowed to deteriorate," he noted. "It's like, if you don't do it our way, we've set it up so you can't do it any other way."[150] At one point, Wilder had considered the idea of an eminent-domain-style takeover of the Carpenter Center from VPAF. It fell flat.

Wilder noted the arts project never held wide public support. "To raise money for the arts center? That's not my priority," he told *Style Weekly*. "[I'm] continuing with the theme I started when I was governor: 'The necessities before niceties.'"[151] If he hadn't raised concerns about the cost of the original arts center plan, the City would have been saddled with an overly ambitious project that private supporters would be unable to fund, the mayor said. Now the battle had finally ended. Everyone went along with the new terms. Farrell's favorable fundraising report was pleasing to the mayor's ears.

The mayor's committee issued its first report in May 2006. Based on an expected $45 million in raised funds, including up to $25 million from Wilder's City of the Future plan, the report first called for renovating the Carpenter Center with improved acoustics, an extended stage house, expanded lobby, concession areas and restrooms, new HVAC systems and upgraded electrical systems, and more seating. Additional funds were later raised for an adjacent 200-seat community playhouse, a jazz and cabaret space, reception and gallery areas, classrooms, and offices.

Wilder told a *Style Weekly* reporter that he had no apologies for how the performing arts project was handled. "Could I have done it differently? Could I have been more mellifluous, uh, softer, said things in – how would you call it – less strident terms? Maybe so. But name me a time when I said something that was incorrect or that my factual basis was off or askew. Or that I maligned anyone."[152]

Wilder again emphasized the City should not take on debt to renovate and expand the Carpenter Center if it did not own it. "The City should not and will not incur debt on property we do not own," he said. "Therefore ... it will be imperative for the structure of the City's involvement to be crafted with this policy in mind."[153] Wilder's committee recommended that the foundation transfer ownership of the land and building to the City and that a public-private partnership could oversee construction and operate Richmond's new cultural arts venue.

Though Richmond's symphony, ballet, and opera were like orphans seeking a home, other concert venues remained available such as the Richmond Coliseum, Landmark Theater, and Dogwood Dell.

Wilder often received requests to officially welcome the big-name acts that were touring through the region. Soul crooner Al Green invited Wilder to drop by his hospitality tent at the Fridays at Sunset season finale. Another time, the mayor introduced the Average White Band at the Second Street Festival in historic Jackson Ward. On occasion, Wilder might even remain on stage and perform as an impromptu backup singer. Performing came naturally to him, a remnant of his youth. A photo from his Korean War days shows him in uniform standing before a microphone, singing to a group of fellow soldiers. He knew how to work an audience.

"American Idol" Elliott Yamin Sings

In 2006, "American Idol" singing contestant, Elliott Yamin, came home to Richmond to perform before a huge downtown crowd. He was one of three remaining finalists, each of whom made a hometown appearance to be shown on the morning news shows. Wilder rolled out the red carpet to welcome him. As the white stretch limo pulled up, he was among the first to greet Yamin, who was accompanied by his mother, Claudette, who had a physical impairment affecting her pace of walking.

Yamin belted out a Michael Bublé tune, "Home," before 4,000 screaming fans who jammed into the downtown James Center Plaza to see him. Wilder presented Yamin with a tiny blue box that when opened, revealed a special gift: the ceremonial key to the city.

"We know that Virginia is caught up in Elliott mania," Wilder exclaimed. "He is an ambassador for all of us, for all Virginians." Adding to the hysteria, Wilder announced he had received a fax from American Idol judge, Paula Abdul, saying that she had chosen the song that Yamin would sing the following night, a tune titled "What You Won't Do for Love," by Bobby Caldwell.

Overwhelmed with the throngs cheering him on, Yamin appeared downright awestruck standing with the mayor. "This is . . . the happiest day of my life," he gushed, as he and Wilder held opposite ends of the silver key for the cameras.[154] Later that day, Yamin met Governor Kaine and threw the first pitch at a Richmond Braves baseball game.

In often unique ways, the Richmond community can be very generous in offering kind gestures of help. That manner of kindness was extended to Yamin. A local dentist sent an email offering to provide free dental work to straighten Yamin's teeth, a sweet gesture.

After Yamin's downtown performance, he was delivered to a downtown restaurant for a series of interviews. A phalanx of admirers swarmed around as he made the short walk from the limo to the front door. The mayor and I were standing at the back of the pack. Seeing the chaos created by the television cameras and autograph seekers swarming around, the mayor suddenly intervened to calm the crowd by cautioning everyone to just slow down. "Make way for the mother," he bellowed, and the crowd immediately began clearing an open path for Yamin and his mother, who struggled mightily to keep up. They made it inside with no further trouble.

"B.B. KING DAY"

Presenting keys-to-the-city was a rarity, and some performers simply wanted the next best thing. When blues guitarist B.B. King came to the Landmark Theater, his manager requested a proclamation that could be read at the start of his show. Citing a scheduling conflict, Wilder punted that task to Sheila Hill-Christian, his CAO at the time. It was a perk that came with the job.

We met B.B. backstage before the show, as he was wheelchaired into the building. He was almost eighty-five at that point and seemed rumpled and frail, yet alert. After we all shook hands and exchanged brief pleasantries, King's son wheeled him off to his dressing room.

When the curtain went up, B.B. slowly walked out on his own to take his chair at center stage. As the applause died down, the announcer introduced Hill-Christian who briskly walked out to read the mayor's words of welcome.

> Whereas: B.B. King was born on a Mississippi plantation in 1925, and later as a young man hitchhiked to Memphis, Tennessee in 1947 to pursue his musical career, playing street corners for spare change and sometimes performing in as many as four towns a night; and
>
> Whereas: Mr. King, one of the most influential guitarists of our time, has had a tremendous impact on the development of modern blues and rock music, influencing such musical greats as Buddy Guy, George Harrison, Eric Clapton and Stevie Ray Vaughan to name only a few; and
>
> Whereas: B.B. King is a living legend and is one of the most honored musicians of our time, as he is a member of the Blues Hall of Fame, the Rock and Roll Hall of Fame and has received seven Grammy Awards as well as the Grammy's coveted Lifetime Achievement Award, the Presidential Medal of the Arts, and has his own "Star" on the Hollywood Walk of Fame; and
>
> Whereas: B.B. King's most identifiable trademark is his beloved guitar, named Lucille, which has been with B.B. since 1949 and is credited as the inspiration that has propelled B.B.

through the course of his illustrious career which has provided much joy to generations of music lovers; and

Whereas: Mr. King and Lucille continue to perform more than 250 concerts per year before live audiences, which B.B. feels is the most essential aspect of being a blues artist;

Now, Therefore, I, L. Douglas Wilder, Mayor of the City of Richmond, Virginia, do hereby proclaim May 11, 2008 as "B.B. King Day" in the City of Richmond and encourage all citizens to join together to recognize and celebrate his musical achievements which represent a lifetime commitment to the love of music enjoyed by so many, both in the U.S. and around the world.

B.B. was smiling, holding the framed proclamation in the air, as Hill-Christian glided offstage amid loud applause mixed with catcalls. She later thanked the mayor for the opportunity to meet B.B.

Close Call: Mayor Almost Knocked Out

With the decision made to renovate the Carpenter Center, the facelift of another downtown venue was already well on its way. However, a peculiar twist of circumstances announcing its rebirth might have proven . . . deadly.

Wilder was invited to speak at a press conference to herald the reopening of the National Theater, rebranded as simply The National. The concert venue featured an open stand-up floor plan with upper rows of auditorium seating. The theater's website offered the rationale for the seat-less floor plan: "We recommend standing for a wide variety of reasons – you can dance, you look taller, you'll have a better view of the stage and any potential new friends you might try to make during the show, it's good exercise and it's just cooler."

An architecturally ornate building on East Broad Street between Seventh and Eighth Streets, the original National Theater opened in 1923 for touring music and vaudeville shows and silent movies. However, it sat empty after 1983 and was later purchased by the Historic Richmond Foundation to save it from demolition. It was the only surviving auditorium of what was originally called Broad Street's elegant "Theatre Row." A bit more history: a consortium of concert promoters bought the building in 2006 for $1.6 million and then pumped another $15 million to modernize the venue for upcoming shows such as

Little Feat and Willie Nelson.

Though the theater's reopening came in April 2008, the owners wanted to drum up some early excitement for what was to come. What better way to do that than arrange for the mayor to speak at your press conference? It was mid-December, and the mayor and I walked over to The National, only a block away from City Hall. He gave handshakes along the way to passers-by who were startled to suddenly see the mayor approaching.

Entering The National that morning, we were given hard hats to wear. With wires hanging overhead and loud hammering going on, some degree of finishing work was clearly still needed. The logistics for the press conference were already laid out for us. A lectern and microphone had been set up in the upper area where the seats were still draped in plastic.

We mingled for several minutes as we waited for the press to arrive and during that time, I noticed the awkward and potentially calamitous arrangement for the speakers. The lectern was situated only a few rows from the outer edge of the balcony, which had a low handrail. I didn't say anything, I admit, but it seemed clear to me that with one good misstep, someone could trip and topple over the balcony onto the main floor below.

The press conference soon began, with a handful of local reporters present. When it was the mayor's turn to speak, he removed his hard hat and reminisced about the theater's long history and the renewed energy coming to downtown Richmond. "When you go into these buildings [downtown], you feel something – a rebirth," Wilder said. "Though it may appear to some to be bricks and mortar . . . when you hear the applause for the people who will perform, it will be more than just for them."[155] The mayor was referring to the vision of the Historic Richmond Foundation in saving the building as a piece of history. Without the foundation stepping in, the showcase building would likely have been torn down.

As the mayor spoke, something suddenly fell from the ceiling and landed smack on the written remarks in front of him. It came down only a matter of inches from his unprotected head. You could hear the thump when it landed. Without missing a beat, however, Wilder held it up in the air with a surprised smile for everyone to see: the brass shell of a fire sprinkler.

Wilder joked afterward that the falling object could have been a failed retaliation for his effort to evict the school board from City Hall only a few months earlier. He laughed as he poked fun at himself. The consequences could have been far different if the mayor had been standing only a foot away, however. The sprinkler shell, while only about the size of one's fist, carried some weight and fell from a considerable height, with some force of speed—fortunately, missing the mayor's head.

Reopening the Carpenter Center, however, remained the big prize for the mayor. His *Visions* newsletter echoed the sentiment of many Richmond arts patrons. In an article titled, "No Time to Waste in Renovating Carpenter Center," Wilder wrote that the project "cannot be renovated quickly enough to meet the needs of our symphony, ballet, opera, and other cultural groups, all of which have suffered immeasurably in both financial and morale terms since the Carpenter Center was shuttered in late 2004."

> In an effort to salvage a failed fundraising campaign, I appointed the Performing Arts Committee in 2005 under the leadership of prominent local attorney Robert J. Grey to make viable recommendations. The Committee's report . . . reflected the collaboration of all parties toward seeking a viable and sustaining solution. The City will spend up to $25 million in renovating the Carpenter Center and will receive title to that property as a result of this enormous investment. I look forward to the renovation groundbreaking this summer and the planned grand opening in September 2009. Our performing arts groups have waited patiently for this long-sought resolution.[156]

Wilder had always favored a scaled-down arts project featuring the renovated 1800-seat Carpenter Center as its centerpiece. The cost totaled $74 million, far less than the $112 million price tag for a more elaborate arts center that he believed had questionable public support. Since its reopening in 2009, the newly christened Carpenter Theatre has served as the home of the Richmond Symphony, the Virginia Opera, and the Richmond Ballet, in addition to national touring acts and local and regional productions. The battle over a performing arts center, an issue the mayor inherited upon taking office, had finally come to an end.

CHAPTER SIX

JUMP-STARTING NEW BUSINESS AND OWNING A HOME

DOWNTOWN'S NEW HILTON HOTEL
& FEDERAL COURTHOUSE

Wilder's economic impact was felt across the city but especially along Broad Street, downtown. He used his power as mayor to jumpstart business and clean up entire city blocks after decades of neglect and decay.

Construction projects in the city totaled more than $2 billion in 2006, according to the city's Department of Economic Development. From the observation deck on the 18th floor of City Hall, one could see five or six cranes scattered across the city landscape on any given day. Two Fortune 500 companies announced plans to build new headquarters in downtown. A new federal courthouse was under construction. Plans were moving ahead for Richmond CenterStage. Up and down Broad Street, dilapidated buildings were being restored or replaced like new teeth in a denture plate.

Wilder had been in office only a few months before he began to question continual delays in transforming the former Miller & Rhoads department store, at 5th and Broad, into a Hilton Hotel. The project had already fallen years behind schedule when the developer could not secure a $70 million construction loan to begin the work. "We have no firm dates at this point," a representative for the Chicago-based developer, ECI Investment Advisors Inc. told *Style Weekly*. "Frankly, it's taken longer than we thought."[157]

Having a top-drawer hotel just across the street from the Greater Richmond Convention Center was deemed essential for luring business conferences and boosting downtown tourism. Lack of hotel rooms had been a major reason Richmond was losing conventions to other cities. "Where's the Hilton?" Wilder asked about ECI's promise to develop the Hilton Hotel. "They've told us every nice thing, every optimistic thing (but) I'm an old-schooler. My thing is let me see what you are talking about."[158]

The mayor wanted ECI to jump-start the project, already on the drawing board for more than four years, by bringing in an additional developer. The jump-start occurred when Wilder arranged for ECI to partner with HRI Properties of Louisiana and Prudential Financial, for what became a $110 million project consisting of a 250-room hotel and 133 condominiums.

In April 2006, Wilder and others announced the redevelopment plan in front of the Miller & Rhoads building, which had been vacant since 1990—after the department store declared bankruptcy. "The face of Downtown Richmond is continuing to improve with today's announcement that work will soon begin to bring to Downtown another quality hotel," he announced. "This new hotel will further enhance the City's popularity as both a tourist and convention destination. In addition, the condominium complex offers overwhelming proof of the growing demand by those who seek the urban appeal of living in Downtown."[159]

Wilder had every reason to be upbeat about the Hilton Hotel project. He resuscitated it. "This [Miller & Rhoads project] was absolutely dead," he told a *Style Weekly* reporter. CAO William Harrell credited the mayor for making the project finally happen. "The mayor drove getting this thing done," he said.[160] The hotel/condo complex opened in 2009. Wilder also worked to reduce hazardous bus and pedestrian congestion on Broad Street where strings of GRTC buses bottlenecked in front of City Hall and the adjacent Library of Virginia. "It's not safe, it's not good, it's not healthy," he told city council, which approved his proposal to redirect several bus routes to lessen the flow.[161]

Another major project underway on Broad Street—which Wilder acknowledged he could not take any credit for—was the new $102 million federal courthouse at 7th and Broad Street. During his second month in office, he participated in a groundbreaking ceremony for the sleek, seven-story building with a massive glass atrium. The new courthouse was described by the *Richmond Times-Dispatch* as "the first of a three-part construction mini-boom likely to make a big difference to downtown Richmond."

"Remember, the federal courts building replaced the most blighted block in all of downtown," Jack Berry, executive director of Venture Richmond, told the paper. "The court building coupled with the CenterStage arts center and the Miller & Rhoads Hilton hotel will completely transform three crucial blocks on Broad Street."[162]

While unable to take credit for the new courthouse, Wilder played a key role in naming it. Senator George Allen sought Wilder's advice in recognizing a Black jurist for the building, and the mayor recommended Spottswood W. Robinson III.[163]

Robinson was a former dean of Howard University Law School, the first Black appointed to the U.S. District Court in Washington and later, to the U.S. Court of Appeals for the District of Columbia Circuit, where he was later named chief judge. He was heavily involved in the U.S. Supreme Court's 1954 Brown v. Board of Education court case that outlawed segregation in public schools. Robinson had mentored Wilder as he was just starting his law practice.

Meanwhile, the local bar association favored naming the courthouse after Robert R. Merhige Jr., who served more than thirty years on the U.S. District Court for the Eastern District of Virginia and rendered high-profile rulings in the early 1970s—such as requiring the University of Virginia to admit women and ordering crosstown busing to desegregate a number of Virginia school systems.

The result: the Spottswood W. Robinson III and Robert R. Merhige Jr. Federal Courthouse, named after widely respected federal judges who played historic roles during the nation's civil rights movement. It opened in 2008.

Elsewhere in downtown, Virginia Commonwealth University was building a $192 million medical center complex near City Hall that would increase the number of units for trauma, neonatal, and cardiac patients. VCU also began construction for a $228 million Monroe Park campus addition that included a new school of business and an expanded school of engineering on the western edge of downtown. The Virginia State Capitol received a $105 million, two-year restoration and reopened only days before Queen Elizabeth's visit to commemorate the 400th anniversary of Jamestown.

Richmond also experienced a tremendous level of private investment. Washington, DC, developer Douglas Jemal invested more than one-half billion dollars in downtown Richmond for projects that included the twenty-three story Central National Bank building and the James Center.

Downtown was beginning to pop with new and trendy art galleries and restaurants. Long-derelict buildings were restored as apartments, condos, and boutique shops. Downtown became a popular destination after years of people mainly staying away. People also were increasingly drawn to the downtown riverfront as a place to live. Construction had begun on Vistas on the James, a 160-unit condo building on the James River, where Wilder purchased a unit. Farther east, a forty-five-acre urban riverfront village called Rocketts Landing was thriving with new residents.

FORTUNE 500s COMING DOWNTOWN

Big business was returning. Philip Morris USA, the nation's number one cigarette maker, announced plans to build a $350 million research and development center at the Virginia BioTechnology Research Park. The 475,000 square-foot center would bring some 500 well-paying science and research jobs into downtown Richmond. The center represented one of the largest private business investments in the city's history, the mayor noted.

"Obviously, you have to have confidence in the city to invest that kind of money," Wilder said about Philip Morris USA, adding that Richmond was chosen over other contenders such as North Carolina's Research Triangle Park. The new research center would revitalize downtown. "Look at what this does for Broad Street," he remarked about the increasing demand for new stores, restaurants, and supporting businesses. "It is not going to be an island."[164] While recognizing the benefits the research center would bring, he could not take credit for the project that was well underway by the time he entered office.

Wilder's impact was immense, however, for another Fortune 500 company that selected downtown Richmond as its new corporate home. MeadWestvaco Corporation, an international packaging and paper giant, announced in late 2006 that it would relocate its headquarters from Connecticut to Richmond with a $100 million office building overlooking the James River. MeadWestvaco would bring at least 400 employees downtown.

"MeadWestvaco's decision to come to Downtown followed fierce competition among neighboring localities who sought to lure this major employer," Wilder said in his *Visions* newsletter. The company noted "all of the energy and excitement of Downtown" as well as proximity to the city's financial district and airport, and the positive impact of Virginia Commonwealth University as reasons for choosing Richmond.[165]

MeadWestvaco's chief executive officer, John A. Luke Jr., recalled the influence that Wilder brought to the table as the company was deciding where to relocate. They were standing together on City Hall's 18th-floor observation deck that offered a sweeping view of the city.

"We looked at the expanse of the city—the biotech park, the new Philip Morris [research center], all that VCU had done . . . . He painted a very real vision of the city that was compelling," Luke said.[166]

Other corporate leaders also took notice of new life in downtown.

"The city is under a transformation right now, particularly in the downtown area," said Thomas F. Farrell, CEO of Dominion Energy, as well as serving as finance chair of the mayor's Performing Arts Committee. "It's coming back to the depth of businesses that are here. It's expanding Philip Morris which just opened its brand new science center, the new courthouse is under construction, the new hotel is going into the old Miller & Rhoads building. There are cranes all over the city. There are apartments being developed in the old tobacco warehouses. A lot of development is going on across the river in Manchester."[167]

Wilder wanted the public to remember his efforts to boost business growth. Two weeks before leaving office, he led the media on a tour of major development projects during his term. We passed by ongoing projects like the Hilton Hotel, the National Theater, MeadWestvaco, and the $60 million Williams Mullen law firm's office tower, as well as the Movieland cinema complex on North Boulevard. We also visited the sites of projects still on the drawing board: a $420 million plan to build a hotel/housing/office development on a sixty-acre tract along North Boulevard and $363 million for a baseball stadium with hotel/housing/offices on an approximate twenty-acre tract in Shockoe Bottom. The fate of those projects would rest on the shoulders of the next mayor, as time ran out for Wilder.

Cleaning Up Broad Street

The tour showed how Broad Street clearly benefited from the City's stepped-up housing code enforcement to reduce blight. Owners were held responsible for the maintenance of their property. Litter, tall grass, and abandoned vehicles were not tolerated. Early on, City inspectors focused on long-empty buildings along Broad at 2nd Street, which is a major gateway into historic Jackson Ward. "We're also using Spot Blight measures to clean up Broad Street, and you only need to look at the extensive renovations now going on at Second and Broad to see what we are bringing about: the kind of positive change that people have long been waiting to see happen," Wilder declared in his 2008 State of the City address.[168]

City housing inspectors could issue a summons on the spot for code violations, which expedited cases going to court. Weekly code enforcement sweeps were aimed at spotting violations that might lead to more serious forms of neglect. Citywide inspections increased from 26,000 in 2006 to more than 47,000 in 2008.

"It is well known that crime and blight go hand in hand, and for years entire neighborhoods were affected and it diminished the health of our entire city," Wilder wrote in his newsletter. "Just as we have done the unthinkable by reducing crime to its lowest point in 26 years and making neighborhoods safer for our citizens, we are enforcing code compliance on property owners across the city so they understand that we will not tolerate neglect."[169]

The City strengthened its vacant building registry to track the condition of 3,400 unoccupied buildings. Compliance procedures would lead to either the sale, rehab, or demolition of properties not maintained. Buildings vacant for twelve months or longer had to be boarded and secured or rehabilitated and made suitable for occupancy. More than 280 buildings citywide received extensive renovations.

The mayor was quick to recognize the growth of minority business. He spoke of "unprecedented gains" among minority businesses and entrepreneurs due to stepped-up support by the City's Office of Minority Business Development. The city's overall minority participation rate was nearly 18.5 percent while the state's rate during the same period was 2 percent, he noted.[170]

The City aggressively promoted commercial development within designated enterprise zones, creating more than $22 million in business investment and hundreds of new jobs in economically challenged areas by offering incentives such as tax abatements, employment grants, and machinery rebates. The city's CARE (Commercial Area Revitalization Effort) program assisted with renovations, security improvements and sprinkler systems, representing $28 million in new investment.

More than 2,500 new jobs came to the city during his term, the mayor said, and he frequently recognized the companies that brought them. The mayor and I attended the grand opening of the Farmer's Foods at Southside Plaza, a major shopping center that had been without a grocery store for more than a year. We visited the Right-Minds advertising agency which the City had wooed to relocate to the upper floors in Main Street Station. In his newsletter, the mayor commended Interactive Financial Marketing Group, LLC, a national online marketing company located in Shockoe Slip, for being named one year as metro Richmond's fastest-growing private company.

The Need for Affordable Housing

Wilder emphasized the "tremendous need" for the availability of housing that was within the means of the average worker. This was one of his top priorities. Richmond had the second highest house prices and rents among six other "peer cities" in the Southeast, according to a Greater Richmond Chamber of Commerce survey.

In his 2007 State of the City address, Wilder noted the average cost of a house in the city was $225,000 and an individual needed to earn at least $58,000 a year to be able to qualify to buy one. "So when I talk about the need to create more affordable housing, I'm talking about meeting the needs of our police officers, bus drivers, cafeteria workers, teachers, secretaries, fire fighters, sales clerks—in short, just about everybody in our local economy, without whose work, our city would not be viable and able to subsist."[171]

Wilder advocated new zoning ordinances and an affordable housing trust fund that could generate additional housing and lead to new mixed-use, mixed-income neighborhoods. He envisioned the conversion of empty school buildings into apartments and condos, offering new opportunities for home ownership.

Expanding ways that people could buy a home would enable them to break free from public housing or other residential pockets of poverty across the city.

"Concentrating public housing in one area has the effect of giving a designation to that area that is counterproductive both to economic development and the highest and best use of publicly owned land," he wrote in a *Richmond Times-Dispatch* commentary. "Affordable and adequate housing has to be addressed on a regional basis. Businesses are concerned with where their workers will live, and providing that venue is more compelling than the specific location."[172]

Wilder established the Interagency Task Force on Community Infrastructure to undertake a comprehensive study of ways to promote home ownership and revitalize neighborhoods. He announced plans for the first phase of a major downtown revitalization plan, called Jackson Place, as a mixed-income, mixed-use housing community with up to 240 dwellings on a five-acre parcel in Jackson Ward. However, the project led by the Richmond Redevelopment and Housing Authority eventually fell apart due to contractual issues.

"There is a dire need for workforce housing," Wilder reminded council in late 2006, when he proposed zoning changes that would encourage construction of additional housing. Council, however, viewed the proposals as a "give-away" to developers. And since the proposals would have required changes to the city charter, some council members suspected the mayor might seek even more sweeping changes. Wilder dismissed what he described as "the absurd idea that if the city charter is reopened for any reason at all . . . then the mayor will run amok."

"You got a better idea, you do it," he countered. "I will get out of the way if I am an obstruction."[173]

The mayor often participated in events to raise awareness of the need for additional workforce housing. In 2007, in his work overalls with hammer in hand, he joined several Virginia legislators at the State Capitol to build window and door frames for a housing project sponsored by Richmond Habitat for Humanity, part of the worldwide organization. The next year, to support "Affordable Housing Awareness Week," he and other city officials volunteered to spend the day putting the finishing touches on new homes being built in the Blackwell community in South Richmond. I recall that while many of us opted for paint brushes, the mayor took on the less glamorous task of standing in a nearly five-foot-deep trench applying glue to connect PVC piping.

In addition to finding ways to increase the housing supply, Wilder understood that city government needed to be more accountable and operate more efficiently. A data-driven performance reporting system called "RichmondWorks" was launched to track and coordinate services provided by city departments. Previously, in many cases, records were not kept electronically or were incomplete and unusable. "It is impossible to improve government efficiency without measuring performance and it is impossible to track results without reliable data," he said. "Almost every business in the private sector does it and our government should be no different. That is why my Administration announced we would 'tear down the silos' between city departments and . . . help make government more efficient and hold top and mid-level managers responsible for employee performance – and RESULTS."

RichmondWorks greatly improved communication between city departments. In years past, especially in areas like Shockoe Bottom, merchants would complain when a road or sidewalk had been redone only to be ripped up a short time later for underground utility work to begin. That stopped when projects were coordinated among city departments.[174]

Wilder was proud that his administration's efforts to improve public safety, streamline local government, and build the local economy were succeeding "—and just look at how our City is booming," he noted. "Even the recent Crupi Report, which was commissioned by the Chamber of Commerce to analyze our city over the past fifteen years, had this to say: 'The City of Richmond is moving from a big little city to a little big city.'"[175]

CHAPTER SEVEN

Demise of the Maymont Bears

A City in Mourning and Anger

"Ashes to ashes, dust to dust…"

The female Episcopal priest stood, resplendent in gold-filigreed garments that glistened in the afternoon sun. She clutched a handful of freshly dug earth, her hand raised toward the sky as she spoke. It filtered through her fingers down into the final resting place of two of Richmond's most prominent residents.

For years, their home had been in Maymont Park, a one-hundred-acre Victorian retreat with manicured gardens and rolling hills, perched high above the roaring James River. They had always been the main attraction at the park's animal exhibit, attracting a half-million visitors each year.

And as they had lived together, so too would they die together. Baby and Buster, Maymont's two 350-pound male black bears, were laid to rest. More than 500 mourners, including some council members, had gathered on this crystal-blue Saturday afternoon, unseasonably warm to be early March.

A quiet calm encased those who came to pay their respects. Many wept openly. Some clutched flowers, stuffed bears, homemade cards, or cameras they used to snap pictures. A makeshift memorial overflowed with bouquets, teddy bears dressed like angels, bear-shaped honey bottles, sympathy cards, and toddler drawings. "We are so sorry you are gone—have fun in heaven," read one sign. Nearby, a giant-sized Winnie the Pooh stood guard. A boy scout troop escorted a color guard and ceremoniously lowered two bronze urns containing the bears' ashes into the ground. Many people stood in line for the opportunity to kneel down for a handful of dirt that they too could toss onto the bronze urns, just as the Episcopal priest had done.

The mayor, sporting a tan safari-like jacket, delivered the eulogy with righteous passion. He had arrived early, greeting the mourners, chatting at one point with police officers mounted on chestnut-colored horses along a scenic grassy knoll just in the distance.

"These bears are making a contribution even in their death, because they remind us that they lived, but they were put to death not by their own kind," he told the gathering. "To see that when they are in their natural habitat, they are not killing, they are not vicious, they are not mean. And when youngsters can come to see that, it encourages them to grow into a life of not killing, not being mean . . . [176] Let us continue to be certain that nature provides us with lessons for how to live."[177]

Wilder's impromptu remarks fired up the crowd with a tone of gospel fervor. He gesticulated with his hands in the air for effect, the heels of his cowboy boots rising upward now and then to boost his frame for emphasis, mindful of how sensitive his words became for those who gently wept.

At the gravesite, tearful mourners were so tightly clustered that local television crews complained they had to squeeze their tripods between the bushes to land a spot to shoot. At times one might almost imagine someone accidentally slipping down into the hole, yet the entire ceremony carried through without any glitches. It was so unlike the chain of events that led to this day of collective mourning.

Two weeks earlier, one of the two bears was lying along the wall of the woodsy habitat when a thirty-year-old single mother and her four-year-old son came to Maymont for a Saturday picnic.

The two ventured to the less-visited side of the habitat where the child scaled a low wooden fence into a restricted area. He had been eating an apple earlier and had the scent of an apple on his hands. The boy then put his hand through the ten-foot chain-link fence to pet the bear. The bear bit the boy's hand before the mother could grab him.

The mother later told the authorities, "The bear was sitting there quiet and calm…not acting aggressive in any way" and that the bear "realized he'd done something wrong and scampered away."[178]

The mother rushed her child to Bon Secours St. Mary's Hospital where he was treated for a light puncture wound, prescribed antibiotics, and released. She reportedly told the hospital nurse that she helped the boy over the outer, lower fence to get closer and had been coming to the same spot at Maymont for years to feed the bears. She later recanted that account, insisting she looked away for only a moment as the boy dashed toward the animal.

The hospital reported the child's emergency room visit to the city health department, which in turn contacted the Virginia Department of Health. State health officials informed the Virginia Department of Game and Inland Fisheries. The situation occurred during the Presidents Day holiday weekend, which hampered prompt notification among authorities. Maymont officials did not learn about the bear bite until three days later. The director of the city health department was not informed until four days later.

No one had thought to notify the Mayor's Office.

This was the first bear bite at Maymont, though the city's housing of black bears was traced back to around 1980 when the first black bears came to live there.

Like generations of black bears before them, Baby and Buster were moved there by the Virginia Department of Game and Inland Fisheries, which technically owned the animals, and licensed to facilities like Maymont to exhibit them. The younger bear came from Goochland County in 1999 as a two-year-old "nuisance" bear. The older one was orphaned and brought to the park as a cub in 1994, settling into its new home before making its public debut in 1995 during Maymont's Bear Family Day.

Visitors to Maymont always wanted to catch a glimpse of the black bears, ages nine and twelve, who enjoyed a good life there. The two-acre exhibit featured a large pond at its center, a rocky cliff, towering trees, and woodsy vegetation that made for a spacious setting to romp or snooze. The park's zoologists knew the animals well, commenting that the younger one liked to climb while the older one enjoyed the water.

Five days after the bear bite, during which some officials were uncertain who should have the final say-so in making a painful decision, the fourteen representatives of state and local agencies and Maymont decided that the bears needed to be tested for rabies. That meant they had to be put down.

Because the mother and child could not identify which of the two bears was involved, both Baby and Buster were quickly euthanized by injection and their brains sent to a state laboratory. An autopsy revealed that both bears had tested negative for rabies. All of this became known only after it was too late to save the bears. The Richmond community erupted in a storm of extreme anger and disbelief.

Hundreds called City Hall, Maymont, and even 911 to express feelings of anguish and disgust. Thousands posted messages of grief on online bulletin boards. News headlines arrived from Washington, DC, Chicago, and beyond. "I have never seen public response to a situation, topic, or issue like this besides 9/11," commented WRVA radio show host Mac Watson.[179]

Wilder learned about the bears after media inquiries began to pour in five days after the child was bitten. He became furious to learn that their headless carcasses had been discarded at an area landfill. Angry and incredulous, he held a press conference to condemn the killings and announce an official investigation.

"The Maymont facility is [designed] to attract kids to have an appreciation for wildlife...to show how animals are our friends," the mayor said. "And this is how we reward our friends?"[180] He noted that his office had never received so many calls on a single issue.

The death of the Maymont bears followed one of the city's most shocking murder sprees that occurred only six weeks earlier. On New Year's Day 2006, Bryan and Kathryn Harvey and their daughters, ages four and nine, were found slain in their Woodland Heights home. Five days later, the bodies of Mary and Percyell Tucker and their twenty-one-year-old daughter were discovered in their home on East Broad Rock Road. The killers were later apprehended in Philadelphia.

The timing of those occurrences led to comparisons in human emotion. A *Richmond Times-Dispatch* commentary noted twice as many angry or mournful comments were posted to its website about the bears as compared with the human murders, referring to "the desensitization we all feel about man-on-man violence, and how complex and flawed human nature seems compared with the seemingly simple and noble lives of animals."[181] The newspaper's editorial offered additional insight:

> The furor over their passing has eclipsed even the outrage regarding the murder of the Harvey and Tucker families. To understand why, one must note more than that the bears were a Richmond institution, which they certainly were. They were Maymont's star attraction, and they had delighted thousands

of children of all ages during their years in captivity. They would have been mourned if they had died of old age.[182]

When asked whether he thought it was unusual for people to be angry and grieve more over the killings of the bears than homicides, the mayor replied, "No, I don't. People recognize immediately the innocence of the bears. We were their hosts."[183] He termed the killings as "reprehensible as well as senseless."[184]

"Our job is to protect them. It's the same horror you have if someone says to an urchin on the street, 'Let me take you home, adopt you, keep you — and then beat you, abuse you, and kill you,'" he said. "We brought these animals in with the understanding they were to be protected and looked after. It's a very sickening, heart-wrenching thing that the bears paid the ultimate price."[185]

A community already in angry disbelief at the death of the bears exploded with unfettered rage after learning about the manner of the bears' disposal.

People were outraged with the mother, the child, the officials who decided the bears' fate, and whoever decided to dump them like trash. "People were saying, 'they euthanized the bears, they should euthanize the mother,'" reported Lite 98 radio talk show host Bill Bevins, who was flooded with calls. "I had to [say], 'Calm down.'"[186]

City Hall sharpened its tone also. In a draft press release titled "Investigation Underway Regarding Euthanization of the Maymont Bears," the mayor pointedly crossed out "euthanization" and replaced it with the word "killing." The mayor announced that the remains of the bears would be exhumed, and a proper memorial service would take place.

Behind the scenes, CAO William Harrell quietly negotiated with Maymont officials to have the animals buried just outside their exhibit home. Maymont is owned by the city while a foundation operates the facilities and maintains the grounds. At first, Maymont officials seemed to balk at the mayor's plans for a memorial there, signaling an indignant air of autonomy. It did not sit well with the mayor. Harrell smoothed over the situation, reminding park officials that the city contributed $300,000 each year for the park's upkeep.

The next day, the mayor announced that a memorial service would be held at Maymont on the following Saturday afternoon. "Like so many members of the public, I share the view that there should be a fitting memorial service and interment for the bears at Maymont Park, where they had lived happily for so many years, and where they had brought such enjoyment for the thousands of visitors who came there to appreciate the wildlife exhibit," he said in a press release. "I want to assure the public that the City intends to thoroughly investigate the actions that led to the most unfortunate killing of these beautiful wildlife animals."[187]

The task of recovering the bodies from the landfill fell to J.R. Pope, the city director of parks and recreation. He spent several hours riding with a backhoe operator sifting through mounds of six-foot-deep garbage. His mission was only successful after detecting a blue tarp that had been used to wrap the animals.

The Virginia Department of Game and Inland Fisheries informed Pope that the bears' remains had to be cremated since they had ingested chemicals that killed them. That's when City officials learned that disposal in the landfall wasn't the proper course to begin with.

The Thalhimer's Gift

Reflective of the Richmond community's generosity (recall the dentist's offer to Elliott Yamin), offers of charity came pouring into City Hall to ensure Baby and Buster would receive a proper funeral.

Loving Pets Crematory offered its services, which was no small task considering the size and weight of the deceased. Nelsen Funeral Home provided the urns etched with each bear's name and image. Booth Memorial Company would create a bear-shaped headstone as an eternal tribute to mark the gravesite. It would be based on the winning entry in a children's design competition. However, Booth's generous offer was no longer needed when one of Richmond's most prominent families contacted the mayor's office with a unique gift.

Days before the memorial service, Charles G. Thalhimer called to invite the mayor to his home in Richmond's affluent West End. He and his wife, Sibyl, came outside in welcome as the mayor's Grand Marquis rolled slowly up the driveway to their Bridgeway Road home.

In their manicured front yard stood a life-size, 400-pound bronze of a bear. As we greeted one another, we quickly assumed the cordiality of first names. Charlie, a kind and soft-spoken man, told us the history of acquiring the bear, saying his children long ago used to play on it.

Thalhimer explained that he wanted to donate the bronze to Maymont, where he and his late wife Rhoda had been major supporters for many years. Having reached the age of eighty-five, he told the mayor that his years of collecting artwork were coming to a close. "I've sort of been collecting over the years," he explained. "Now that I'm getting older, I'm de-collecting."

Charlie said he paid $45,000 for the statue years ago but the same piece would cost $75,000 today (then 2006). The four-and-a-half-by-five-foot bronze, by sculptor William H. Turner of Virginia's Eastern Shore, ended the need for a bear tombstone design contest. So instead of a headstone, Booth Memorial agreed to make a stone marker to honor Thalhimer for his generosity. It would be placed at the foot of the bear statue.

After I finished snapping photos of the group standing beside the bear in the Thalhimer's front yard, Charlie and Sibyl invited us in to see their home. The rooms were decorated with paintings, sculpture, and other works of art. Tasteful surroundings, indeed. As our tour began, we were introduced to a uniformed maid who stood by, smiling yet shy. I don't recall her name, but I do remember something Charlie said. "We've had her thirty-five years." Looking back now, perhaps he said it was forty-five years? I can't be sure, but I do recall the length of time seemed sufficient to represent one's entire career providing for a wealthy family.

As we toured the home, Charlie and Sibyl—both genuinely welcoming and gracious—had something to say about each room. They described how, some months before, the dining room ceiling had collapsed due to a plumbing leak. It created such a mess that the children insisted the couple go to stay at Sibyl's apartment in New York City while repairs could be made. I recalled thinking, okay, this is the way wealthy people handle calamity. The children whisk their parents out of the way until normalcy can be restored.

Earlier, Sibyl had given me her card in case I needed anything when Charlie wasn't available. I later noticed it showed a New York City address, at the prestigious One Fifth Avenue co-op skyscraper, located not in midtown Manhattan at Central Park but further south, at Washington Square Park in Greenwich Village.

As we were walking through the house admiring this and that, Charlie tried to give the mayor a bread-box-sized bronze elephant. He was simply trying to de-collect, after all. The mayor declined. Later,

Charlie again tried to give a piece of art to the mayor which he accepted: a small but valuable bronze of a Remington-style horse, by a British artist whose name I don't recall. "I feel like a thief," the mayor said in astonished appreciation as Charlie handed it to him. The piece sat on his desk for some time after our visit with the Thalhimers.

THE MAYOR'S INVESTIGATION

Back at City Hall, an internal investigation was piecing together what had happened after the bear bite.

Five days after the child was bitten, more than a dozen state and local officials met at Maymont to discuss options recommended by the U.S. Centers for Disease Control and Prevention: kill the bears to test for rabies; quarantine the bears for observation; or start the child on rabies shots. Richmond's public health director, Dr. Janice Carson, was the highest-ranking city official at the meeting. She later explained she had recommended that the child take the rabies shots, but that state officials had insisted on testing the bears for rabies. She said state health officials had told her that euthanizing the animals to test for rabies was considered the "gold standard" and was urgent.

Early in the meeting, Maymont's executive director asked for a show of hands for euthanizing the bears, and no one raised their hand. After much consideration, though, the "reluctant and heart-wrenching decision" was made to test the bears for rabies, according to the city's thirteen-page investigation report. It indicated those at the meeting unanimously determined "that the best interest of public health would be served by euthanizing the animals to determine whether or not the child needed to be vaccinated."

As that meeting was underway, the child's mother had called Carson for information about having her child take the rabies shots because she "didn't want anything to happen to the bears," according to the report. She asked Carson for information about the vaccine to determine whether she would give it to her child and agreed to follow up by noon that day. However, when the two spoke again only a couple of hours later, Carson told the mother that the decision had already been made to kill the bears.

Carson later said that state game officials even had their plans in place. As soon as the decision was made, the Virginia Department of Agriculture transported the brain tissue to the lab for sampling, and that the lab had been put on notice to be ready, she said.[188]

The city's report described the health department's notification process as "grossly inadequate."

"City health department officials would have well been advised to notify City leadership prior to making any decisions relative to the bears as it related to the child," the report said. "There was no one person clearly in charge of making the final decision at the meeting and consideration of the mother's opinion and preferences was not at all incorporated into the decision-making process.

"Maymont's public information and emergency protocols should specify that the City Administrative leadership should be considered when decisions of this nature are brought to the table," read another excerpt. In addition to reprimanding the involved officials, the report criticized the lack of cooperation by the mother during the inquiry process and assured the public that two new bears would be brought to Maymont.

Alternatives other than killing the bears did exist. "The behavior of local and state officials made matters worse," said the *Richmond Times-Dispatch* in an editorial titled, "Why Bears Matter." The article continued, "They carried out what appeared to be a hasty decision to have the bears killed so rabies tests could be conducted, even though (a) rabies seemed unlikely, (b) rabies inoculations are no longer painful, and (c) other alternatives that did not involve killing the bears might have sufficed. Public officials are supposed to be more deliberative."[189] The city's report found that the child did not need stitches, and neither the hospital nor a pediatrician follow-up visit ever mentioned the need for taking rabies shots.

Carson, who had been with the city for twenty months, lost her job for not notifying the mayor or CAO Harrell about the situation. A city press release announced her departure as a "key personnel decision." Unlike other separation announcements, hers did not include a quote from Harrell expressing thanks for her service. Carson, however, refused to become a scapegoat. "As the former director of the Richmond City Department of Public Health, I will not accept the blame nor full responsibility for the deaths of the bears at Maymont Park," she wrote in an op-ed in the *Richmond Times-Dispatch*.[190]

The Richmond SPCA also investigated the situation. SPCA executive director Robin Starr's report noted that none of the officials was an expert on black bears or rabies in black bears. Citing a national expert at The Humane Society, the report said a better choice would have been to treat the child for rabies and quarantine the bears for a reasonable period of time.

"The failure to consult with the Mayor's office is most perplexing," the SPCA report said. The decision to dump the bear bodies in the landfill "exacerbated the public's immense anguish over this occurrence," Starr wrote, adding that the participants in the decision to kill the bears reportedly didn't know they could have had the bears' remains cremated instead.

The mother, identified only as "Julia" in media reports, went virtually underground during the turmoil. She became embroiled in a Child Protective Services court hearing and hired prominent local attorney Michael Morchower to represent her. Across Richmond, she was vilified with contempt and seen by many as unfit to be a parent. Conspiracy theories evolved as a result of her conflicting accounts of what had happened. She hired Morchower when she heard that "Richmond Mayor L. Douglas Wilder called for an investigation into the incident and into whether [I] was negligent as a parent."[191]

The city's report said the mother's actions violated Maymont's safety measures and did not reflect vigilant care for the child's well-being. City officials had wanted to interview the child as part of its investigation to determine whether the mother could have prevented her son's injury.

Morchower and Tony Spencer, another prominent attorney, represented Julia on questions of inadequate parental supervision during the two-hour closed hearing. Richmond Juvenile and Domestic Relations District Court Judge J. Stephen Buis ruled the child was adequately cared for by his mother. No evidence of child abuse or neglect was shown. The case was closed.

"This is a wonderful mother who has a wonderful relationship with her child," Spencer said. "The family unit prevailed in this case. It was an accident. A one-time accident," said Morchower.[192] "We've had 100 murders in the city of Richmond over the last two years, and the two bears have generated more interest and more concern than all of the murders we've had combined," he told the *Washington Times*. "For an accident of this nature to generate this level of hostility towards the mother is beyond my wildest imagination."[193]

Julia, the boy's mother disguised in large sunglasses and a broad floppy white hat, avoided reporters after the hearing by exiting the court building separately from her attorneys. Having caught hell from all corners for what had occurred, she simply wanted to disappear. And who could blame her for that.

Maymont's New Star Attractions

Soon a new bear would be coming to Maymont—and he needed a name.

The mayor's announcement of the arrival of a new black bear brought cheers from the Richmond community. It helped to fill the void left by Baby and Buster's needless killing. For a community still healing from grief, the news imbued a measure of celebratory salve. Little more than two months later, a black bear arrived at Maymont, compliments of state game officials. When he was found months earlier, the male cub was approximately six months old, either abandoned or orphaned, and weighed a mere fifteen pounds.

With the upcoming introduction of the now nourished sixty-pound cub, the mayor announced a children's contest to recommend a name for Maymont's newest addition. "Though in the very early stages of restoring the Maymont exhibit to what it had been," the mayor said in a press release, "I did want the public to be aware of the diligent efforts underway to see that the black bear exhibit can once again serve as a popular attraction for the thousands that visit this beautiful park each year."[194]

Before his formal debut, the new bear needed to acclimate to his new home for six weeks in the park's off-exhibit den. During this time, the bear was taught to become comfortable with its habitat so that once allowed outside into the exhibit area, it understood to come back to its enclosure at night for feeding.

Meanwhile, the bear naming contest throttled into full swing. We received more than 400 suggested names from across Virginia and even Maryland. A panel of student judges would decide the winner. The new bear's name would be announced at the time of its introduction to the public. Although the naming contest was intended for children, many entries were sent in by adults who could not resist the urge. Maymont's newest occupant was christened "Phoenix," and like the mythical bird that rose from its own ashes, the chosen name reflected the story of resurrection and beauty, much like restocking the bear exhibit itself.

The debut of Maymont's first replacement black bear was celebrated at an all-day "Bear Affair" festival held there in June. Local television personality Lisa Schaffner warmed up the crowd of some 400 spectators as the mayor and Governor Kaine chatted amicably on the stage, waiting their turn to speak.

"The bear is a beautiful, rare and unique thing," the mayor told the gathering. "It's about life and coming back." When the mayor announced the name, Phoenix timidly peeked out of his den and hid behind a tree for a few minutes. He scoped out his noisy audience before scampering up the hill. The mass of standing families moved promptly over to the viewing wall that offered windows for small children to see the bear's every movement. Many adults stood on their tiptoes to catch a view. Other children were perched atop parental shoulders, pointing, and applauding at the sight of the animal. By this time, sections of the bear habitat perimeter had been fortified with a hedge of thorny Barberry bushes, additional security fencing, and visitor warning signs in English and Spanish. "This is a wonderful story. The bear was all alone in the world, and now it will have all these friends," Governor Kaine told the crowd. "It's great to be able to celebrate Maymont's newest addition."[195]

Next came an unannounced feature of the celebration: the unveiling. A cloth had been ceremoniously draped over a large object near the bear exhibit. To close the program with dramatic flair, an announcement was made, and the cloth was pulled away to reveal the life-size bear statue. It was located just across from the gravesite. Charlie was beaming when the mayor publicly thanked him for his generosity in donating the statue, and recognized his late wife, Rhoda, as well. Both had been major supporters of Maymont over the years.

When Phoenix got a new buddy to keep him company months later, Wilder promptly announced that another new bear-naming contest would begin. As before, children across the greater Richmond area were encouraged to send in names along with an explanation of why theirs was the best choice. More than 300 entries arrived, this time coming from as far as South Carolina. A panel of high school students judged the names based on criteria such as creativity and originality. Two local youngsters, ages nine and ten, shared the winning name: "Midnight." "I think the young black bear at Maymont should be named Midnight because both bears are black," one child printed in big block lettering.

Midnight's debut came during another bear ceremony at Maymont. The twenty-one-month-old male bear from Madison County weighed about 130 pounds and was acclimating to the exhibit for a few hours each day. Midnight and Phoenix appeared quite compatible together romping in their expansive woodsy digs. Minutes after Midnight's name was announced, Phoenix appeared and playfully awoke the still-sleeping newcomer—to the delight of the small group of students, teachers, and parents who attended the event. "Maymont now serves as a wonderful home for these two bears which visitors will be able to enjoy for many more years to come," the mayor announced.[196] At the close of the ceremony, Maymont presented Wilder with an honorary certificate proclaiming him a "Bear Buddy for Life."

Today at Maymont, the bear statue has a nose rubbed shiny from the playful children who climb all over it, just as Charlie's kids did in their own front yard. As one sad chapter closed, a new, happier one opened.

PHOTOS

Mayor Wilder's impact on city council is depicted in this editorial cartoon by Gary Brookins. The mayor was one of Brookins' favorite subjects, resulting in more than two dozen cartoons.
(Courtesy: Gary Brookins)

On the campaign trail, Wilder promised to streamline local government—and the extent to which he took action is reflected in this editorial cartoon by Gary Brookins.
(Courtesy: Gary Brookins)

Mayor Wilder was grand marshal of the Hull Street Christmas Parade in 2006. Police Chief Rodney Monroe escorted him along the parade route because the horse seemed skittish and ready to bolt.
(Author's Collection)

Mayor Wilder speaks at a rally by the Alliance to Conserve Old Richmond Neighborhoods (ACORN) to protest the state's plans to demolish the Murphy Hotel in Downtown. The hotel was torn down in 2007.
(Author's Collection)

"American Idol" singing contestant, Elliott Yamin, receives the key to the city from Mayor Wilder before performing before a massive downtown crowd in 2006. *(Author's Collection)*

Mayor Wilder honored blues guitarist, B.B. King, with a proclamation announcing "B.B. King Day" when he performed in Richmond in 2008. Chief Administrative Officer Sheila Hill-Christian read the proclamation before the start of the show. *(Author's Collection)*

Mourners toss a handful of soil on the graves of Baby and Buster, the Maymont Park bears that were killed and tested for rabies after one of them bit a four-year-old child in 2006. More than 500 people attended the memorial service with a eulogy by Mayor Wilder.
(Richmond Times-Dispatch)

Mourning the deaths of Baby and Buster, the star attractions at Maymont Park's animal exhibit, is reflected in this editorial cartoon by Gary Brookins. The Richmond community erupted in a storm of extreme anger and disbelief after learning what had happened to the bears.
(Courtesy: Gary Brookins)

The mayor visits the home of Sibyl and Charlie Thalhimer to admire the bronze bear statue that was given to Maymont Park as a tribute to the memory of its black bears, Baby and Buster.
(Author's Collection)

Mayor Wilder, Democratic senatorial candidate Jim Webb and I stop for lunch during the campaign. Webb narrowly defeated incumbent Senator George Allen.
(Author's Collection)

As Mayor Wilder greeted Queen Elizabeth, he graciously extended his right hand to shake hers as his left hand gently touched the back of her elbow. Though meant as welcoming and innocuous in the moment, the gesture represented a breach of royal etiquette.
(Joseph Sohm/Shutterstock.com)

(Author's Collection)

Editorial cartoonist Gary Brookins portrays the royal couple's visit to Richmond with a passing reference to Wilder's method of "cleaning house" in city government. *(Courtesy: Gary Brookins)*

Mayor Wilder enjoys a Richmond Braves playoff game at The Diamond with Mike Plant, executive vice-president of the Atlanta Braves, in 2007. The quandary over whether to build a new stadium for the Richmond Braves ended with the team's decision to relocate to Georgia.
(Richmond Times-Dispatch)

During a three-hour gig as guest host on Jimmy Barrett's WRVA morning show in 2007, Mayor Wilder promoted his vision to develop a public marina on the James River, among other city topics.
(Richmond Times-Dispatch)

Standing in Libby Hill Park during "Richmond Day" on May 24, 2007, Mayor Wilder and London's Richmond-upon-Thames Mayor Marc Cranfield-Adams take in the famous James River vista that gave the city its name.
(Author's Collection)

Mayor Wilder and others prepare for a groundbreaking ceremony for the "Richmond Riverfront Section" of the Virginia Capital Trail in 2007. The fifty-two-mile trail for cyclists and pedestrians connects Richmond with Jamestown along the scenic Route 5 corridor.
(Author's Collection)

Only days before the state's senatorial election in 2006, Mayor Wilder campaigned for Democratic candidate Jim Webb (at left) at Virginia Union University. Joining them are Gov. Tim Kaine, then-Sen. Barack Obama, and former Gov. Mark Warner.
(Richmond Times-Dispatch)

CNN's John King interviews Mayor Wilder about Barack Obama and presidential politics in February 2007. The interview was taped in the mayor's office, as I sat off-camera at his desk.
(Author's Collection)

Mayor Wilder and top aide Harry Black attend a city council meeting in March 2007. The council rejected Wilder's recommendation to appoint Black as the city's acting chief administrative officer.
(Richmond Times-Dispatch)

Mayor Wilder's selection of Sheila Hill-Christian as the city's new chief administrative officer was unanimously approved by council, leading to this banner headline in the *Richmond Free Press*.
(Author's Collection)

Police Chief Rodney Monroe's success in community-oriented law enforcement earned him a national reputation—and job offers from other cities. A month after this headline ran in the *Richmond Free Press*, Monroe accepted an offer to become the new police chief for Charlotte, NC.
(Author's Collection)

Accolades poured in after the mayor announced he would not seek re-election. Many noted his lengthy career of public service, as reflected in this tribute by Gary Brookins.
(Courtesy: Gary Brookins)

Two weeks before the presidential election in 2008, Barack Obama drew a full house at the Richmond Coliseum, with nearly 13,000 people in attendance. Another 7,000 swarmed outside, listening to him over loudspeakers.
(Richmond Times-Dispatch)

CHAPTER EIGHT

THE MAYOR TOUCHED THE QUEEN

PREPARING FOR THE ROYAL ARRIVAL

The phone call came unexpectedly, especially since City Hall was closed that afternoon.

"Linwood, is that you standing at the window in your office? The Secret Service are saying you better get away from that window, or they will shoot now and ask questions later." The voice belonged to the city's emergency management director, Ben Johnson. His tone was serious. Little did I know that more than a dozen sharpshooters were stationed along the roofs of downtown buildings overlooking the Virginia State Capitol, just across the street from City Hall.

May 3, 2007 was not your average Thursday. Queen Elizabeth II and Prince Philip would soon arrive for a grand ceremony to commemorate the 400th anniversary of the founding of Jamestown, England's first permanent settlement in North America.

The carefully planned event called for the queen to greet thousands of well-wishers and tour the 219-year-old, Jefferson-designed State Capitol, newly refurbished over a two-year period. It reopened only days before her arrival. Her Majesty also would address a special joint session of the Virginia General Assembly, the oldest continuous lawmaking body in the New World.

Richmond was the royal couple's first stop on a six-day visit to the U.S., their first in sixteen years, that included visits to Colonial Williamsburg and Jamestown. Of course, they would also make the most of their trip by slipping in some other activities, such as dining at the White House with President George W. Bush, laying a wreath at the World War II Memorial in Washington, DC, and attending the Kentucky Derby.

Some 7,000 people came to see the queen in Richmond, with hundreds standing in line for hours on that cool, drizzling morning, some since dawn. The city's bus system provided free shuttles into downtown since nearly a dozen streets had been closed off the night before.

Security fencing was set up in concentric rings on the lawn, enclosing access among groups of credentialed guests. Uniformed and plainclothes officers roamed through the crowd, looking for anything suspicious. State and city downtown offices were closed that afternoon so employees could go to the Capitol or stay at home to enjoy watching the queen on television. That was the official "spin." Yet there was a hidden reason: as Johnson told me later, it's much easier for sharpshooters to monitor buildings when they are empty.

So, when the sharpshooters noticed me standing at the window of my fourth-floor corner office at City Hall, which faced toward the State Capitol, Johnson sprang into action and called.

I asked him if I could remain in my office as long as I sat at my desk and stayed away from the windows, and he relented. Still, sitting at my computer, I was a bit shaken by the thought that the back of my head could be in the crosshairs of a gun held by a sharpshooter. I fixated on some strange JFK assassination thoughts I could not shake.

Sitting obediently at my desk, I watched the televised arrival of the gleaming black limousine bringing Her Majesty and the Duke of Edinburgh up the driveway and to the steps of the Governor's Mansion, where the front door opened on cue, to be greeted by Governor Tim Kaine and his wife, Anne.

For Wilder and everyone else, the arrival of British royalty provided a unique respite from otherwise seemingly mundane topics of the day, like building new schools or approving the city budget. Preparations for the royal arrival had been underway for months, with a heavy emphasis on the choreographed protocol. Buckingham Palace and the British Embassy had dispatched about fifteen advisors to consult with the Governor's Office about the rules for playing host to the queen. The State Department even sent a consultant who specialized in foreign dignitary ceremonies and appropriate gift-giving.

Days before the event, I participated in a mock rehearsal on the Capitol grounds so that I could brief the mayor on protocol to follow. As one would expect, the arrangements for a visit by Queen Elizabeth are timed precisely to the minute. British protocol is British protocol, after all. Though her entourage arrived at the Governor's Mansion at 3:30 p.m., invited guests were strictly required to be there by 2 p.m. or they would not be allowed in. At 2:30 p.m., the Secret Service locked down the entire Capitol Square grounds as a security precaution for the queen's arrival.

Wilder was among the dignitaries waiting inside the Governor's Mansion. Joining him on a select guest list were former Virginia governors, the current U.S. Senators and the chief justice of the Virginia Supreme Court, and their spouses. Wilder was accompanied by his daughter, Loren. She had served as surrogate First Lady when her father was governor, so she knew the role well.

The plans were laid out in painstaking detail and in strict order. Everything must be just so. As stated in the confidential preparation plans:

> After the Governor enters the Mansion with Her Majesty and His Royal Highness, he will begin making introductions to pre-set clusters of guests. The cluster assignments will be given to you by Amy Bridge, Mansion Director, upon your arrival at the Mansion. Time allotted for each cluster is approximately two minutes. The Queen will remain at the Mansion for 12 minutes. It will become apparent when it is time for HM/HRH/GOV/FL to begin moving towards the door to leave.

What followed outside was a traditional part of the queen's public appearances: the "walk-about." She spent fourteen minutes walking with Governor Kaine around the State Capitol to greet thousands of cordoned-off well-wishers who had waited for hours. Many held floral bouquets and cameras for the special moment.

Security officials jumped to attention at one point when some high school football players rushed up to the rope to hand the queen an autographed football. She calmly accepted the gift and kept moving down the line.

People screamed and applauded wildly as Her Majesty made her way, collecting her gifts and smiling brightly as her white-gloved hand wobbled in the air. I took some degree of pity for her lady-in-waiting who struggled with the numerous bunches of flowers (and the football) handed off by the queen.

Behind them came Prince Philip escorted by First Lady Kaine, who described different things along the way. At one point even the Prince took part in helping collect the many bunches of flowers in their glistening plastic wrappers. Bound by protocol, the Prince always walked at least two steps behind his wife, though that day he was trailing much farther, appearing to enjoy the spirit of the welcoming crowd and his conversation with the First Lady.

A week before, the Governor's Office had sent several documents outlining royal etiquette and protocol on topics such as how to address the queen, to stand when she enters a room, and when it was proper to shake her hand. I passed all of that information along to the mayor.

One rule of etiquette Wilder and others had to always uphold was to "be in place." Just as the invited guests had to be in their place for the queen's "cluster chats" when she arrived, they also had to make sure she was safely out of sight—doing her walk-about—before they could plan their next move: dashing off by alternate route to the other side of the State Capitol, to be in their designated place before the queen arrived there for the ceremony to begin.

The Mayor's Touch

As Kaine walked with the queen, he maintained an appropriate social distance. After reaching the South Portico of the State Capitol, they stopped to observe a ceremonial dance performed by Virginia's Indian chiefs. Then they headed to where Wilder stood, waiting to be presented. As she approached, however, he dashed over to be next to his daughter, briefly turning his back to the queen (another royal no-no). The queen shifted course toward his new location. Wilder greeted her by extending his right hand to shake hers as his left hand gently touched the back of her elbow.

Wilder touched the queen's elbow! C-SPAN captured the moment.

Based on the royal protocol information we were given in advance, the violation was clearly evident: "It is proper to shake hands if either the Queen or Duke of Edinburgh offers an extended hand. It is not appropriate to touch the Queen or Duke, except to shake hands when they have offered theirs."

Other than that faux pas, innocent as it was, Wilder and his daughter followed the script. Loren handed her father a small, beautifully wrapped box with royal blue silk ribbon, which contained the key to the city. He handed the box to the queen, who looked down at it thoughtfully for several moments.

Prince Philip then quipped to Loren, "Is that the key to the city? You might want to give it back. If that is the key to the city, how ever will he get back in?"[197]

Wilder laughed loudly and playfully grabbed the Prince's upper arm, prompting the queen to look up from the gift she was holding and smile at the mayor. Wilder then extended his hand to shake the Prince's, as if to reassure him that he only meant well with his burst of enthusiasm. The entire exchange with the Royals lasted about a minute.

The mayor's exuberant touch upon the queen did not create too much of a stir. However, *Style Weekly* could not resist commenting on Wilder's breach of protocol: "The royal visit of Queen Elizabeth II to Virginia may have been the gala event of the year. Faced with real royalty, our governors got giddy: Tim Kaine looked like a goofy-grinned prom date with his thumbs-up mug, and Doug Wilder nearly caused an international incident when he grabbed the Queen's hand for a hearty handshake."[198]

Leaving Wilder, she moved forward to shake hands with the Indian chiefs who had lined up to meet her. Then, the eighty-one-year-old British monarch and forty-nine-year-old Virginia governor slowly ascended the two dozen granite steps of the South Portico—offering no handrail—to enter the building. Their spouses followed, as Wilder and other participants watched from below.

Oliver Hill's Key to the City

The queen slowly walked past layers of roped-off well-wishers inside as she made her way toward the lectern where she would speak. As planned, she stopped for the governor to introduce her to civil rights icon Oliver W. Hill, frail and blind in a wheelchair, who sat waiting for her.

Kaine later described the touching moment when she gently clasped his hand and spoke to him.

"I am so honored to meet you," she told him.

"The pleasure is all mine," Hill replied.

"You know I am so warmly welcomed in Virginia," she continued.

"You're going to have to come back real soon," he enthused.

Hill had turned 100-years-old two days earlier. At his birthday celebration at a downtown hotel later that week, attended by 1,000 guests, Wilder recounted what Philip had jokingly said in reference to the key. He then presented Hill with his own key to the city and poked fun at himself for his way of shaking up City government. Wilder said, "And I can tell you Oliver, that there are those who will say to you, 'Keep it and use it to fix it so I never will be able to get back in.'"[199]

After the queen entered the building with Kaine and was safely out of sight, Wilder and other dignitaries dashed back through the building by an alternate route to take their seats in the historic assembly chamber—and be in place—before the queen arrived to speak.

Her remarks focused on how modern times had embraced social change and inclusion, and she emphasized a respect for cultural diversity. She contrasted the occasion with her visit to Virginia fifty years earlier, for the 350th anniversary.

"Over the course of my reign and certainly since I first visited Jamestown in 1957, my country has become a much more diverse society just as the Commonwealth of Virginia and the whole United States of America have also undergone major social change," she said. "The melting pot metaphor captures one of the great strengths of your country and is an inspiration to others around the world as we face the continuing social challenges ahead."[200] A standing ovation followed her seven-minute address.

Unknown to the public was the extent to which Kaine and his staff strategized with the queen's advisors on all aspects of the impending royal visit. Three months earlier, they huddled on how to address media inquiries about the queen's itinerary that, if not skillfully handled, might create a frenzy in the British press. One news outlet already quoted a Secret Service official in Louisville, Kentucky, who confirmed the queen would be there the same weekend as the Kentucky Derby. The queen's representatives insisted that Kaine's office make no comment, referring those questions instead to Buckingham Palace and the British Embassy. Explained an embassy advisor, "This is done very much for security purposes, but also avoids critical or mischievous media picking holes in the programme before we can even get it off the ground."[201]

Kaine and his staff also agonized over the queen's speech planned before the General Assembly, coming less than three weeks after the Virginia Tech massacre in which thirty-two were killed and seventeen wounded by a deranged sniper. The Associated Press even carried a story that the queen had already planned to meet with some of the Virginia Tech survivors. That news report caught Kaine's staff off-guard because it had not yet been publicly disclosed.

Due to the raw sensitivities of the recent Virginia Tech massacre, Kaine's office was given the opportunity to edit the queen's speech and emphasized the degree of cultural change and diversity since her visit in 1957. It recommended nuanced changes that included toning down her remarks about slavery. References about Wilder and his being the "grandson of slaves" were dropped completely. The queen only alluded to slavery near the end of her remarks, when speaking about the 200th anniversary of the United Kingdom's parliamentary act to abolish the transatlantic slave trade.

After the speech, she met for about eight minutes with Virginia Tech faculty and students, including three students who had been wounded. One student gave her a bracelet with thirty-two polished stones, one for each person slain, that bore the school's colors of maroon and orange.

The entire scripted event moved in clockwork order. The only hiccup occurred earlier that day, causing a brief delay, when the queen's entourage arrived at Richmond International Airport. The moveable steps were too short to reach the door of the plane and the red carpet wasn't properly unrolled. She remained in the plane waiting for things to get straightened out.

As schedules go, the queen's entire visit in Richmond from start to finish lasted a total of seventy-three minutes.[202] Having viewed the event on my office computer and knowing it had just ended, I stood up from my desk and could see the queen's fifteen-motorcycle, twenty-plus vehicle motorcade moving along Interstate 64, heading east toward Colonial Williamsburg. By that point, I didn't think the Secret Service sharpshooters cared very much about how close I stood next to the window.

Within an hour, the royal couple appeared in an open horse-drawn carriage traveling down Duke of Gloucester Street, the main street in Colonial Williamsburg, lined by thousands who watched and waved.

CHAPTER NINE

GAME OVER FOR THE RICHMOND BRAVES

RENOVATION PLANS UPSTAGED

It seemed everyone was on board to keep the Richmond Braves baseball team from leaving the city. The only question: how could it be done? Build a new ballpark? And if so, where, and how much, and who would foot the bill?

Others wanted to renovate the existing 9,500-seat ballpark, an aging sports facility that had become known for its structural cracks, falling chunks of concrete, and lack of modern amenities. Christened "The Diamond" when it opened in 1985, the city's ballpark lost its luster over time. Braves officials described it as the poorest-grade facility for any AAA minor league team in the country. The ongoing debate—whether to build or renovate—had begun well before Wilder became mayor. The discussions continued with a long series of hits and misses along the way.

In 2003, ballpark renovation became the focus, as the city and neighboring Chesterfield and Henrico counties committed to spend $18.5 million to spruce up The Diamond. That applecart was disrupted only a month later, when a private group of local businesspeople and baseball supporters proposed building a new $58 million stadium in the city's downtown.

The proposal to build a new ballpark quickly derailed the agreement to renovate the old one. A group called the Richmond Baseball Initiative was considering three locations: Shockoe Bottom, just east of downtown; along the Canal Walk near Ethyl Corporation south of downtown; or in the Manchester district, south of the James River.

Several Chesterfield and Henrico officials balked at the proposal for a new ballpark, explaining their funding commitment was only for renovation. A new ballpark would require a renegotiated deal. Some county officials said that a new ballpark should not even be built in the city but in their own area, where open land was more widely available. Still, the business group privately briefed city council on its proposal. And city council, in turn, gave nearly $20,000 for an architectural and planning company to evaluate the three locations.

Only a few months later, the Richmond Braves made its desires known for a new stadium, as well. Braves officials had lost interest in continuing to play at The Diamond, though having initially agreed to stay once the site was renovated. Instead, they now wanted to investigate the possibility of a new downtown stadium rather than lock into renovating the old one. All along, though, team officials underscored their commitment to remain in Richmond. That's what everyone was hoping for: to keep the ball team from leaving the city.

The Richmond Baseball Initiative later presented plans for a new ballpark in Shockoe Bottom. It would anchor a large development including restaurants, retail stores, trophy office space, housing, and a hotel. Feasibility studies could take up to a year.

Meanwhile, county officials complained that the Braves' decision was putting their credibility at stake and their funding commitment effectively on hold. They pointed out that any delay would only increase the cost of renovations. A new stadium would require a new deal. Yet more time would be needed before any final decisions could be made.

The concept of a "village development" featuring a new ballpark took full steam in the coming months, however, ballooning into a $330 million project that would be funded privately by Global Development Partners LLC, with the help of a community development authority created by the city. The new development, to be called Market Village, would feature 1.2 million square feet of mixed residential and commercial space. New historic-styled buildings would fill in vacant spots between existing buildings that would surround the ballpark. Planners envisioned boutique shops and other retail space on the ground floor, with 1,200 apartments and condos on the upper floors. Parking would be either behind buildings or underground. Historic landmarks such as the Farmers' Market and Main Street Station would be within easy walking distance.

Yet, as can happen with a spectacular development vision, it proved not meant to be. The village project collapsed in late 2005. Time to start over. Wilder began to push his own proposal: a new $40 million ballpark at a nearby site known as the old Fulton Gas Works, an eleven-acre tract owned by the city at the bottom of Church Hill. The plant operated until the 1950s to convert coal into gas for heating homes. A Fulton baseball stadium could be built at no net cost to taxpayers because real estate taxes, admissions taxes, and other stadium revenues should be able to cover construction costs, the mayor pointed out.

Anxious for a new stadium, the Richmond Braves shared its excitement in a letter to Wilder in January 2006. The letter from Mike Plant, executive vice president of the Atlanta Braves (which owns the Richmond Braves), encouraged the mayor to believe there was a ballpark solution in sight. It read:

Dear Mayor Wilder:

After several productive meetings with your staff, I am writing to reiterate that the Braves intentions are to stay in Richmond. While we have not yet finalized an agreement to date, I am encouraged with the progress. In the weeks ahead we pledge to work with the appropriate individuals in developing a Memorandum of Understanding which identifies the responsibilities of each party, the thresholds for performance and a timeline which allows us to play our 2008 season opener in a new stadium.

The new stadium site proposed presents some great opportunities. However, along with those opportunities come challenges that must still be addressed with city staff and others. I appreciate the effort you and your staff have made to identify an opportunity for the Richmond Braves to continue to be part of the City of Richmond's future development plans.

Mike Plant

A month later, Wilder sweetened arrangements by announcing that the developers of the nearby Rocketts Landing on the James River would help pay for a ballpark as well as a marina. Richmond would not have to raise money for a new ballpark, he said, and funding from neighboring Chesterfield and Henrico counties would not be required. The mayor had long advocated developing the city's eastern riverfront for public use. Along with the growing Rocketts Landing residential development, he believed the stadium project and marina could greatly help to transform the area.

After receiving Plant's letter on wanting to remain in Richmond in a new stadium, he continued to wait for a Memorandum of Understanding. It would spell out the issues that the City and Braves would need to resolve before construction could begin. The Braves' letter suggested an MOU could be coming within weeks; however, nothing seemed to be happening.

Mayor "Smokes Them Out"

It was now time to issue a press release about the matter. The headline said it all: "Atlanta Braves Organization Reneges On Plan to Support New Ballpark in Richmond." It was the mayor's first public comment on the Braves' inaction to proceed with an MOU.

> By late 2003, notwithstanding plans to renew its lease at The Diamond which was to be refurbished and, then later, shifting direction by expressing a desire for a new downtown ballpark, the Braves now remain no closer to having a new home than before.
>
> Despite the engineering-related and other studies that we have provided to make this deal work, the Braves organization is now being unresponsive to the City's desire to accommodate the team with a new stadium in the Fulton Bottom area.
>
> The Braves need to explain why they are suddenly balking at the good-faith efforts extended to them, for several years now, by the City.[203]

Privately, the mayor growled, "We had to smoke them out. We need some answers on this."

Plant, whose letter had encouraged Wilder, seemed indignant. "I'm just blown away by these false representations. He [the mayor] said we misled the citizens of Richmond, and I don't think we've done that," he told the *Richmond Times-Dispatch*.

The mayor's press release did achieve its desired effect of smoking out information. Plant said the mayor had already been informed about major issues that needed to be worked out before an MOU could be signed. That included questions about highway access to the site, parking, the possible presence of buried toxic waste, how the project would be financed, and what to do about a creek that ran through what would be the middle of the playing field. Information provided by the City was far too sketchy for the Braves to commit, he said.

Wilder, for his part, said the city couldn't wait forever for the Braves to decide what to do.

"Will we be looking for other teams to come? If necessary," he said. "Are we depending on the Braves to come to fulfill what needs to take place in Fulton Bottom? No. Will we welcome the Braves if they want to come? Yes. But there's a limit to everything, and the limit here today is that we have said that we have done all that we know how to do."[204]

While not pulling the plug on a new Fulton ballpark, the Braves soon reached out to Chesterfield and Henrico. The Braves were sold on having a new ballpark surrounded by shopping, entertainment venues, and apartments or condos, which had been a key part of earlier proposals. Team officials asked what the counties might have to offer. Some early interest was shown for the vacant Cloverleaf Mall at Midlothian Turnpike and Chippenham Parkway, just west of the city limit. County leaders spoke of the need for a regional funding arrangement. Ultimately, nothing happened.

If the Braves left the city, it would mark the end of a half-century tradition of playing minor-league ball at the site of The Diamond. Team officials said that a new stadium was needed to create more revenue, noting that the team ranked 10th in attendance in the fourteen-team International League and was losing $1 million a year.

By mid-2006, Wilder announced his support for The Diamond for the future of baseball in Richmond, ending speculation about other possible locations. Time was running out. "After receiving much input from our citizens on the issue of a new baseball park, it has become increasingly clear to me that The Diamond is the most logical choice in continuing to serve as the venue for baseball in our region," he said in a press release. "In consideration of many factors, such as centralized location and highway access, I am convinced that The Diamond is the very best option available."[205]

As the city's lead negotiator for the ballpark, the mayor had a major task before him. Within weeks he met with the regional partners: Henrico County, Chesterfield County, and the Richmond Metropolitan Authority which owns and operates The Diamond. On the other side of the negotiating table was Mike Plant, the Braves' point man to handle discussions with Wilder. And Plant had to answer to his higher-ups, as well.

Ballpark construction, either new or refurbished, had to begin so that deadlines could be met for upcoming baseball seasons in Richmond. The Braves knew this, the mayor knew it, but nothing firmed up in terms of a written agreement. All parties would have to agree on how much to contribute toward a new stadium, to keep the project moving ahead for the opening season in 2008. Yet, having many seats at the table hindered any ability to make quick decisions. While the mayor made sure the City's economic development and planning staffs were ready to shift into high gear, a lot of other moving parts had to be coordinated to be able to achieve anything. Still, everyone wanted to keep the Braves in Richmond.

Building a New Ballpark

By year-end 2006, Wilder announced a grand vision to bulldoze and redevelop the entire area at The Diamond site and build a new ballpark. The concept of a "village" of shops and offices surrounding a sports arena enticed the Braves. That's what the team had sought during earlier, failed negotiations.

The Braves had forced the City's hand to redevelop the Boulevard corridor by refusing to sign a long-term lease to continue playing at the old ballpark. One of its complaints was the ugly industrial area next to the playing field, used for decades by the City to store maintenance vehicles and other equipment. The sixty-acre swath had long been overlooked due to its gritty, back-street nature, though it represented the largest tract available for development within the city limits. Relocating the City's maintenance operations elsewhere and opening up the tract for new development could have a transformative impact.

The mayor knew the clock was ticking. This was his last and best chance.

"They (Braves) want to play in 2008 in something new," Wilder told a *Richmond Times-Dispatch* reporter. "We can't play around. We don't have idle time. We have to hit it."[206]

New discussions were taking place, though largely below the radar. When it became apparent there wasn't enough time to build a stadium for the 2008 season, the mayor worked with the Braves for a short-term lease extension at The Diamond as an agreement was being reached for a new stadium. The local paper splashed a photo of the mayor and Braves' Plant in September 2007 enjoying a play-off game in a Diamond luxury box. Things were looking up. Wilder, caught by a reporter on his way out, said discussions had been "very productive." The Braves later agreed to sign a lease for up to three years, through the 2010 season, to allow time for a new ballpark to be built.

Among the regional partners, however, questions remained about funding and whether to renovate the ballpark or build a new one. A lot would have to happen—and quickly—before the ceremonial shovels could break ground to get things started. When the City again announced plans in January 2008 to build a new, 8,500-seat stadium near the old one, Braves and county officials complained they had not been briefed in advance. Moving hurriedly to this point, the City had already sought bids to demolish the old ballpark. Another factor that hindered negotiations was Time Warner's pending sale of the Atlanta Braves (and its farm team, the Richmond Braves) to Liberty Media. Internal corporate decisions had to be made before the Braves could firmly proceed with any plans to remain in Richmond.

Negotiations then stalled over a long-term lease, even as the Braves reportedly offered a $15 million, twenty-year lease they were willing to sign to stay in Richmond. The *Richmond Times-Dispatch* said the team had offered to pay five times as much rent for a new stadium along with other concessions, but still could not get the regional partners to agree.[207]

The City chose a national developer to create a master plan for the old ballpark site. This large tract on the Boulevard could be reconfigured with roadways to the new stadium, likely with a new hotel and plenty of land for shops and ample parking. Another nineteen-acre tract could become available by relocating a state-owned facility near the ballpark. The mayor felt certain he could get Governor Kaine's buy-in on that.

Remaining at its current location, offering interstate highway access, seemed ideal.

THE BRAVES DECIDE TO LEAVE

Within days of the City unveiling its master plan to redevelop the ballpark area, the news broke: the Atlanta Braves decided to move its Triple-A farm team to Gwinnett, Georgia, about forty minutes outside of Atlanta. The Gwinnett County Board of Commissioners approved a $5 million deal to buy a twelve-acre parcel to build a new ballpark for the Braves. The team would soon become the Gwinnett Braves. The move reflected an accelerating trend to relocate farm teams near their major league parent.

Looking back at Mike Plant's comments in the local media, it became apparent to some that he had always been playing a game of cat-and-mouse with Richmond. Just weeks before announcing to leave, the Braves were still working with the City. "We're still at the table, at this point in time," Plant told a reporter.[208] Local media coverage reflected a changed tone in recent months. Braves officials increasingly pointed out things they disliked about the old ballpark—as well as the City's planning process for a new one.

Richmond and its regional partners were stunned by the Braves' announcement. Many officials were quoted in the paper expressing their frustration that the team was leaving. Others noted no agreement had been reached on whether to renovate the ballpark or build a new one.

Plant called to personally inform the mayor that afternoon after the Gwinnett commissioners voted. He said his organization had been involved in discussions for two years with Gwinnett County about building a new ballpark. Chief Administrative Officer Sheila Hill-Christian and I listened carefully as the mayor spoke with Plant on the phone, which was placed on speaker. It was a brief and solemn phone call, punctuated by our occasional raised eyebrows by what we heard as we looked at each other.

We immediately issued a press release headlined "Richmond Braves Involved With New Ballpark Plan In Georgia For Past Two Years." It read:

> Mr. Mike Plant, executive vice president of the Atlanta Braves, this afternoon notified Mayor L. Douglas Wilder that his organization had been involved with Gwinnett County, GA officials for the past two years in planning a new ballpark there.
>
> Richmond officials had been approached by baseball teams as recently as two months ago, but did not actively pursue the opportunity because they believed they were negotiating in good faith with the Richmond Braves.
>
> Given recent developments, the City will pursue all op-

tions and has already received calls from at least two organizations.

There will be a baseball team in Richmond.[209]

Approached by local reporters, Wilder said he was not angry, but surprised and disappointed by the Braves' decision. He later acknowledged the Braves' departure had damaged the public's perception of him. Reportedly the Washington Nationals had been interested in coming to Richmond, but nothing came of it because the City had been waiting for the Braves to make a decision.

Plant described the Braves' reasons for leaving in this way: "It was delay, lack of clarity on financing and this opportunity coming along. Between June and January, I talked with someone [at the City] for 45 minutes. I rest my case."[210]

Hill-Christian took issue with Plant's assessment. "Only just a week before the word leaked out, the Braves had notified the City of Richmond in writing on January 7 that *the Braves are still supportive of a stadium located on the Boulevard site,*" she wrote as the guest columnist of the mayor's *Visions* newsletter. "Bottom line: local officials in our region had been negotiating in good faith with the Braves, never expecting what would come about."

She also spoke about the future of baseball in a video segment. Her calm demeanor reinforced what the mayor had already said: the Braves secretly negotiated a deal to relocate. "I was with the Mayor when a senior Braves official personally telephoned with the news about leaving Richmond," she said. "During that phone call, he disclosed that the Braves had been involved with the Gwinnett ballpark plan for the past two years."[211]

Henrico County's top official also came to Wilder's defense about the length of time required to plan and redevelop the area around The Diamond. While acknowledging the Braves' frustration with the pace of the work, Henrico County Manager Virgil R. Hazelett said, "They had accepted that timetable. They understood what was going on."

City council, which was not involved in the negotiations, became equally frustrated. "What the hell are we supposed to do? This was the mayor's project," Council President Pantele told a reporter.[212] Council issued its own press release with Pantele noting, "As we work towards a replacement team, we hope that the City Administration will learn from this experience."[213]

Richmond had a problem on its hands in getting a replacement team. While the mayor continued to proclaim that Richmond would have a new team, there was little he could do to make that happen.

For the better part of 2008, the city was prohibited from trying to lure another team by the International League, which owned the territorial rights to Richmond, until the Braves left. Any franchise talking to Richmond officials without permission could face a $25,000 to $50,000 fine from Minor League Baseball.

If a new stadium in Gwinnett was not ready in time for the 2009 season, the Braves still had the option to renew its lease agreement to play at The Diamond. So, the City's hands were tied. The chairman of the Richmond Metropolitan Authority criticized the Braves, noting they had insisted on at least a two-year lease renewal. "It's certainly clear now what their intent was," said RMA's James L. Jenkins. "They were trying to cover their bases to keep us from cutting them short in case their facility was not ready."[214]

Just two weeks after the Brave's announcement, Wilder expressed his frustration during a wide-ranging interview with the *Richmond Times-Dispatch*. The subject of the Richmond Braves' departure certainly came up.

"Tell me what we could have done, or what I should have done, not we, what I should have done. I think the Braves made up their minds some while back, early on, that they wanted a new stadium," he said. "If someone would tell me what it is I should have done, I'd like to know. No one has yet told me."[215]

The Atlanta Braves notified the RMA in September that it was terminating its management agreement to use The Diamond. Just the night before, the Braves played what turned out to be its last game there in a 9-3 win over the Norfolk Tides.

Wilder pushed, prodded, and cajoled many stakeholders in seeking a ballpark deal to benefit the city. City staff made a scramble to put all of the parts together, but it could not happen soon enough. Approaching the end of the year, the mayor knew time had run out, on his watch. Ironically, the national developer in charge of the master plan recommended that a new ballpark should be built in Shockoe Bottom instead of at The Diamond site. The entire matter would confront the next mayor.

While the Braves' departure freed the city and its regional partners to pursue a new team, attracting another Triple-A franchise was out of reach. No Triple-A teams were looking to relocate. Class AA and Class A leagues, though, eagerly expressed interest in coming to Richmond. Despite Wilder's assurances, Richmond did not have a baseball team in 2009. Baseball returned to Richmond the following year. The Diamond became the home of a Class AA team named the Flying Squirrels.

CHAPTER TEN

Mayor Fights for a Public Marina

"The View That Named Richmond"

Wilder had big dreams when it came to the James River. He battled those who sought to commercialize the riverfront for economic gain by building luxury condos to be enjoyed by a privileged few. Looking back, it's clear that without the actions he took to help preserve public access to the river, the James might not look the way it does today.

He envisioned the City developing a riverfront park east of downtown that would include a public marina featuring tourist attractions such as tall ship festivals. "There is nothing like a sunset on the James," he said, referring to the river views from his condo in Shockoe Slip as well as from his riverfront home in Charles City County.[216] To fulfill his dream, the mayor wanted to preserve an almost ten-acre stretch of open riverfront land consisting of three adjacent parcels. The City already owned one of them, but the others would need to be acquired from private owners.

It became a lightning-rod topic—historically and politically—when a developer in 2006 had proposed building a $160 million high-rise condominium complex on the largest of the private parcels. The project, called Echo Harbour, would gobble up more than half of the open waterfront.

But Echo Harbour would not only restrict public access to the river. The proposed twelve-story condo towers also would block the historic view of the James from the Libby Hill Overlook that gave Richmond its name, due to its striking geographic similarity to the London borough of Richmond-upon-Thames. Historic preservationists were soon up in arms.

149

The condo project was also financially linked to a member of city council, Bruce Tyler, whose architectural firm represented the Echo Harbour developers. The mayor and others quickly accused him of a conflict of interest. Wilder kept Echo Harbour before the public eye. To alert the public and build opposition to the project, a press release titled "Developer of Controversial Waterfront Project to Address Planning Commission" was issued two weeks in advance of the January, 2007 meeting.[217] Many more press releases would follow in the months ahead.

The mayor wanted the City to purchase the other privately-owned parcel, held by Lehigh Cement Company, as the centerpiece for the park. Next to it was the City-owned Intermediate Terminal site, where he envisioned a seventy-three-slip marina that could accommodate a variety of watercraft including dinner cruise ships from the Hampton Roads area. He wasn't alone in wanting to maximize the waterfront. Next to the Intermediate Terminal to the east, the Rocketts Landing residential development announced plans to build its own 150-slip private marina. Wilder sought a joint venture to share operational costs, such as for a harbormaster, fueling stations, and bathrooms, to transform the area as a maritime tourist attraction.

RICHMOND'S 400TH BIRTHDAY

Wilder's idea of a riverfront park and marina received a boost when Richmond commemorated the 400th anniversary of Jamestown as the first lasting English settlement in North America and the Jamestown settlers' visit to what would later become known as Richmond. British Captain Christopher Newport led a group that reached the falls of the James some eleven days after establishing Jamestown. To celebrate the anniversary, the mayor declared May 24, 2007, as "Richmond Day" to kick off a weekend festival featuring live music, dance performances, living history storytelling, a Richmond Symphony evening concert, and a "400 Candle Blow-Out" fireworks display over the James.

More than 50,000 people came to the river to see a replica of the Godspeed, one of three ships that carried English settlers from London to Jamestown in 1607. Three other ships—the schooners Lady Maryland, Virginia, and Pride of Baltimore II—were also open for free tours. The festival continued at nearby Libby Hill Park, where one could see the historic river view resembling its namesake in England. Even the mayor of Richmond-upon-Thames, Marc Cranfield-Adams, came to town for the occasion. He stood with Wilder at the park that overlooked the James to admire "the view that named Richmond," as coined by William Byrd II in 1737.

The mayor's proposal gained another boost of interest months later when Wilder and corporate leaders held a groundbreaking ceremony for the "Richmond Riverfront Section" of the Virginia Capital Trail. The park and marina would complement the City's segment of the fifty-two-mile hiking and biking trail that connected Richmond with Jamestown along the scenic Route 5 corridor.

In October 2007, after more than a year of design reviews and meetings, the mayor held a press conference at the Intermediate Terminal site to announce plans to build Richmond's first public marina. He ceremoniously signed the paperwork seeking approval from state and federal authorities. The targeted completion date would be the summer of 2009. The mayor introduced an ordinance to council seeking authorization to begin negotiations to purchase the Lehigh parcel. Council's approval would be required for any proposed purchase agreement as well.

The marina's $6 million cost would more than pay for itself through utility hook-up fees, totaling more than $9 million, once the Rocketts Landing riverfront community was fully developed, the mayor said. However, news reports estimated total costs at more than $17 million after making additional improvements near the marina. That included about $5 million to realign state Route 5 out of a flood-prone area and $4 million for environmental cleanup to prepare the City's nearby Fulton Gas Works property for redevelopment. To cover those costs, the City and the Richmond Redevelopment and Housing Authority would sell thirty acres in the area for about $11 million.

Still, some council members, including Tyler, questioned the mayor's plan. "What sense does it make for the city of Richmond to be in the boat business?" he asked during a council meeting.[218]

BUILDING PUBLIC SUPPORT

Wilder received a significant shot of support when one of the city's most prominent corporate leaders urged council to invest in the public marina and riverfront park.

"As you consider your decisions about to be made on the riverfront . . . please balance the long-term benefit to our city vs. the short-term gains . . ." of the Echo Harbour project, grocer magnate James

E. Ukrop wrote in an email sent to council, with a copy to Wilder and two other city officials. "By investing in the marina and park site, you will not only create more public access to the river, you will also not lose the magnificent view of the river from Libby Hill (one of our city's most valuable assets)."[219]

Wilder openly expressed his own view about the Echo Harbour project. "We have made it clear that we're not interested in any of these high-rise apartments on the river," he told the *Richmond Times-Dispatch*.[220] Council, however, delayed acting on the mayor's proposal for months until more financial and engineering information became available. "We don't know the scope. We don't know what market we're targeting," explained Councilman Martin Jewell.[221]

Leery of the marina project, council even removed any reference to a "public marina" from the Lehigh purchase ordinance and made a point to include this caveat:

"No obligation or payment of public funds shall be incurred or made for the development of a public marina on or adjacent to the real estate described in this ordinance."

The newly added language effectively terminated the mayor's plan to build a marina. To counter council's action, Wilder launched a full-blown public relations campaign that blasted council for attempting to sell the riverfront to developers instead of preserving it for the public. It began with strong language in his *Visions* newsletter, with a headline that read: "It's Your River, Richmond, But Not For Much Longer."

> Council's own argument in meetings has been they want to leave options open to see what developers may offer for this [Lehigh property] and surrounding land – yet this now prohibits the City from exercising any options on land it currently owns!
>
> Curiously, there is no restrictive language by Council that applies to the *other* property adjacent to Lehigh: the proposed Echo Harbour condominiums. This potential development is represented by Councilman Tyler's architectural firm, as shown on the company website.
>
> Other cities such as Charleston, Louisville and Portland have created incredible riverfront parks. Our Council members and others have visited these cities and always talk about how we should emulate their successes.

Now, as we face the last opportunity to preserve and develop a masterpiece within our own park system, Council members have chosen to further delay my proposal and altered the language so that part of the land might be sold at a later date.

The mayor encouraged citizens to contact their council representative "and let them know you want to protect the river for <u>ALL</u> of Richmond."[222]

A few days later another release, titled "Mayor Wilder to City Council: Don't Sell Riverfront to Private Developers," warned of council's upcoming plans to kill the mayor's proposal.

"This is the City's last opportunity to preserve the open riverfront parcels in the Downtown area," Wilder said. "If our citizens wish to maintain these few remaining parcels of land for the public's enjoyment and not for the private developers, then they should immediately contact their Council representative before it's too late."

In addition to reminding the public that Tyler's architectural firm was involved, the release unearthed new conflict-of-interest dirt surrounding the situation. "Developers associated with the Echo Harbour project have made sizable political contributions to Council members, such as Council President William Pantele, Council Vice-President Delores McQuinn, and Bruce Tyler."[223]

The city's press office used every media platform available to promote the mayor's plan. The marina project was featured on the city's website for weeks. A video of the mayor's press conference announcing the marina aired repeatedly on the city's public access cable channel. The topic was among the mayor's daily radio messages airing on WRIR. The mayor promoted the riverfront park and marina during his three-hour spot as guest host on Jimmy Barrett's WRVA morning show.

Arrangements were made for the Schooner Virginia, a modern replica of an early 20th century pilot vessel, to return to the Intermediate Terminal one weekend to give free tours, serving as a reminder of what Wilder envisioned as a maritime tourist attraction in the city.

The riverfront park and marina proposal proved to be one of the mayor's most effective examples of an integrated PR campaign designed to influence public opinion and build support. The mayor's call to action paid off, as he noted in his newsletter:

"Just a few weeks ago, citizens responded to the *Visions* newsletter about protecting the City's riverfront for a public park instead of private development. Your calls and emails were heard loud and clear and legislation that had been sitting idle for seven months was suddenly, unanimously approved [by city council]."[224]

Tyler had already written to counter the mayor's statement that "no Council Members have made any attempt to meet" with his administration on the subject. He attached an email he had sent to Hill-Christian asking for a meeting. Tyler's letter read in part:

> As I have indicated publicly, the proper development of the James River is a critical piece to the future development of the City of Richmond. However, I believe the approach you have chosen is not in the long-term best interest of the City of Richmond, its taxpayers, and its citizens.
>
> I trust you will make yourself and your staff available to discuss this issue in a timely manner. I look forward to meeting with you.

Wilder's chief of staff, Sandra R. Robinson, sent a smack-down response to Tyler a few days later. It read:

> Through your letter of May 9, 2008, you prove once more that this City Council is incapable of articulating its own vision for the development of the City of Richmond. Instead, you continue to pick holes in plans laid by this Administration.
>
> The City, through its administration, has been trying to finalize a purchase of the Lehigh cement company for almost three years. Those efforts have included protracted and difficult negotiations with the property's owners and the state: all for the development of the James so that it can remain enjoyed by everyone—regardless of financial status. With developers tripping over themselves to gain approval for development plans that seal off access to all except those who purchase one of their high-priced condominiums, this has not been an easy feat.
>
> In the process we have provided presentations, offered tours, and answered City Council's questions. The information has been provided, it has not changed since provided, and it will not, at this point, be repeated.
>
> If you believe that you know of a "better approach" to develop the James at the site where the Mayor proposes a public

marina and the state wants to construct a bike trail, then articulate and develop that plan. The City has waited more than 400 years for the public marina, with no one doing anything to bring it to fruition for the benefit of the public. That said, the ethics of good and sound government should prevent you from further articulating the cause of your client (the developer of Echo Harbour) as is illustrated on your company's website (a copy of which is attached). To have to remind any elected official of that in these days is puzzling.

Sandra R. Robinson

The battle lines hardened between council and the mayor over the riverfront park and marina proposal. Wilder briefly floated the idea of using eminent domain to acquire the Lehigh property. That idea went nowhere fast as he continued to criticize the Echo Harbour project.

"Sadly, the prevailing mindset among many people here in Richmond is to often defer to the developers and overlook what few remaining opportunities we have for truly serving the public good," he lamented in a publicized letter to Joseph P. Riley Jr., longtime mayor of Charleston, S.C., which had taken strong measures to preserve its own riverfront.

INFLUENCE OF THE DOWNTOWN MASTER PLAN

Another city initiative, already underway, greatly escalated public support to maintain the open waterfront on the James.

In mid-2007, the city's Department of Community Development launched the formation of a new Downtown Master Plan to reflect the city's long-term vision for creating a more vibrant quality of life there. Based on extensive input from citizens and businesses, the master plan served as a blueprint for future development of Richmond's downtown and riverfront. Downtown was already becoming a sought-after destination as one of the city's fastest-growing residential areas.

"A Master Plan is a guide for localities to use in making future decisions," Wilder wrote in a *Richmond Times-Dispatch* commentary. "As Rachel Flynn, the city's director of community development—who has ably overseen the Master Plan's development—has repeatedly noted, 'It all starts with a city having a firm vision in place for what it wants to become.'

"I made it clear, and our city officials have insisted, that what was needed was 'the people's plan' because our citizens are voicing an unprecedented degree of interest in what they want our downtown to become," the mayor continued.

"Many cities across America have already bettered themselves—e.g., New York, Chicago, Charleston, Washington, D.C.—by purchasing property to create riverfront parkland for public recreation, by investing in environmentally friendly mass transit for traveling convenience, and by establishing design standards to create neighborhood quality-of-life enjoyment that we all want."[225]

The Downtown Master Plan, shaped by twenty public input sessions involving more than 800 citizens and stakeholders, was adopted unanimously by city council in October 2008, though council continued to ponder the issue of balancing property owner rights with the master plan's goals. When council approved final changes to the Downtown Master Plan in July 2009, the plan gave the eastern segment of the James River an "urban center area" designation that allowed for buildings to be no taller than six stories.

The Downtown Master Plan reflected strong citizen support to preserve public access to the James River, as well as other measures to make Downtown more livable. The plan focused on seven guiding principles:

- James River: create more recreational access to what was described as Richmond's "great, wet Central Park" and preserve views of the river by limiting building heights.
- Urban Architecture: require new construction to conform with the scale and character of downtown's historic architecture.
- Variety and Choice: establish zoning options for mixed-use development to create diverse, inclusive downtown neighborhoods.
- "Green City" Landscape Design: create an integrated system of park areas, with an ambitious program to plant new trees and greenery at sidewalks and median planting strips.
- "Traditional City" Transportation: promote walkability, offer more mass transit choices such as bus rapid transit, and restore two-way traffic patterns.
- History: promote the city's unique history through aggressive historic preservation measures that include additional cobblestone streets.
- Economic Diversity: provide mixed-income housing and retail

opportunities so residents at all income levels can fulfill their daily needs within their general neighborhood area.

Wilder had left office by the time council approved purchasing the Lehigh parcel, which the Downtown Master Plan had recommended. The Lehigh property, combined with the adjacent City-owned Intermediate Terminal, offered almost a quarter mile of riverfront property that could be developed for public use.

Over time, the Echo Harbour project encountered additional issues that threatened its viability. The developer filed a $5 million lawsuit against the Richmond Redevelopment and Housing Authority for attempting to renege on selling two small lots that were needed to provide emergency vehicle access to the low-lying riverfront property. At Wilder's insistence, RRHA tried to invalidate the sale by returning the developer's $23,400 deposit, but the sale later went through.

Even overcoming that hurdle, the Echo Harbour developer had to provide specific details on other issues such as potential flooding, relocating a five-foot-wide sewer line, and estimated water consumption before the project could be presented to council for consideration.

The developer also balked at the need for extensive engineering studies. Serious technical issues would first need to be resolved, so that the only question before city council would be whether the project was appropriate for the site, said Flynn. "We're factfinders," she told a reporter. "If we're not even clear on the facts, then that's just sloppy work that you forward to a public body."[226]

The Echo Harbour project never materialized into the luxury riverfront condos envisioned by its supporters. Grand architectural renderings were eventually shelved and largely forgotten.

The controversy was put to rest in 2021 when a national non-profit called The Conservation Fund announced plans to purchase the five-acre property and place it under a conservation easement that ensured the historic views of the James River, as well as public access, would remain in perpetuity. With the addition of the Echo Harbour land, the amount of open James River frontage virtually doubled, to approximately nine acres.

When the land purchase was announced, Richmond Mayor Levar Stoney said, "[The deal] includes a 350-foot dock that will provide deep water access to the James River for recreational activities."[227] The dock is fundamentally sound and usable after minor repairs, officials said.

The James River Association announced plans to build an environmental education center on one acre of the parcel, while the remaining four waterfront acres were transferred to the city as Dock Street Park as part of the James River Park System. Acquisition of the land, finalized in 2023, also allowed for the completion of the city's segment of the Virginia Capital Trail, the fifty-two-mile trek connecting Richmond with Jamestown, that could be relocated from a busy city street to a pathway along the park.

Though Wilder's vision of a city-owned marina dissolved, his actions were highly instrumental in helping to preserve "the view that named Richmond" as well as the public's unfettered access to the open riverfront.

CHAPTER ELEVEN

ON THE CAMPAIGN TRAIL

POLITICAL ENDORSEMENTS

For those seeking political office, Wilder's endorsement was considered influential as well as newsworthy. He never felt Democratic Party-bound to make an endorsement. Sometimes he didn't make one at all, which could be interpreted by some as a quiet nod to the Republican candidate. "It's one of the most popular parlor games in Virginia politics: guessing who, if anyone, will get former Democratic Governor L. Douglas Wilder's endorsement," wrote a *Washington Post* reporter.[228]

In the U.S. Senate race in 2006, Wilder endorsed first-time Democratic candidate Jim Webb over incumbent Senator George Allen, a Republican seeking his second term. Wilder's announcement was carried in the *New York Times* and *Washington Post* as well as in newspapers across the state. Polls showed the Allen-Webb race in a virtual dead heat.

Allen made the traditional rounds in search of votes at the annual "Gold Bowl" football match between Virginia Union University and Virginia State University. Wilder, already sitting in the bleachers with *Richmond Free Press* publisher Raymond Boone and Police Chief Rodney Monroe, spotted Allen and headed farther up, leaving an open seat next to Boone. A *Richmond Free Press* article noted that Boone said he looked around and saw George Allen coming. Allen then spent nearly half an hour with him "apparently seeking a *Free Press* endorsement. Meanwhile, Mr. Wilder observed from above, chuckling. Fans quietly observed the entire episode in amazement."[229] Allen had hoped to reach Wilder but couldn't. "Mayor Wilder's endorsement, anyone would love to have his endorsement," Allen later told NBC12.[230]

Before making an endorsement, Wilder typically reverted to his long-held playbook of interviewing candidates who sought his favor. He had his list of questions. He sought "succinct reasons" for why they should receive his endorsement. He performed this ritual with the Virginia gubernatorial candidates during his first year as mayor. Democrat Tim Kaine got the nod over Republican Jerry Kilgore. For Webb, the exercise paid off. But as usual, Wilder's endorsement came only a matter of days before the election. He had a history of holding tight to his cards until late in the game. Only a few days after the football game, at a City Hall press conference with Webb by his side, the mayor gave his blessing along with the commitment to campaign for him. He predicted that Hampton Roads and Richmond would be the "battlegrounds" and "a lot will depend on the turnout in those areas."

Wilder said the country was "moving down the wrong road," citing the war in Iraq as a waste of money. "I think the Iraq war has been wrong from the beginning. We've been in this terrible quagmire for four years. The American people have been sold a bill of goods.[231]

"Look at what a person stands for today and how their views help to make a better Commonwealth of Virginia on behalf of all of our citizens. Mr. Webb understands the need to put this country back on course."[232] In addition to campaigning for Webb, the mayor coached him on campaigning. Privately, he suggested Webb should exude more spontaneity because his demeanor came across as "wooden."

Wilder extended Allen the courtesy of contacting him before the press conference, to let him know an endorsement would not be coming. "I want to tell you where I'm heading but under no circumstances will there be any demonizing of you," he told Allen by phone before the press conference with Webb. "I will just say positive things about you. My personal feelings haven't changed for you."

Wilder wanted to reassure him that the politics would not get dirty. Allen had directly succeeded him as governor of Virginia. They were bonded as members of a distinct club, where respect was given and returned. Wilder and Kaine had even more in common: both had been Richmond mayors and Virginia governors, though in reverse order.

The week following the endorsement, Wilder and I attended an outdoor campaign rally for Webb on the grounds of Virginia Union University. The crowd had grown to nearly a thousand before the speeches finally began. The election was only a few days away. While boosting voter support for Webb was the intended purpose, everyone knew the big draw would be a U.S. senator from Illinois by the name of Barack Obama. He was still two years away from winning the presidential election. Highly popular, he had not yet even announced his candidacy, but everyone knew he would. He also returned to Virginia as a featured speaker at the Jefferson-Jackson Dinners in 2007 and 2008, drawing massive audiences to the annual Democratic Party event.

Before the mayor and I left City Hall for the short ride to the VUU campus, I purchased two copies of Obama's latest book, *The Audacity of Hope*, to bring with us. It seemed a prime chance to get the autograph of a future president. Wilder seemed almost giddy when he saw what I had done. One book for him. One book for me—both to be signed by the author.

As people gathered outside for the rally, their breath shaped in the brisk morning air, the VIP crowd remained in a nearby university building where a holding room offered light refreshments. In addition to Webb, the gathering included Governor Kaine and his wife, Anne, former Governor Mark Warner, Congressman Bobby Scott, State Senator Henry Marsh, and State Delegate Donald McEachin. Everyone was milling around, waiting for Obama to arrive. When he did, the mayor sprang into action by getting the books autographed. Obama wrote a lengthy passage in the mayor's copy that began: "To Our Leader." I shook hands with Obama, who seemed very relaxed and was smiling as he worked the VIP crowd. By sheer luck, someone had a camera and snapped a photo of us, with me looking business-like in a coat and tie, and him wearing a jacket with an open-collar white shirt.

When it was time to go outside for the speeches to begin, the crowd roared as Obama appeared on the stage. Later that day, Wilder's security detail took us to Norfolk State University for another Webb campaign rally. The mayor, wearing a stylish orange leather coat, would speak. We were running late, so the driver was gunning it and tailgating, almost running the car ahead of us off the interstate. The mayor had to tell him to slow down.

A few days later, Webb won the election, very narrowly, against Senator Allen.

Campaigning for Obama

Getting Obama's autograph at VUU wasn't the first time the two charismatic politicians had met. Obama introduced himself to Wilder at a

Washington Correspondents' Dinner shortly after being elected to the U.S. Senate in 2004. "I was very impressed with him – nice looking guy," Wilder said. "He came over to *my* table, as a matter of fact. He said very nice things – how he had been inspired by what we had done in Virginia, and it meant a lot to see that take place. And he wrote something similar to that in the book when he autographed it," Wilder told *Politico* in 2007.[233] Obama was inspired that Wilder, as a Black man, had been elected governor, and cited him as a role model.

Propelled by Black politicians like Shirley Chisholm and Jesse Jackson who helped pave the way, Wilder and Obama understood the complexities of running for president. When Wilder briefly ran in 1991, he gained high marks among early focus groups in New Hampshire until they learned he was a Black man. By Obama's campaign, sixteen years later, views on race had softened. Obama acknowledged the change in the book he autographed for us. "Whatever preconceived notions white Americans may continue to hold, the overwhelming majority of them these days are able – if given the time – to look beyond race in making their judgments of people."[234]

Wilder agreed. "I think absolutely that the nation is ready," he said. "People change."[235] Still, he cautioned that his own experience should be a reminder that the concern would not go away completely. "Let's not kid ourselves again. The issue of race will not disappear, but I don't think it will predominate," he told the *New York Post*.[236] Though he had not yet endorsed Obama, he said Obama's style reminded him of his own. Both men downplayed the issue of race while running for office. Neither ran as a Black candidate, but simply as a candidate who happened to be Black. "(Obama) doesn't use race as a badge, nor does he consider it a barrier," Wilder said.

Wilder took issue with those who questioned whether Obama was "black enough" in his views and whether he spent adequate time seeking support within the Black community. Wilder called the "black enough" criticism "inappropriate," claiming it was due to "the pimping of race."

"What is blackness?" he asked. "Is it the way you talk? Do you got to say, 'Dey this, dey dat.' Or the way you dress? Or is it the forgiving of certain things? What is black enough? Is (Jesse) Jackson black enough? Is (Al) Sharpton black enough?"

During his statewide races, Wilder said some "were accusing me of not spending enough time in the Black community, not recognizing that 85 percent of the vote was not in that community. Where was that criticism coming from? Some of the Afro-American community. They ultimately were supportive. But they were questioning the strategy."[237]

Running for national office, Obama also could be targeted by other Black politicians in other ways as well.

". . . I told Barack and Michelle Obama in a Washington gathering, early on, I said the biggest problem that you may encounter in this trek is going to be overcoming the doubts and the fears and suspicions of your own people," Wilder said during an interview with NPR's Michel Martin.

"I said, but don't be dissuaded by that because it won't be from the people themselves, from the grassroots, it'll be from those who think they are the top and they should be the ones that pass judgment of who is next prepared to lead. Pay no attention to that, do what you should do, and he's done that."[238]

Wilder elaborated on his advice to Obama in an interview with *Politico*.

"Certain black leaders would believe that you have to go through their prism: 'If I lay my hand on you, you're okay,'" Wilder chuckled. "So many people have made a living off of the pimping of race. I told him when he runs, one of his big problems he would have is with the African American leadership, as such. He didn't question it. He said, 'I think I know what you mean.'"[239]

He referred to it as a "crabs in the basket" mentality that basically means "if I can't have it, neither can you." Like crabs trapped in a bucket, they're all striving to get out at the same time and consequently, none can escape. In the same manner, members of a group can work against each other so that no one achieves a level of success beyond the others.

By late 2007, Wilder still lavished praise on Obama but was not yet ready to formally endorse him. "I've been tremendously impressed with Obama," he told *Politico*. "He has the ability to be a uniter, more so than she [Clinton]. I think the country is tired of the 'us' and 'thems.'" Still, *Politico* cautioned, "Wilder enjoys political gamesmanship and has a history of withholding favor, so his future intentions remain unclear."[240]

Wilder had always been vigilant that his endorsement not be taken for granted. "Anyone with even a passing familiarity with Virginia politics and Wilder's role in them knows Wilder likes nothing more than withholding his nod, forcing months of personal wooing and press reports about his intentions," observed the *Washington Post*.[241]

Sometimes the media jumped the gun. *Jet* magazine incorrectly reported Wilder had endorsed Obama in late November 2007. It drew the mayor's immediate response. A press statement titled "Mayor L. Douglas Wilder Indicates Position on Presidential Candidate Endorsement" read: "A report by *Jet* magazine (November 26, 2007) stating that I have endorsed Sen. Barack Obama for President is incorrect. While I previously have said kind things about the senator, I have made no endorsement of any candidate at this time."[242]

Wilder finally endorsed Obama on January 4, 2008. "Our country needs a leader who can unite and inspire our citizens, a leader who can see things with a fresh eye, and a leader who can move beyond the parochialisms of the past. We need a leader whom people want to rally around with the confidence that positive change is on the way. Senator Barack Obama brings forth all of these qualities. I am tremendously impressed with him . . ." He planned to campaign for him across the country "to the fullest extent possible that my schedule will allow."[243]

Hillary's "Hissy Fits"

Wilder instinctively knew how to make headlines, such as when he spoke of Hillary Clinton having "hissy fits" on the campaign trail. "Hillary's reactions to things conjure up images that are not necessarily the healthiest in terms of hissy fits or reactions because of emotions, like the crying and the weeping and then forgetting somewhat that she did that," he said in a *Bloomberg* interview.[244]

That same day he also told CNN that Clinton's "hissy fits" reinforced the stereotype of a woman's emotions. While not exactly a nice thing to say, it made the national news. "Well, did you see it? People describe things differently. Sobbing. Wiping away tears. But the whole thing is, look, wait a minute, if you say you're strong, I'm tried and I'm tested, be strong. Be tested. Don't weep and cry about it. You don't have to do this. You can quit any day you want to.

"But if you stand up to it, measure to the task. And that's what I'm saying. Be the candidate rather than the woman. Be the candidate rather than a person of race. This is what the American people are looking for. Someone who speaks for all of them."

Wilder also said Obama faced more difficulty as a Black candidate than Clinton did as a woman. "What he has to do is to understand that it's difficult for some people to come to grips with that. And he can't attack anybody. And particularly for an African American man to attack a white woman, it's not going to be accepted. Let's face it. And I've always said stay above the fray, deal with the issues, concentrate on moving America. And he's done just that. I've never once heard him talk about running to make history because he's an African American or a member of a minority group."[245]

The mayor warned Obama about the dangers of trusting the accuracy of voter opinion polls. They could vary greatly from actual election results, especially when a white candidate runs against a non-white candidate. Often, the mayor's interviews referenced the "Bradley Effect," which describes when some white voters will intend to vote for the white candidate but tell pollsters they are either undecided or likely to vote for the non-white candidate, so as not to be labeled as racist. It was coined after Los Angeles Mayor Tom Bradley, an African American who lost the 1982 California governor's race despite being ahead in the polls.

Some political analysts called it the "Wilder Effect" because a similar situation confronted him in 1989, when he won the race for governor by a razor-thin margin (less than one-half of one percent), though election-day exit polls showed him with a ten-point lead. For the 2008 presidential election, though, Wilder predicted a reverse of the Bradley Effect. He expected many Republican and independent voters to publicly say they would support John McCain while quietly voting for Obama due to pocketbook issues. The nation's economy was tanking during the general election campaign.

"I'm not naïve enough to believe that racism is gone," Wilder told CNN's John King during a taping in his City Hall office. "On the other hand, I think the nearest thing to there being a candidate who could cross that is Obama. The burden is on him to say, 'Look, I'm not running as an African American. I'm not running for history's sake. I'm not running for anything other than to be the best possible person to lead this country.'"[246]

When Obama competed against Clinton in the New Hampshire primary, the polls suggested he would win by thirteen points. Instead, Clinton beat him by three points. "He should never have believed those New Hampshire polls, and I think now he recognizes that," Wilder said. "Even if he gets the nomination and heads into the fall with an apparent lead, the election will be closer than any polls will suggest."[247]

The mayor often criticized Clinton's explanation of her 2002 vote authorizing the Iraq war. "If Hillary had said to the American people,

'Look, I made a mistake. If I had known what I know now, I would have never supported the Iraq war.' If she had it to do all over again, she would have never made that same mistake again. If she had done that before, Barack Obama would be nothing," he told the *Corriere della Sera*, a newspaper in Milan, Italy.

Wilder also spoke of Clinton's "polarizing" personality. "The question keeps coming about Hillary, as polarizing as she is: Would she be the best candidate? She's fine one on one. But when there's a group, she's a little drawn, a little reserved, and somewhat testy – not relaxed. People would probably disagree, but today, I think Obama would have the best chance of winning in a general election because he doesn't carry any baggage."[248]

In a *New York Times* commentary titled "No Exit," Wilder wrote:

> Hillary Clinton's campaign was done in by a sense of entitlement and hubris. There is no greater evidence of that than the fact that, three days after the final two primaries in the campaign for the Democratic presidential nomination, she had yet to gracefully acknowledge her defeat. By waiting so long, she threatened her future stature within the Democratic Party. The question now should not be, "What about Hillary?" but rather, how does Mr. Obama plan to win and to lead – with or without Mrs. Clinton.
>
> —L. Douglas Wilder, the mayor of Richmond, VA, and the former Democratic governor of Virginia.[249]

After Obama secured enough delegates for the party's nomination, NPR's Michel Martin of "Tell Me More" asked Wilder what was going through his mind at seeing history take place.

"I couldn't have been more proud of him and the pride is registered because at no time has he ever failed to acknowledge that it was not a personal victory for him, but a victory of aspiration for a lot of people, for a lot of dreams, for those who fought for him to have that opportunity, for the destroyed souls of people many generations here before who were denied. And yet people who fought and did the things to change the patterns and the minds and the opportunities for him to have this single opportunity, and it was as if all of those people were there enjoining in this expression."

Wilder said he saw a lot of himself in Obama. Some thirty years older, he was guiding and protective, enabling Obama to reap the benefit of his decades of political experience.

"...he never indicated that he was running to make history. He was running to be elected. He was running to show qualifications and he dared to say, 'Look, I don't need anyone to tell me when my time is. It's whenever I determine it to be my time.' I saw so much of me in him that – I have said that to him. I mean, we joke about it when we talk on occasions."[250]

In a commentary Wilder wrote for the *Wall Street Journal*, he described Obama as "a forceful voice on the American scene who will be our agent for meaningful change – a voice committed to carry our nation to greater heights and to heal the divisions within our country. Unlike any other candidate, he inspires so many people of every description to step up and say: Yes, we can."[251]

During the months leading up to the election, Wilder's popularity with the press flourished. Just as he had set a historic "first," Obama's candidacy now sought to do the same. Wilder was ready to speak. Giving interviews came easily to him. He needed no coaching. When filmed in a studio, he knew to remain focused directly on the camera and maintain an elder statesman's smile. It worked.

Phone calls were coming in from the producers of some of the biggest names in network news: NBC's Andrea Mitchell. CBS' Nora O'Donnell. MSNBC's Rachel Maddow. CNN's Wolf Blitzer. Fox's Tucker Carlson. The *Washington Post*'s Courtland Milloy. The *New York Times*'s Jeff Zeleny. CNN's Glenn Beck. Sirius-XM Satellite Radio's Tim Farley. MSNBC's Chris Matthews. Voice of America's Howard Lesser. American Urban Radio Networks's April Ryan. MSNBC's Joe Scarborough. NPR's Mara Liasson. Sirius-XM Satellite Radio's Keith Murphy. Syndicated radio personality Michael Baisden.

Bob Schieffer of CBS' "Face the Nation" and Wilder hit it off so well that he was a featured guest three times on the Sunday morning program.

International media also showed great interest, with interview requests from across the globe: CBC Radio One. Euronews. Korean Broadcasting System. BBC London News. BBC Scotland. Ireland Radio. TV New Zealand. National Public Radio – Italy. Tokyo Broadcasting System. Angolan TV. *Berliner Zeitung* newspaper in Berlin. *Asahi Shimbun* newspaper in Japan. *La Croix* newspaper in Paris. News outlets in Russia, Denmark, and Kenya. The mayor was interviewed twice by Al Jazeera, the first English-language news channel headquartered in the Middle East.

Wilder's video interviews often took place in the broadcast studio in the basement of the General Assembly Building, located across the street from City Hall. Though viewers at home wouldn't know, it was an unexpectedly cramped yet functional space, with a single-view camera facing a lone chair. An image of the Virginia State Capitol served as the backdrop, a far more serene view than the ceiling pipes and hanging wires one would actually see off-camera if there in person.

It was time for yet another interview and I laughingly recall how, as we jaywalked across Broad Street toward the studio, the mayor, for no apparent reason, suddenly broke into a mild trot. No traffic was coming in either direction. To keep up with him, the security officers who accompanied him everywhere began to speed up, and so did I. Looking back, I could only imagine how silly the spectacle of four grown men scurrying across Broad Street that sunny afternoon must have been.

Wilder's interviews on Face the Nation required more preparation than the basement studio could provide. CBS taped Wilder in his office by remote feed, amid a phalanx of camera equipment. As he was being interviewed "live" in his office, I was watching and taping the show from my office two floors up.

After the interview, he joined me to watch the program. He laughed thunderously at certain segments of it, completely tickled with how it played. It happened to be Easter Sunday, so he invited me to join him at an elegant brunch at the Monument Avenue home of Don Baker, a former *Washington Post* reporter who authored the Wilder biography, *Hold Fast to Dreams*. Baker's well-dressed assembly of guests casually mingled, sipping from champagne flutes, smiling sedately, and eating daintily from the fine French china. As the mayor greeted a string of old friends, I was striking up impromptu conversations with friendly strangers. We didn't stay long, but it was an unexpected treat to enjoy Easter brunch in such an opulent setting.

The Second Black Governor

Even before Obama was elected president, Wilder witnessed another trailblazing moment he eagerly wanted to see. It involved a Harvard-educated attorney in Massachusetts named Deval Patrick who in 2006, became the second Black to be elected governor. It took seventeen years for someone to follow in Wilder's footsteps. "Thank God – at last! I'm so glad it took place," he gushed to the Associated Press. "I had thought it would happen in 3, 4, 5, 6, or 7 years, but thank God it's now happened."

News coverage about Patrick invariably mentioned the connection with Wilder as a political milestone. "Being No. 1 means nothing until you know there is a No. 2, to show that there are dreams and hopes and opportunities available to all individuals," Wilder wrote in a *Richmond Times-Dispatch* commentary. ". . . I took tremendous comfort in the confirmation of my long-held belief that my election as governor was not some sort of aberration that could never happen again."[252]

Wilder had campaigned for Patrick. He contributed to his campaign and had others send money. He later attended his inauguration. The two met again when Patrick gave the Charter Day address at Howard University and was presented an honorary doctorate by Wilder, who served on the Howard University Board of Trustees and decades before, had obtained his law degree there. (It would take another sixteen years before Wes Moore of Maryland became the third elected Black governor, in 2023.)

Now Wilder was focused on Obama's campaign—and the milestone it represented. Early on, Wilder encouraged him to campaign broadly in rural and traditionally Republican areas, just as he had done when he ran for statewide office. "I was asked not to campaign in the rural areas, but I knew that's where the white votes are. And I knew that to win, I had to get out there because Virginia had the smallest African American voting population of any southern state, representing only 15 percent of the vote in Virginia."

Wilder did not want Obama to repeat the campaign mistakes Tom Bradley had made. "Remember that Bradley did not have overwhelming support among African Americans because they said he was not spending enough time in Oakland compared to San Francisco. They never forgave him for that," he said in a CNN interview.

Wilder advised Barack not to just focus on the cities but to also campaign in rural areas and particularly in suburbia. As Wilder had suggested, Obama barnstormed across Virginia with campaign stops in conservative cities like Chesapeake and Roanoke as well as smaller areas in Southwest Virginia. He also campaigned in the predominantly white, conservative town called Chester, some 20 miles outside of Richmond. The stop was part of a three-day swing through traditionally Republican communities of the rural South.

Standing in the green expanse of a pine grove at the John Tyler Community College campus, with a huge U.S. flag draped between the trees as a backdrop, Obama spoke about the economy, the Iraq War, and the need for a "new direction" to some 300 voters seated at picnic tables. It was an intentionally small-scale, invitation-only campaign appearance.

"The American people are still checking me out, because I am relatively new," Obama told the crowd, adding the closeness of the race "shouldn't be a surprise to anybody. . . John McCain has been in the public eye for 25 years."[253]

The bucolic setting conveyed a grass-roots type of hometown rally where organizers hoped "to create an impression of proximity between candidate and citizen," as described by French photographer Jean-Robert Dantou, who covered the campaign.[254] For Obama, who stood jacket-less with fastened tie and rolled-up shirtsleeves, the laid-back country setting prompted him at one point to jokingly tease the crowd, "Who brought the potato salad?"[255]

Obama returned to Richmond two weeks before the election, where he drew a full house at the Richmond Coliseum, packed to the rafters with nearly 13,000 people. An additional 7,000 swarmed along several blocks outside, listening to him over loudspeakers.

Though we were only a couple blocks away, the throng of people necessitated our arrival by car. In no time, the mayor's Grand Marquis swooped past the barricades and into the underbelly of the aging facility. We were led to a room where a cluster of state delegates and others waited. Many handshakes later, Obama asked the photographer to speed up the obligatory group shots. He seemed very serious and focused as he autographed a tabletop of photos of himself with this person or that, each photo labeled with a stickie indicating the name to inscribe. Then, we were escorted to our seats. The mayor was taken to the other side of the stage, while I was led to a seat that had Richmond Council President, William Pantele, on one side and *Richmond Free Press* publisher, Raymond Boone, on the other. Talk about strange bedfellows.

The mood among the overflow crowd was electric. Amid continuing roars, Obama wasted no time tearing into GOP vice-presidential candidate Sarah Palin's remarks implying that some parts of the nation were more American than others. CNN's latest poll gave him a ten-point lead over McCain. "There are no real parts of the country and fake parts of the country," Obama proclaimed. "There are no pro-America parts of the country and anti-America parts of the country. We all love this country, no matter where we live or where we come from. Black, white, Hispanic, Asian, Native American, young, old, rich, poor, gay, straight, city dweller, farm dwellers, it doesn't matter. We're all together."[256]

Obama said he could win the election by acquiring 270 electoral votes without Virginia's 13, but that he was determined to win over voters who had voted Republican in past presidential elections. "This state is in transition," he said. "Obviously the success of [former Gov.] Mark Warner and Tim Kaine and [Sen.] Jim Webb indicates that Democrats can win statewide, but it's going to require everything we've got to pull this out."[257]

Wilder, an invited guest whenever Obama came to Richmond, could see that Virginia had become a critical battleground. "Nothing I've suggested he hasn't done," he told BBC Radio News. "I hope that that will follow and that he will pay no attention to the polls. Virginia is a microcosm of America, in my view. All people want are good jobs, a good education for their kids, and to get the most they can. If he wins in Virginia, he will win the election."

ELECTION NIGHT

Nearing the end of the campaign, the mayor averaged nearly a half dozen interviews each day. On election night, just as the polls were closing, NBC's John Yang interviewed him for its "Race for the White House" program on the floodlit grounds of the state capitol. Since it was way too early for voting returns and we had time to kill, the mayor suggested watching the television coverage together at his nearby condo at Vistas on the James.

His home looked like a page out of *Architectural Digest*. The terrace offered a spectacular view of the river below. A plush red velvet sofa shaped like a pair of lips filled a corner of the living room. The work of art was called "Marilyn's Lips," the mayor told me. A round coffee table could be elevated by hand to become a dining table. A beautiful bar opened from the kitchen, where I happened to notice an incense burner that needed dumping.

As we watched the political commentators on the flat screen, with the two security detail guys sitting expressionless to the side, the mayor suggested it was time for a drink. First came a champagne, followed by a Virginia wine. The mayor held up the second bottle to read the label. "Umm, the Kluge vineyard … must be from an old girlfriend," he hummed, joking perhaps, or maybe just trying to get a reaction out of me. It wasn't unusual for the mayor to occasionally toss out a zinger like that, to see the person's response. Feeling a tad tipsy by this point, I knew enough to keep my mouth shut.

Of course, the mayor was referring to the Kluge Estate Winery and Vineyard, established by a statuesque, Iraqi-born Briton named Patricia Kluge. She had been romantically linked with Wilder when he became governor in 1990. She was the estranged wife of John Kluge, a media mogul estimated at one time by *Forbes* magazine to be America's richest man, with more than $5 billion. She and John were the largest financial supporters of Wilder's campaign, hosting elaborate fundraisers at their 45-room country manor in nearby Charlottesville. Later, the media gave gossipy reports about Wilder's use of a state helicopter to visit her there, as well as getaway sightings of the couple in Nantucket and Virginia Beach.

By mid-1990, the *Washington Post* cracked the egg with an article titled, "In Richmond, Romance Rumors Fly." It began like this:

> The rumors have been bubbling in this city for weeks, tantalizing but unconfirmed, and for the most part unpublished: Is it really true that Virginia Gov. L. Douglas Wilder is romancing Patricia Kluge, estranged wife of the nation's richest man?
>
> The rumors aren't confirmed, but during the past several days enough circumstantial evidence has been amassed that most reporters and assorted other capital gossips feel comfortable venturing their private conclusions: Something is definitely up.[258]

I cannot recall if we finished the bottle from the Kluge Estate, but it seemed the wine was every bit as smooth as the mayor.

As the early Virginia returns trickled in, McCain was leading by a wide margin. We sat in a moment of silence before realizing that the votes in northern Virginia had not yet been reported. It brought a sigh of relief to both of us. With Obama's victory increasingly apparent, we dashed off to the evening's next stop: The Camel restaurant on Broad

Street. The Grand Marquis rolled up to the curb, where we hopped out to find a boisterous, standing-room-only crowd celebrating inside.

NPR cell phoned for an impromptu interview, but the crowd was so noisy we had to retreat to the quietest place we could find: the men's bathroom. Wilder spoke for only a couple minutes, at one point sitting on the closed toilet seat until he realized how comical that must have looked. Soon enough, someone banged on the door to get in and mayor sliced his hand through the air for me to ignore it. With the interview concluded, it was back to the partiers. CNN called the election for Obama at 11 p.m., noting critical key wins in Virginia, Pennsylvania, and Ohio. The forty-seven-year-old drew 365 electoral votes and 53 percent of the nation's popular vote, while his seventy-two-year-old opponent received 173 electoral votes and 46 percent of the vote. It was the first time that a Democratic presidential candidate had carried Virginia since 1964.

Soon the politicians at The Camel took turns praising Obama's victory. They were introduced individually, in terms of political ranking. After some state delegates spoke, Wilder took his turn to congratulate the first Black coming to the White House. The crowd went wild. From there we went to Mike Byrne's restaurant in Shockoe Slip for a nightcap before calling it a monumental day.

Media requests poured in the next morning for Wilder's reaction. The mayor described Obama's election as "a catharsis. It's spell-breaking, in terms of being able to say to any child in America, 'You can be anything you want to be,'" he told NPR. "It doesn't matter whether you're rich, or whether you're selected, or whether you're Asian, or African. It doesn't matter. You're an American. And what we say by words is now matched by deeds - at the highest possible level. And excuses can't be tolerated: 'Oh, I can't do this,' or 'We can't do this.' No, no, no. That's *forboden*. That's gone."[259]

Wilder attended Obama's inauguration, accompanied by his daughter, Loren. Both he and Governor Kaine were honored guests at Virginia's Inaugural Black Tie and Blue Dominion Ball, held at the Smithsonian National Air and Space Museum's Udvar-Hazy Center, with music by the Commodores.

In the weeks leading up to the inauguration, some speculation surfaced that Wilder might be appointed to an ambassador post somewhere, but nothing ever materialized.

CHAPTER TWELVE

MAYOR BOOTS SCHOOL BOARD OUT OF CITY HALL
(FOR ABOUT SIX HOURS)

THE MOVE BEGINS

It was a twilight summer evening, perfect for a City Hall lockdown. All the necessary ingredients came together to make for a banquet of chaos. Take the brewing frustration of a mayor, mix it with the continued inaction of a school board, add a heaping helping of moving vans ready to load, toss in a dash of alleged pornographic web-surfing, and top with dozens of police officers stationed throughout.

Welcome to Richmond City Hall on Friday, September 21, 2007.

Around 7 p.m., a caravan of trucks arrived at City Hall with 150 movers ready to begin. The time had come to relocate the Richmond school system offices, as the mayor had promised to do, from the upper six floors of City Hall to 3600 West Broad Street. Everything had to go: furniture, file cabinets, computers, and phones for more than 170 school system employees.

City police officers, in charge of securing the building, had already begun clearing out members of the public who were milling in the lobby. Orange cones and yellow tape blocked the doors to keep people from entering. Police brandished handcuffs, threatening to arrest reporters and any others who might try to enter. Sidewalks were cleared of curious bystanders.

As the moving vans lined up along three sides of the block, police guarded the entrances so the movers could begin dismantling the contents of the school board offices. They brought in dollies and hand trucks, loads of flat boxes, and other packing supplies.

Still inside and unwilling to leave, however, a quorum of school board members huddled for an emergency meeting on the 17th floor. As city police were trying to clear out the lobby, I saw one school board member make a dash for the elevator to get upstairs. School Superintendent Deborah Jewell-Sherman also attended the meeting, but at least one school board member complained to local broadcast reporters that she had to wait ten minutes before being allowed inside to join them.

Meanwhile, the movers had begun their work.

That night's sudden eviction should not have come as a complete surprise to school officials, as the mayor had sought to relocate them from City Hall for more than two years. Even before his swearing-in, Wilder advised them to plan to leave. He had delayed the timetable for their relocation several times, at their request.

The mayor viewed relocating the school offices as a cost-saving move. Approximately $1 million a year could be saved if city departments, paying to rent office space elsewhere in downtown, were housed instead in City Hall. Additionally, the mayor said the proximity of departments in City Hall could lead to more efficient service delivery to residents. Because the student population had dwindled over several decades, he also believed the school system did not need offices that took up six floors of space at City Hall. Instead, he had his staff secure office space for school officials in a suburban area of town that offered ample parking space as a convenience for parents meeting with teachers.

Despite the mayor's rationale for relocating, however, school officials did not want to leave City Hall and were angered by the police-monitored manner in which the move was carried out. School board member Carol A.O. Wolf came down to the lobby to insist that police allow the public and reporters to attend the emergency meeting underway. "Go ahead and arrest me," she told police officers who ignored her plea.

School Board Chairman George P. Braxton also came downstairs and announced, "We're having a public meeting. Can I take a member of the press with me?"

"There is no public meeting," Assistant Police Chief Ray Tarasovic responded. Reporters were turned away.[260]

Police Chief Rodney Monroe, on the street overseeing the operation, explained the situation to a nearby reporter. "If the School Board wants to have a public meeting, no one is stopping the School Board from having a public meeting. But this building, City Hall, is closed to the public . . . I recognize that this is a very tense environment.

"I am not here as an attorney to try and interpret what's right and wrong. That's for the courts to determine. The Richmond Police Department is just here to carry out its responsibility in ensuring public safety during this particular move." Monroe later said Deputy CAO Harry Black had asked for police officers to oversee the operation.[261]

Wilder was not there. He spent the evening at the dedication of the Main Street Station Plaza in Shockoe Bottom, gamely dancing to the band and sporting a festive blue glow stick around his head. He was given a vivid red sash to place around his shoulders, prompting him to joke: "I am a bit of a target tonight. I better take this off."[262]

Approached by a reporter as he was leaving, he replied, "Two years – it's over. Enough is enough. It's happening tonight because 3600 is ready."[263]

Plans for the eviction had been arranged a few days before, and the mayor called a handful of key staff members together to discuss what he was planning. At first, the mayor posed the question rhetorically as to whether a forced eviction was a wise action to undertake. Black questioned the move. "Can it be sustained?" he asked. No one gave him an answer, as I recall. At one point I piped up to say that since the mayor had repeatedly threatened to relocate the school board, it was finally time to act.

The plan was set. I left the meeting with my marching orders. As press secretary, I would handle the media. As the movers were hitting their stride, I emailed our press release to alert the media. Next, I would go out onto the street to read it for the news cameras and take questions.

> The relocation of the school system offices from City Hall to an alternate location has been discussed over and over, for some two years now. Several extensions have been made during this time. Both through numerous meetings and by written correspondence, the School Superintendent even indicated her desire to have the school system offices move to an alternate location.
>
> The Mayor wrote a letter to the School Superintendent in early August that office space was planned for the school

system's relocation to the 3600 Building on West Broad Street. The Mayor notified the Superintendent that this office space would be available as of September 1, with the completion date to be no later than September 30.

Having seen no indication that the school system intended to be out of City Hall by September 30, the action being taken—beginning tonight and continuing through the weekend—is aimed to minimize any disruption for the school system personnel who can resume work at their new offices, with their furniture and equipment, as of Monday, September 24.

As a result of the relocation of the school offices to their new location, the City will save approximately $1 million dollars annually now being paid by several City departments for office space in various areas of Downtown.

As soon as the City Hall space is prepared and ready, City departments will be brought into the space left vacant by the school offices. The proximity of the City departments coming to City Hall will not only save $1 million annually, but also produce greater efficiencies in the delivery of municipal services to our citizens.[264]

Standing out in the street, I noticed City Hall was eerily aglow from the huge klieg lights that had been set up to assist the movers. The grand illumination attracted curious passersby who stopped to look, but police officers shooed them away. I could hear a bizarre recording of tropical birdcalls coming from down the street, which seemed like some sort of psychological warfare technique designed to distract matters. Overall, the eviction had been well-planned; city officials even had to wear printed name badges to get around.

After reading the press release, I was surprised—and relieved—that the reporters' questions were softball. I promised reporters another on-the-street press conference the next morning and then retreated to my City Hall office. Just before 9 p.m. the school board and superintendent, along with a few council members, left their emergency meeting in City Hall and gathered on the sidewalk. They stood in a tight circle as a show of solidarity. The board voted to retain State Senator Henry Marsh as legal counsel to seek an emergency court order to stop the movers.

Fortunately, my earlier appearance didn't collide with theirs. I had already left City Hall to join some friends at an Oktoberfest party at

Benedictine High School near my home. German beer helped me escape the anxieties of the day, and my thoughts quickly shifted from a situation that I was no longer tracking.

I learned the next morning that Marsh had an emergency hearing with Circuit Court Judge Margaret P. Spencer around midnight. She issued a temporary restraining order to stop the eviction. The movers reversed course and started bringing furniture and computers back into City Hall.

The next morning, I met with a handful of reporters who, again, did not press me with hard questions. I wanted to keep the mood casual, so I wore a golf shirt rather than the standard coat and tie. I basically repeated the mayor's objectives for conducting the move. It was over in about twenty minutes. Meanwhile, the mayor would soon be arriving to give a lunchtime speech at the National Federation of Press Women conference at the Richmond Marriott, only a few blocks away. He opened his remarks with veiled references to what had just occurred at City Hall. He joked about the name tags shaped like a sheriff's badge that some attendees were wearing, adding he was glad there wasn't a new sheriff in town. "Some things that are happening around here would make one suspicious," he quipped.[265]

Caught by reporters, Wilder explained that the real question was, "Who runs Richmond?"

"If I have the authority, I need to know that, and if I don't, I need to know that. I will continue to assume that I do, but I will abide by all lawful decisions."[266] He said he was not informed of the media's exclusion from the school board meeting when he received his last update at 2 a.m.

The act of forcibly relocating the school board came only days before Wilder's imposed September 30 deadline. With school officials showing no sign of planning to leave, the forced move-out took place. Now, packed boxes sat waiting to be reopened. With office cubicles needing to be reassembled and computer wires strewn about, school officials denounced the mess. Door locks had been broken. Confidential student records spilled onto the floor.

The failed eviction produced banner headlines in the *Richmond Times-Dispatch* for several days to come. With front-page announcements such as "Wilder Fulfills Threat To Evict School Offices"[267] and "Uncertainty Pervades City Hall Amid Turmoil,"[268] newspaper sales must have surely picked up.

Council members offered quick condemnation. "A very orchestrated military attack," chimed Councilwoman Ellen Robertson. "Inexcusable and a disgrace to our city," declared Councilman Chris Hilbert. "It was just butt-ugly," agreed Councilman Martin Jewell. "The police were used as the personal army of the mayor. We can't have a government that is in effect a Third World junta," warned Council President William Pantele.[269]

The Computer Porn Investigation

Pantele had topped the news cycle that morning when the press office issued a news release headlined, "Porn Site Visits Discovered on Council President's Computer."

This was only the first bombshell of the day.

"The City's continuing investigation of inappropriate usage of City equipment now indicates a pattern of 'porn site' usage on the City Hall computer located in the office of Council President William Pantele. Deputy Chief Administrative Officer Harry Black has forwarded these findings to Police Chief Rodney Monroe for further investigation.

"I am sure that the Police Department will be meeting with the involved parties to further investigate this evidence to ascertain whether criminal activity has occurred," Black said. An investigation of alleged abuses involving City equipment among employees had been ongoing for nearly a year, the release added.[270]

Wilder later said the timing of the release was coincidental with events later that day. Yet the text, carefully written, was damning. *Style Weekly* said it "stopped just millimeters from directly accusing City Council President William Pantele of . . . a pattern of 'porn site' visits" using his computer log-in.[271]

Only later did I learn that it was the day of Pantele's 16th wedding anniversary.

The police department also issued a news release about the use of city equipment linked to pornographic material. That release, which did not mention anyone by name, said the "sole purpose of the Richmond Police Department's involvement is to determine if any sites visited or images downloaded contain child pornography."[272]

Pantele said he was unaware of any misuse and that others knew his username and password. He kept an unlocked council office, and his log-on password was on a Post-It note on his computer monitor.

"It's just not a secure environment," he acknowledged.[273] "If it weren't so serious, it would be laughable. I have no idea what this is about."[274]

A week later, the police investigation concluded that no city computers—neither Pantele's nor any others—had been used to visit sites that contained child pornography. Still, there was substance to the investigation, which identified the personal log-ons of more than one hundred employees from at least ten city agencies who had frequented porn sites.

As news cycles go, the press release about Pantele was quickly buried by actions occurring later that day. Our second press release was issued at 4:18 p.m., indicating that City Hall would close at 5:00 p.m. and reopen at 7:30 a.m. Monday. The sudden announcement only fueled rumors already swirling that a forced move might soon be coming.

Earlier that afternoon, school system employees had begun taping flyers marked "No Trespassing" and "Confidential Records—Accessed by Authorized Personnel Only" on their office doors, computers, and file cabinets. Others taped a copy of council's ordinance permitting the school system to remain in City Hall.

Knowing for more than two years that Wilder wanted them out—and anticipating the worst—several school employees including the school superintendent disclosed they had begun the school year with a stripped-down office by removing their personal items, the *Richmond Times-Dispatch* reported.

As the day unfolded, another salvo was launched to rattle council. It wasn't announced publicly, as with the allegation against Pantele. Instead, it was only known among a select few at City Hall.

The city council liaisons received a phone call from Deputy CAO Harry Black's office to schedule an appointment to interview for their job. Months before, they were told to reapply with Black for their job or face termination. All of them did reapply except for one, who was fired. Employee interviews were later postponed, as the mayor appealed the issue to the Virginia Supreme Court. Nothing would happen until the matter was resolved. "No hiring, no firing, no anything," the mayor said at the time.[275]

A Little Backstory

In the aftermath of the failed eviction, a crossfire of accusations and questions about legal authority continued to dominate the news.

Marsh was in court challenging whether the mayor could ignore ordinances authorized by council that allowed the school system to remain in City Hall. Marsh grilled Black who, at the mayor's direction, had arranged the move and gave the order to close City Hall. He was peppered with questions about student confidentiality, safe record-keeping, and criminal background checks for the movers.

Court testimony by City Economist John Wack contradicted earlier estimates that the City would save $1 million if the school offices relocated. The first-year savings would be $866,000, he said. But that did not include $2 million for renovation, moving expenses, and furniture or equipment for the school system's new office at 3600 West Broad Street, nor the $550,000 in annual rent.

Council called on Judge Spencer to make the mayor and Black repay the cost for office space that sat empty because Black had signed the lease without its approval. Also arranged without council's approval was the estimated cost of the move, which varied from $250,000 to $450,000.

Ironically, it wasn't the first time 3600 West Broad had been considered. The school board intended to relocate there in 2006, but the mayor objected, according to David Ballard, the retired school board chairman. He added that CAO William Harrell said the school system could remain in City Hall until it could find a permanent home. However, city and school officials remained at odds on the next step. Because several schools operated with noticeably small numbers of students, the mayor believed the school system could benefit by consolidating the student population into fewer schools and using a closed, surplus building rather than renting office space. School officials discussed that option, but ultimately did not agree.

In September 2005, however, two years before the eviction, the school board expressed its intent to vacate City Hall. The resolution read:

> Whereas, The School Board of the City of Richmond, Virginia (the "School Board") is charged by the Virginia Constitution to carry out its duty to provide for the public education of students in the City of Richmond (the "City"); and
>
> Whereas, The School Board is charged with the duty to provide adequate office space sufficient for its employees to carry out the administrative functions of the School Board; and

Whereas, the School Board's administrative offices have occupied several floors of Richmond City Hall ("City Hall") since the building's completion in 1972; and

Whereas, since 1972, the School Board has occupied its office space in City Hall without a written lease with the City; and

Whereas, each year since it began its occupancy of City Hall, the School Board has paid, on an annual basis, rent in [an] amount equivalent to its proportionate share of building maintenance costs, utilities, security and parking; and

Whereas, each year since it began occupancy of City Hall, Richmond Public Schools has received funds from the City in its annual budget to cover the cost of housing its Administrative Offices;

Whereas, RPS will most certainly incur additional cost in finding comparable housing for its Administrative offices;

Whereas, the cost of moving the Administrative offices was not anticipated in the 2005 budget;

NOW THEREFORE BE IT RESOLVED by the School Board of the City of Richmond, Virginia that it is in the best interests of the School Board, its employees, and the students and parents of Richmond Public Schools to relocate the administrative offices of the School Board to a facility separate from City Hall;

BE IT FURTHER RESOLVED that the School Board shall consider all reasonable options and will relocate its Administrative offices upon receiving the commitment from the City Council for funding of all expenses associated with the move and future rental payments.

Two months later, the school board voted to negotiate a lease for up to 70,000 square feet of office space at 3600 West Broad, but still could not meet the mayor's January 1, 2006 deadline, and would need until mid-April to relocate, Ballard said. The school board also asked the City to pay up to $3.4 million for the move and about $745,000 in annual rent.

Wilder rejected the proposal outright. "That request is denied because you had sufficient time, almost a year, to do what was necessary to be done," he wrote. "Now, it surprises me that you say that with your request not only can you not move, but it will take approximately $4 million for you to do that. That is not acceptable."[276]

School Board Deadline Kept Slipping

Wilder continued to push the school board to leave City Hall. Even before taking office, he said they needed to go. A July 1, 2005 deadline was extended to January 1, 2006 and then to July 1.

The school board had considered relocating to Richmond Technical Center, Whitcomb Court Elementary School, some empty downtown bank buildings, a vacant supermarket building on Jefferson Davis Highway, and the Main Street Station train shed.

A crossfire of hand-delivered correspondence continued between the mayor and school superintendent. In a September 30, 2005 letter Wilder bluntly wrote:

> So that there will be no misunderstanding, I want you to know that our administration for these purposes, will be dealing directly with you. We need to know where you would like for the properties of the school system to be relocated when the vacating process begins, so that the premises will be vacated by January 1, 2006.
>
> I say that our administration will be dealing directly with you because I have been told by the City's real estate agent that other persons have been saying different things.

More months elapsed and the move-out deadline slipped again as school officials understood they could remain in City Hall until getting a permanent new home as part of the mayor's City of the Future plan.

The mayor wrote to CAO William Harrell and City Real Estate Services Director Jane Ferrara on December 18, 2006 concerning the school system's plans to move.

> As we are quickly approaching the New Year, Richmond Public Schools ("Schools") needs to be reminded that the City intends to relocate the departments it has been operating off-site, e.g., Utilities, Economic Development, and Juvenile Justice, back to City Hall. To prepare for this transition, Schools will be moved out of the building. As contemplated, this move

should occur no later than June 30, 2007—after the academic year has concluded.

I would hope at this late date Schools has been working with you in the selection and renovation of its new home. If that has not been the case, you might also remind Schools that its cooperation with the City will ensure that its transition out of City Hall is smooth—for it is certain. Until this project is completed, I will seek regular reports from you as to your progress.

School Superintendent Jewell-Sherman, who was copied on the mayor's letter, responded to Harrell the next day and copied the mayor and school board chairman.

The Mayor indicated his expectation that the City Hall administrative offices of the Richmond School Board be vacated by Saturday, June 30, 2007. As I shared in a telephone conversation with you yesterday afternoon, my recollection is that the last correspondence from your office concerning a move was in February 2006. Additionally, we met to discuss the possibility of a new administrative office site on October 11, 2006. Subsequently, we have conversed about this matter one other time when consultants were to meet with you in the City. During these discussions, the June 30, 2007 timetable was never mentioned. Rather, the earliest date contemplated during our discussions was the summer of 2008.

Internal school system communications showed that Jewell-Sherman had been warned by her own staff that time was running out. A February 15, 2007 letter from assistant superintendent Thomas E. Sheeran recapped meetings held in 2006 and early 2007 between school and city officials and included this warning:

With the date of June 30, 2007 looming over us like the "Sword of Damocles," I feel it is necessary to provide these reference points so you and School Board members can see how this issue has evolved over time.

More months passed.

In May 2007, Wilder wrote to remind Jewell-Sherman that he was

MAYOR BOOTS SCHOOL BOARD OUT OF CITY HALL (FOR ABOUT SIX HOURS)

waiting for more information about the school system's plans to leave City Hall.

> In our last conversation relative to moving, you said the Richmond Public Schools ("RPS") might need an extra couple of months past the June 30, 2007 deadline to be completely moved out of City Hall. Though I did not readily agree to your implied request, I also did not reject it outright. In fact, I waited for you to provide a more specific timetable by which the request could be evaluated. You never provided that timetable, nor any other specific that could relate to your general request.
>
> For almost two years, RPS has known that the City Administration intended to reclaim the City Hall offices that RPS had been renting. During this time, City Administration has made every reasonable effort to assist RPS in finding a suitable new home that would meet its purposes. The City offered to retrofit existing unused school buildings for RPS, and had at one point discussed purchasing a building for RPS's uses...all to effect RPS's smooth transition out of City Hall. Those efforts were greeted with both dilatory actions and communications by RPS staff.
>
> For these reasons, be advised that the deadline for RPS to vacate its City Hall location remains June 30, 2007, as City Administration will be relocating its offsite departments to this space. The City stands ready to cover all reasonable expenses that we will incur in assisting in RPS's move.

In a June 22, 2007 letter, Jewell-Sherman informed the mayor that she had been working with city staff to consider a commercial space, a renovated Armstrong High School, or relocating to the Onslow Minnis Building in the city's East End. She indicated the planned June 30 move-out deadline could not be met. She asked for a sixty-day extension, with the new move-out date of no later than September 30.

> (City staff) noted that an RPS move from City Hall to an alternate site may take approximately 60 days from the decision point to our actual occupancy elsewhere. While this would not meet your desired June 30, 2007 deadline, it would

be in keeping with our mutual desire that RPS vacate City Hall expeditiously.

Wilder responded the next day:

From what I have been told, 3600 W. Broad Street is the intended relocation spot for Richmond Public Schools' offices. You should therefore make arrangements to start the process of moving, as that is where we intend to have you located.

. . . As you know, I never agreed with nor had any conversation about the option that would have required the City to spend millions of dollars to renovate Armstrong School (which fortunately you rejected and never reported to your Board). Moreover, I knew nothing about the Onslow Minnis School other than what had been reported in the press.

I have not given you any specific time beyond June 30 for moving, nor do I do so now. Please consider this as notice that the June 30, 2007 remains the date – and 3600 W. Broad the place. If when you have started that process, let me know, then we can determine how much more time will be needed. (We are all aware that this move is temporary until you and the Board can determine where you will be permanently located.)

Fireworks erupted the following week when the superintendent notified the mayor that the school board wanted to renovate a building on its own, rather than go to 3600 West Broad Street.

Excerpts of Jewell-Sherman's June 28, 2007, letter to Wilder:

I write to reiterate that the School Board and I share your desire that we find an acceptable solution for relocation of RPS administrative offices.

I also write to bring you up to date on the School Board's most recent actions. During the June 27, 2007 meeting of the School Board's Operations and Facilities Committee, Committee members voted to forward a recommendation to the full School Board at its Monday, July 2, 2007 meeting. The recommendation will be to have the School Board approve the pursuit of partnership opportunities to renovate an existing RPS building or property through the Public Private Education Act (PPEA). A key benefit of pursuing such a strategy for our relocation is that the cost will be within market rates, thus demonstrating fiscal accountability to the citizens of Richmond. Additional benefits are that this strategy will necessitate only one move of the administrative function and will provide for a permanent location.

Wilder's scathing response arrived the next day:

I am in receipt of your latest letter dated June 28, 2007 and I must say that I am appalled at your duplicity. You meet with me and say one thing; you meet with my representatives and say one thing; you tell me that you are making recommendations to your Board; and then, you send me something that clearly would be cost escalation at its highest by dealing with the PPEA. Its purpose is to make money, while our purpose is to save it.

I have determined that there is far too much administrative space allocated for schools that represents a duplication of services which should be consolidated.

I have suggested the need for you to have Schools close its existing unused facilities and relocate your Administrative Offices into one of those surplus buildings, yet, you have chosen to ignore that option. I will not be recommending to the Council any such expenditure that will envision such a proposal.

Accordingly, and as I have said, your temporary location will be at 3600 West Broad Street. I do not intend to argue this matter any further. You continue to waste the taxpayers' dollars and I am not going to condone that. Your people are stating that you do not have money to feed the children or the money to pay for your utilities on time, yet now you have found hundreds of thousands of dollars to pay for moving expenses. I have tried to be cooperative with you for the past 2 ½ years, yet to no avail. I am going to save money and not waste it any further.

Later that day, we issued this press release to sway public opinion:

Mayor Reiterates Call for School Administration to Vacate City Hall

We are prepared to see that the Richmond School Administration relocate its offices from the six floors of City Hall that it now occupies. The School Administration will move to a temporary location and, as such, the expenses associated with that move should not be exorbitant.

It's appalling that one-third of City Hall continues to be used by School personnel for a student population of only 23,000 students, with this personnel occupying the same amount of space as decades ago when more than 50,000 students attended the public schools. By consolidating administrative functions and eliminating duplicate services, the School Administration should not need as much space as it has had in prior years.

When you factor the current expenses that City departments are paying in rent at various Downtown locations, it's a sound business decision that these City departments should be housed at City Hall, which will save more than $5 million over the next five years.

While the determination for an eventual, permanent location is the prerogative of the School Board, it is apparent that utilizing one of its surplus school buildings should be among the most practical options to be considered.[277]

Wilder's concern about getting office space for City departments became so strong that he even floated a proposal with Governor Kaine to repurchase the old City Hall from the state. The handsome Victorian granite building stood conveniently across the street. However, that idea quickly went nowhere.

On August 8—well past the June 30 deadline he had demanded—Wilder again extended the move-out deadline in another letter to the school superintendent:

Having sent you several letters regarding the temporary relocation of the Richmond Public Schools ("RPS") offices, and having heard nothing definitive from you regarding your plan(s), please be advised that the City of Richmond has entered into an agreement to lease space at 3600 West Broad

Street for the temporary relocation of RPS' administrative offices. That space will be available as soon as September 01, 2007, the day on which RPS should begin its transition there from City Hall. (RPS' move from City Hall should be complete by no later than September 30, 2007.) As previously represented, the City will cover all reasonable expenses that it will incur in assisting in RPS' move.

The next day, the mayor did not hear from the school superintendent, as he might have expected. Instead, he received a letter from the school board chairman (entire text shown) reminding him of council's newly passed ordinances that allowed the school offices to remain in City Hall:

Dear Mayor Wilder,

I have had an opportunity to review your letter addressed to Dr. Deborah Jewell-Sherman, Superintendent, on August 8, 2007 (see attached letter). On behalf of Richmond Public School Board, I wish to thank you for your efforts to secure a location for the Richmond Public Schools School Board and Central Administrative Offices.

However, pursuant to City Council Ordinance #2007-161-157 adopted on June 25, 2007, the Code of the City of Richmond was amended to add Section 26-12, which covers the uses of City-owned real estate. This section provides City Council with the expressed "power to control and regulate the use and management of all City-owned real estate" and that "no use of City-owned real estate shall be changed except by ordinance adopted by the City Council." See attached Ordinance.

In addition, City Council Ordinance #2007-191-178, adopted July 23, 2007, specifically notes that you are to enter into a lease with the Richmond Public Schools to permit the district "to continue to use the space that Richmond Public Schools currently occupies in City Hall, 900 East Broad Street." The lease is to be executed within 30 days from the July 23, 2007 timeline. See attached Ordinance and Lease.

Given that background, the letter sent to Dr. Deborah Jewell-Sherman seems out of place and contrary to the law.

As such, I must inform you that the school system does not plan to relocate its administrative offices from City Hall by September 30, 2007. Further, the School Board awaits receipt of the lease document for our legal review and approval as to form.

I will be happy to meet with you to discuss any concerns you might have regarding our use of space in City Hall. Again, thank you for your continued attention to the needs of Richmond Public Schools.

Sincerely,

George P. Braxton

Wilder would have none of it. He vetoed the June 25th ordinance that gave council the authority to lease office space at City Hall. Council President Pantele said he was trying to "keep the peace" when he proposed the measure.

Council's ordinance on July 23 directed the mayor to execute a lease allowing the school board to remain in City Hall for up to five years, at a rent of $10 per year. Relying on a legal opinion by his chief of staff and legal counsel, Sandra R. Robinson, Wilder declared that ordinance invalid and said council had no power to order him to do anything.

With the city administration and school board squaring off for a showdown, the time came for the mayor to set a few cards on the table—and keep a few others for the ready. In his August 30th press release titled "Major Advantages Gained by School Board's Relocation from City Hall," the mayor laid down two of his cards—they were actually attachments to the press release. The first was a copy of the lease agreement for 50,000 square feet of office space at 3600 West Broad Street. The contract, at $550,000 per year and renewable for four years, was signed by Black on behalf of the City, though he had not obtained council's approval. The second was a two-page legal summary prepared by Robinson that explained why council's two ordinances were unlawful.

The press release noted that for the past two years, the mayor had extended the departure timetable several times at the school system's request. It was only six paragraphs—fairly standard in length, but the fifth paragraph would prove to be the most ominous:

The relocation is set to occur during the month of September, as had been communicated by letter to the School Superintendent earlier this month.

Three weeks after that press release, the eviction began: a line-up of moving vans circled City Hall, waiting to be loaded. Organized and methodical, the process moved swiftly under police guard. Wilder had no second thoughts about the eviction. After the school board obtained the temporary restraining order to stop the eviction, the six-packed truckloads of disheveled school belongings were returned to City Hall, waiting to be unboxed and put back in place.

"I don't regret what happened. I regret that it had to happen," Wilder explained, indicating it was a question of authority. ". . . The move has more to do with bringing those entities [city departments] within the city government under the direct involvement of the mayor," he told a reporter.[278] The only thing that went wrong with the eviction was that Deputy CAO Harry Black had allowed school board members and school officials to enter City Hall for an emergency meeting, he added. With the building closed to the public, he said no one should have been allowed inside.

The public—and even those who knew him best—were surprised by the attempted eviction. "I never thought he'd really do it," said Paul Goldman, the mayor's longtime ally who had resigned following news reports about his outside political consulting work. Having left his position as a senior policy advisor at City Hall, he resurfaced as an occasional critic of his former boss.

An assessment of Wilder's management style, offered two years earlier, summed up his modus operandi as a public servant to the people: "Government with Wilder at the helm is always a thrill ride. Trouble is, while the trip's in motion, it's hard to tell whether the car is on the track or barreling into the abyss," commented longtime *Virginian-Pilot* political reporter Margaret Edds.[279] Having written a book about Wilder's trailblazing election as governor fifteen years earlier, she knew him well.

Months after the failed eviction, a *Richmond Times-Dispatch* editorial offered further perspective.

Just how much authority remains to be sorted out. There are different ways to go about that; Wilder prefers the World

Wrestling Entertainment approach, with bright lights and braggadocio. That doesn't automatically make him wrong on any particular debating point, but it does predispose many residents to view his claims with a jaundiced eye.

Then again, residents should have expected fireworks when they voted for him. And Wilder's approach is not necessarily less desirable than one in which the city's decisions are made quietly, behind closed doors, by a handful of influential but unelected patriarchs and padishahs. A little case-rattling can be healthy in a hotbed of social rest like Richmond.[280]

Meanwhile, on the Monday after the eviction, the mayor's public schedule continued in full force as if nothing unusual had happened. Reporters swarmed around him at an anniversary event in historic Shockoe Cemetery. As a Colonial fife and drum corps reenactment marched across an open lawn, Wilder reiterated that the real issue was determining who held the authority to do what.

No one quite knew what to expect at Wilder's next face-to-face meeting with city council on October 1, coming only ten days after the move-out and move-back-in. The local media anticipated fireworks. They failed to spark. The mood was overtly pleasant, with a sense of tension just beneath the surface in view of what had happened.

During the hour-long meeting, Wilder talked about issues like drainage, affordable housing, and the city's public works department. He briefly pointed to the need to agree on city charter changes that he and council could propose to the General Assembly for approval. They did not discuss the school board fight. Instead, the mayor put a rosy face on it. "I thought the meeting was very positive and we need to have more where we ask questions of each other. It's not necessary that we agree," he said.[281]

In an earlier media interview, Wilder explained, "You can't allow temporary disagreements to come between you. If that were the case, my God, nothing would get done in this country, nothing would get done in this state." Others viewed the situation more sternly. Council President Pantele responded to Wilder's remark by saying, "I think what has happened in this city has gone pretty far beyond a temporary disagreement."[282]

The Mayor's Sinking Popularity

In the aftermath of what some people termed "the City Hall fiasco," Wilder's popularity plummeted. The *Richmond Times-Dispatch* flashed a huge photo of the mayor with the front-page headline: "City Hall Turmoil: Support Drops for Wilder." While 79 percent of voters supported him in the 2004 election, only 35 percent said they would re-elect him after the attempted eviction, the newspaper poll said. Of the 500 registered voters surveyed, 49 percent said they would replace him if a new election was held. Wilder's attempt to relocate the school system drew even more opposition. Two-thirds of respondents said he had overstepped his authority, and 56 percent said the mayor's office should not be given any additional power.

Responding to his poor showing, Wilder issued a statement: "As we all know, polls are a snapshot of a current period of time, and for that reason I have consistently said throughout my political career that the only polls that really count are those that are taken on Election Day. That has been and still is my position."[283]

Around this time Wilder, in a *Richmond Times-Dispatch* commentary, wrote that the city charter did not give council the authority to lease City Hall office space to the school system; instead, that authority belonged to the mayor and chief administrative officer (CAO). The mayor summarized his position:

> The overarching issue, of course, is whether the City Council can exercise executive power conferred on the mayor by the people simply by passing an ordinance.
>
> When the City Council decided to bypass the executive and to negotiate contracts on its own, and then to direct the mayor to execute them, it prepared a recipe for chaos. The charter places administration in the hands of the mayor. When the council tries to take over the day-to-day administration of the city by passing ordinances controlling the minutiae of administration, the letter as well as the spirit of the charter has been violated.[284]

Despite his legal explanations, however, the public sting of his actions was felt in other ways. His sinking popularity was highlighted when he was booed in mid-October at the Second Street Festival, which draws thousands of people each year to Jackson Ward. As he came onstage to introduce the Average White Band, the booing began, mixed with a smattering of applause. Wilder held up his hands, unsuccessfully, as if to quiet the crowd, then welcomed the band and walked off the stage.

Wilder later told the *Richmond Free Press*, "I anticipated some of it. And I was not surprised by any of it. This type of thing goes with the territory. And no one ever promised me a rose garden. This job is not for the faint of heart."[285]

Not long afterward, he hosted a string of well-attended community Town Hall meetings where he was heartily welcomed. Wilder hosted several of these during his term, as they confirmed his often-stated belief that "the people are always ahead of the politicians." Using the recurring theme of "Action, Access, and Accountability," the meetings encouraged citizens to ask questions and Wilder's department heads were on hand to answer them. Any question was fair game, with the exchanges keeping the city directors on their toes.

Soon, the mayor took a giant step to redeem his public image, one that won broad public support—including unanimous approval by city council.

CHAPTER THIRTEEN

ARRIVALS AND DEPARTURES

"LOVE AFFAIR AT CITY HALL"

Two weeks after the failed eviction, Wilder held a City Hall press conference to announce he had selected a new chief administrative officer (CAO). Sheila Hill-Christian was no stranger to Richmond government, having served as an assistant city manager, a department head, and as chief of staff to the city manager. She later became executive director of the Richmond Redevelopment and Housing Authority, and more recently, held the plum position of director of the Virginia Lottery.

In making the announcement, Wilder disclosed he had met with Governor Kaine for his approval to offer the CAO position to Hill-Christian. Kaine obliged and Wilder thanked him "for agreeing to 'sacrifice' a talented member of his Administration in order to help this City continue to move forward."

Seated next to Wilder at the press conference, Hill-Christian said, "I guess in many ways, all roads have led to this. I've had some wonderful opportunities at both the state and local level and now I have the opportunity to work for another great individual and someone I've admired for a great number of years. So, despite the fact that I had a job that was lots of fun and people liked getting those big checks from me, to have the opportunity to come here and work for Mayor Wilder was an opportunity I couldn't refuse, and I look forward to it."[286]

She replaced William Harrell, who resigned after two years to become city manager of Chesapeake, Virginia, his hometown. He had quietly borne the brunt of the mayor's frustrations many times during his tenure as CAO and submitted his resignation only one day before he would have been fired.

"Do you know how much more time he had?" the mayor later asked me, holding up one finger in the air. "One day." Though considered an administration "insider" as press secretary, I had not actually witnessed the level of discord that must have existed between the two. I listened but kept my silence.

When announcing Harrell's departure months before, Wilder said Harry Black would serve as the acting CAO until he could be confirmed by council. It was a position Black wanted. A skilled administrator, he dutifully led initiatives the mayor had requested. However, Black's lightning-rod skirmishes with council—school funding, staff hiring, and the failed eviction—had left their mark. Twice, Wilder nominated Black to become the acting CAO, and each time, council rejected him.

"More Tit for Tat," the title of a *Richmond Times-Dispatch* editorial, summarized the conflict. "The Richmond City Council's decision not to confirm Harry Black as acting chief administrative officer for the city comes as no surprise. Black, hand-picked by Doug Wilder, has been the mayor's key lieutenant in a series of confrontations with the rest of city government that have bitterly soured relations between the branches."[287] The editorial also criticized council for basing its rejection on Black's lack of experience and qualifications, adding that he was far more qualified for the job than the former city manager, Calvin Jamison.

The mayor acknowledged what he termed a "personality clash"[288] between Black and the council, adding that council had the right to reject his nomination. "The acting capacity of Mr. Black was such that the confirmation may have been continued indefinitely," he explained. "City government can't act in a vacuum like that."[289]

Hill-Christian meanwhile swept into her new position like a burst of spring air. "Love Affair at City Hall: Hill-Christian Embraced by City Council," declared a banner headline in the *Richmond Free Press*. She was unanimously confirmed and received a standing ovation as council members lined up to shake her hand. "I'm happy for you," commented Council President Pantele after the vote. "I'm really happy for us."[290] At the time, the mayor was visiting universities in England and Russia as a cultural exchange guest of Virginia Commonwealth University President Trani.

Hill-Christian's top priority would be to improve communication between the mayor's office and city council, she said. While acknowledging "I'm not a miracle worker," she promised to help build a better relationship between the mayor and council.

Black remained as the city's deputy CAO and chief financial officer, handing over his other administrative duties. Of Hill-Christian's appointment as the new CAO, he said, "I support the decision. I believe it's the right decision."[291] At the time the mayor announced his selection of Hill-Christian, he commended Black for "his significant contributions to the City, and we continue to have complete recognition and respect for his strong talents and qualifications."[292]

While the fence-mending at City Hall brought a collective sigh, Circuit Court Judge Margaret Spencer issued two rulings that sliced some of the muscle from the city's strong mayor. Wilder did not have the authority to ignore a city ordinance directing him to lease the upper floors of City Hall to the school system, she ruled, and he had overstepped by trying to evict the school board. Wilder said he would appeal the judge's decision to the Virginia Supreme Court.

After the attempted eviction, Wilder sought to prove to the public that School Superintendent Deborah Jewell-Sherman had been preparing to leave City Hall. His *Visions* newsletter featured the school superintendent's entire June 22, 2007, letter where she wrote, ". . . I have clearly demonstrated my wish and that of the School Board to secure an alternate site that would allow us to carry on our critical educational mission and to vacate our City Hall office space as soon as feasible."[293]

Jewell-Sherman appeared to give every assurance that the school system would be moving. It had already spent nearly $700,000 to relocate its IT department from City Hall into renovated space at the Richmond Technical Center in the city's Northside.

School System Involved in Plans to Move

Not until months later did the local media obtain internal government documents revealing the school administration was more deeply involved in leaving City Hall than previously assumed.

Style Weekly published an exposé titled "Did Schools Help Plan Attempted Move?" that provided a bombshell perspective about actions leading up to the eviction. It read in part:

City documents and inter-office communications obtained through multiple Freedom of Information Act requests indicate that school officials not only knew about the planned move, but also were initially involved in negotiating the lease for the 3600 W. Broad St. building where Wilder tried to move them. They also helped develop the timeline to move school offices out of City Hall by Sept. 30.

Wilder's frustration and his big-stick tactics in attempting to evict schools are still considered inappropriate by many, but it's since become clear he had reason to believe schools were complying with his directive to move to 3600 W. Broad St.

Style Weekly also disclosed the school administration's cat-and-mouse demeanor regarding its plans to move:

> (School Board Vice Chairwoman Lisa) Dawson says that "to some extent there was some [playing] chicken" between the School Board and Wilder. She says the board told Sherman and administration officials that 3600 W. Broad St. negotiations were a legitimate delaying tactic to stave off attempts to force the School Board to vacate City Hall. She says the School Board was aware that negotiations were ongoing for 3600 W. Broad St. well into the summer.[294]

By then, city council had approved an ordinance allowing the school system to lease office space at City Hall. Wilder viewed the *Style Weekly* article as vindication of his efforts to get the school system to move. His newsletter, headlined "Truth Crushed to Earth Shall Rise Again . . . Because No Lie Can Live Forever," featured excerpts of the *Style Weekly* exposé published in early January 2008.[295]

CITY COUNCIL INVESTIGATES

Council established an ad hoc committee with subpoena powers to investigate the failed move—and the questions flowed. How much did it cost? Where did the money come from? How was the money spent? Where were the emails, meeting notes, and correspondence about the planned move? Where were the records of requisition orders for expenses and who authorized them? Those questions hung like a heavy cloud over the Wilder administration well into its final year. Deputy CAO Harry Black was planted squarely in the council's crosshairs while CAO Sheila Hill-Christian dealt with much of the fall-out.

As council's investigation was taking shape, Wilder continued to push for meetings with council to agree on City Charter changes that clarified the authority of the "strong mayor." Some officials, however, were privately fearful that "opening" the charter during the General Assembly session could lead to unexpected revisions that might further expand the mayor's authority.

Since charter change proposals must be presented on the assembly's opening day [early January], the mayor favored discussions with council in November and December so they could agree on revisions to recommend. But he knew time was running out.

Meanwhile, the mayor continued to push for new school construction. He met with Hill-Christian and Council President Pantele about a plan to engage the school superintendent. The mayor sent a letter seeking her list of old schools to phase out, with timelines for that to happen. He also asked that she prepare a "corrective action plan" to address the city auditor's recommendations that could save up to $20 million a year.

Even as inroads were sought for new schools and another round of city budget battles was warming up, Wilder moved ahead with a range of other initiatives at that time:

- Developing a new Downtown "master plan" to guide future development
- Creating a public park and marina on the James River in the city's East End
- Completing the first phase of $20 million drainage improvements in Shockoe Bottom
- Creating a new storm utility program for drainage improvements across the city and more equitable consumer water rates
- Finding a new baseball team to replace the Richmond Braves

One issue that would not go away, however, was the aftermath of the failed school board eviction. Hill-Christian soon found herself in the ring, taking punches on where the money had come from to do it. Council's investigative committee, led by Councilman Chris Hilbert, was seething that it had not received key information such as moving expense records, planning documents, emails, and the minutes of internal meetings. "The people are entitled to have answers related to what this cost them and how the decisions were made," he declared.

"This was a traumatic event for the civic fabric of this city."[296]

The mayor challenged the city auditor's preliminary report that questioned the legality of the city administration transferring $500,000 within the city budget to relocate the school board. As the auditor spoke, the mayor periodically interrupted him to criticize his findings as incomplete or misleading and to complain that he was exceeding his role by discussing the legality of using the City funds. "His mission is not to pass judgment – it's to present the facts," the mayor scolded.[297]

Some committee members began to challenge the mayor about his role during the meeting. "The purpose of this hearing is to get the report," said Councilwoman Ellen Robertson. "The intent is not for the purpose of the cross-examination of information. He [the mayor] will have plenty of time to do that and we hope to set up the process so we can question the information." Wilder shot back that the city charter gave him the right to speak. "When I appear with City Council, I appear with the words of the city charter that enable me to speak and I don't have to wait, Ms. Robertson, to participate."

Wilder blasted the auditor's report, stating sharply that council's investigative committee can "do what it wants to do," but he thought the school offices were moving after already relocating its IT department to a new location. "This administration is not afraid of anything," he declared. "We did what we did because we were led to believe the Schools wanted to do it. The Schools started it. They started moving."[298]

Council issued a "subpoena duces tecum" to request information related to the move. Wilder then issued a press release criticizing the investigative committee's work as "misguided and premature in light of the fact that as late as its meeting today, the committee members were still trying to make arrangements . . . to view the documents it suggests (by issuing the subpoena) that it does not have.

"Coupled with the City Auditor's December 17th admission that he himself did not know whether he had received all of the documents for which he had asked, there is no factual basis for issuing the subpoena," the mayor continued. "It is apparent that the committee is not aware of its legislative prerogatives and if anything speaks to an abuse of authority, this is clearly an example."[299]

Council's investigative committee later decided to request a detailed list of documents related to the aborted eviction instead of demanding them by subpoena. A *Richmond Times-Dispatch* analysis of records provided showed a gap in emails from Sept. 7 to Sept. 22, covering two weeks before and one day after the eviction. No minutes of meetings were provided, though a confidential briefing paper mentioned some meetings involving Black's office. Also missing were records showing who had authorized thirty-five expenditures related to the move.

In a letter to the committee, Hill-Christian explained that Black and his budget director, Rayford Harris Jr., had decided to transfer $500,000 from a budget account designated for the Battery Park flood cleanup to an empty account titled "Interim Transition Costs of New Government" that had been used to set up the strong mayor form of city government three years earlier. However, she refused to sign a legally binding certification that the City administration had provided all of the requested documents, noting she did not work for the City at the time of the eviction and was not involved in the move.

Council reacted with harsh words. With the legality of the money transfer in question, Councilwoman Robertson called Hill-Christian a "criminal,"[300] a description she recanted several days later. Council President Pantele used the term "money laundering."

"Based on what we know now, members of the administration essentially appropriated a dead account and filled it with money and used those monies as they saw fit – thus circumventing the processes of the public procurement act," he said.[301]

Hill-Christian defended the money transfer because both accounts were the same type, listed as "nondepartmental," and the transfer was possible because specific funds had not been itemized by council. In a letter to Hilbert, she declined the committee's request to question selected City employees, pointing out that the "spirit of cooperation is being strained by repeated reports of Councilmember Bill Pantele's potentially slanderous charges of 'money laundering' (most recently reported in Style Weekly).

"Therefore, in light of Mr. Pantele's recent allegation, as well as previously reported threats of potential criminal prosecution, I can no longer in good conscience direct City employees to voluntarily present before your committee to answer questions," she wrote. "As you know, initially I said I had no problem doing so; however, it has become clear that this request is simply subterfuge.

"Accordingly, I will gladly prepare a written response to the questions in your letter. And, if you should require further information upon receiving the written responses, the Administration will provide it if it is in our custody."

She backed off from her offer two weeks later, after learning that the committee had discussed the possibility of seeking a criminal investigation by Richmond Commonwealth's Attorney Michael Herring. "My understanding is that there has been a discussion about sending this to a prosecutor," Hill-Christian told *Style Weekly*, "and I cannot ask people without legal representation to make statements that could be used against them."[302]

The investigative committee's report later found that the failed eviction cost taxpayers nearly $1 million and included a "willful failure to comply with the budget ordinance."[303] The key questions of who planned the eviction and who authorized paying for it went unanswered, Hilbert acknowledged. The report said the City administration had turned over spreadsheets of vendor and labor costs as well as purchase orders, invoices, contracts, and other correspondence, but committee members said they could not arrive at answers based on the information they received.

Expenses related to the eviction totaled nearly $975,000, according to the report. That included more than $400,000 in vendor payments and another $320,000 for leased office space. City purchases were approved by people without authority to do so. Black had not obtained council's approval to lease office space, the report said. The two-week gap of missing emails was described as "particularly noteworthy."[304] The report made no recommendation on pursuing legal or disciplinary action.

Council President Pantele later sent the report to Wilder, asking "that all monetary transfers and expenditures not made in compliance with the city budget laws be reversed and that the accounts be reconciled."[305] Wilder, however, wrote back that he disagreed. He planned to take no action because the case would be appealed to the Virginia Supreme Court.

Employee Car Allowances

Another thorny situation Hill-Christian had to handle involved the City's policy on monthly auto allowances. She found herself in the uneasy position of having to defend the mayor while explaining the need to reprimand a director.

The mayor was chauffeured daily in a city-owned Grand Marquis by his security detail, a level of protection that Police Chief Monroe had insisted on. Meanwhile, the City's emergency management director, Benjamin Johnson, was among more than three dozen city employees receiving a monthly car allowance. Like the mayor, he used a city-owned car instead of his own.

Johnson's situation was reported anonymously to the city auditor, who sent his findings to Hill-Christian. "Using the city vehicle while receiving an auto allowance appears to be a dishonest action that caused the city financial loss," City Auditor Umesh Dalal wrote. "A disciplinary action for said dishonesty needs to be taken."[306]

Johnson was assigned a city car when hired in 2003 as well as a $500 monthly car allowance, plus a parking space for his personal car, Dalal reported. Johnson had received the allowance for nearly three years before turning in the city-owned Ford Explorer.

Johnson resigned in April 2008. His departure was announced in a late-day press release that also disclosed the mayor's plan to reimburse the City for the $700 monthly allowance he had received since summer 2005. Copies of the mayor's $25,900 reimbursement check and a City collections receipt were later sent to the press. The check was prepared in the handwriting of his secretary, Ruth Jones, with Wilder's signature at the bottom. The press release went on to note that Wilder had received no cost-of-living increase in his $125,000 annual salary since taking office and had rejected a council-approved $25,000 raise in 2005.

Hill-Christian was placed in the difficult position of explaining how the mayor's circumstances were different than Johnson's. Her press statement described the difference:

> Normally we avoid discussing personnel matters to protect the privacy of any employees; however, since Mr. Johnson has made public statements despite our attempts to protect his privacy, it appears it is necessary to make clear that it is not accurate to compare Mr. Johnson's situation with that of the Mayor.
>
> When an employee has been aware of a problem for some time and has had multiple opportunities to rectify it yet does not, they may find themselves in a situation similar to Mr. Johnson's. When the issue of the car allowance was brought to the Mayor's attention, he took immediate corrective action.

Again, we thank the auditor for bringing this matter to the City's and the media's attention.[307]

Johnson later told the *Richmond Times-Dispatch* that Hill-Christian had forced him to resign. He voluntarily repaid the $16,500 in car allowances he had received.

Wilder, when asked during a media tour touting his City of the Future projects, told reporters he did not know he had been getting a car allowance. "I never knew," he told them. "I never knew when it started . . . I haven't received a check since I've been here, to put in my hand. My checks are all deposited. Bottom line is you either got to believe I know or I don't know, and I just tell you, I don't know."[308]

The situation became all the more embarrassing because the mayor's proposed budget included a 14 percent increase for car allowances. Recent audits also showed the City administration could not clearly track the number of city cars driven home at night nor properly monitor employees' use of city gas cards. Council later abolished auto allowances as part of employee compensation.

Despite the headaches Hill-Christian endured, sometimes there were lighter moments that offered a respite. She and I often met together with the mayor to chart out the activities of the day. One morning, I couldn't help but notice the mayor wearing a huge gold nugget of a ring featuring a king's crown with three large diamonds set in onyx. I commented that he had a new accessory, pointing to my ring finger. The gesture immediately prompted him to tell us the history of the ring.

He passed it over for us to try on as he explained it was Muhammad Ali's third heavyweight championship ring that we were placing on our finger. Ali gave it to Wilder as a gift at the time of his historic election as governor. Inside was inscribed, "To Doug Wilder with respect." It was the only time I saw him wear that ring.

Three Surprise Resignations

With budget negotiations in full swing, the mayor again sparred with city council over funding levels and in particular, proposed cuts for the police department.

Meanwhile, Police Chief Monroe continued to be courted by other cities, this time as one of three finalists to become police chief in Charlotte, NC, which had a department twice the size of Richmond's.

The *Richmond Free Press* said, "For his outstanding success in fighting crime in Richmond, Police Chief Rodney D. Monroe has built a national reputation for effective, community-oriented law enforcement" and "is unsurprisingly a wanted police chief by cities wrestling—more unsuccessfully—with hard crime issues."

Wilder held a press conference to praise Monroe's accomplishments. He also claimed that council would be to blame if Monroe decided to take the new job. To counter Wilder's accusation, council unanimously passed a resolution praising Monroe's work in achieving the city's lowest crime rate in twenty-six years and encouraged him to remain as police chief in Richmond.

Wilder juggled funds each year to make sure Monroe received what he requested to run his department. Since Monroe had come to Richmond, his budget requests totaled $22.3 million, yet council reduced that amount by more than $4.3 million, with the mayor having to make up the difference.

Tensions reached a tipping point when council again wanted to cut the mayor's proposed funding for the police department. Council also wanted to pay for a performance audit of the department's operation. Speculation over what would happen ended in clockwork fashion. In the first of two press releases issued on May 15, 2008, the mayor asked council to restore Monroe's funding.

"I am calling upon the Council to reject its proposed amendment to cut $385,000 from the Police Chief's budget and also to reject its amendment to spend $200,000 for an unnecessary [performance audit] investigation of the Chief and his Department," Wilder said. "I know that I speak for the vast majority of the citizens who don't believe this shows an appreciation for his valuable services."[309]

The second press release, issued later in the day, was clear but terse. Setting the scene for suspense and drama, a Wilder trademark, it consisted of two sentences:

"The Chief informed me late this afternoon that the City of Charlotte had extended an offer to him to become its next Police Chief and that he had accepted that offer. I will have further comment tomorrow."[310]

Monroe's decision to leave Richmond immediately dominated the local news. Less than twenty-four hours later, Wilder dropped his own bomb: he would not seek re-election.

His mind was made up, though he had given no indication this was coming. Only three months earlier, a *Richmond Times-Dispatch* editorial noted, ". . . Wilder left little doubt that he remains the force to be reckoned with in City politics but gave no hint about whether he intends to seek a second four-year term this November. He did give the impression that he's neither tired nor ready to retreat into quiet retirement."[311]

Still, a time of reckoning comes that all politicians ultimately face. It was time to step down and reflect on what had been accomplished. Wilder had plenty to show for his four years in office. "As the first elected Mayor under the City's new form of government, I have set the course that will continue to produce meaningful results even as I now announce my leave from this office at the end of the year," he said in a press release. He commended the "unprecedented gains in public safety" under Chief Monroe, a wave of new businesses coming into the city, and advances in public education. "In terms of improving public education here, we have succeeded in cracking the shell to now allow for meaningful dialogue that will address the issues facing our school system and our youth."[312]

He informed the city directors during a staff meeting that morning. He had seven months left in office and would be seventy-eight on his next birthday. The thought of continuing as mayor for another four-year term—a 24/7 job involving almost daily friction with council and the school board—was clearly a consideration for a person his age.

But there was more to it than that. Wilder had privately informed Monroe two months earlier that he would not run again. He wanted Monroe to take advantage of any career opportunities that might interest him. The opening in Charlotte presented good timing for Monroe to climb higher in an already-successful career.

During the staff meeting, Monroe spoke of the difficulty in leaving Richmond. The mayor warmly commended him for everything he had done to reduce crime. He then disclosed that he would not seek re-election. The room fell dead silent. The meeting ended on a lighter note as the mayor and others congratulated Monroe. Soon after, I issued a press release to inform the public. The next day, the mayor's decision to retire was carried in newspapers across the country.

The *Washington Post* praised Wilder for a political career that broke racial barriers. Its editorial, titled "The Audacity of Mr. Wilder," spoke of his ability to chart a path where others like Barack Obama could follow. "Silver-tongued, cunning, by turns brash, prickly and suavely charming,

Mr. Wilder made excellent copy for journalists while managing also to be a fine governor," read the editorial which also described him as "fiercely independent by nature."[313]

Numerous politicians sang Wilder's praises. Virginia Attorney General Robert F. McDonnell, one of several state leaders issuing a press release, noted: "His legacy is much larger than the individual achievements and actions that comprise his nearly 40 years of public service. His legacy is that of a statesman, who broke through old barriers, eschewed tired labels, and constantly sought new and better ways of governing."

Also sorry to see him go was the media. Without fail, reporters could count on him for an interesting story in the next day's paper. "L. Douglas Wilder's departure from the mayor's suite in Richmond City Hall should leave local news gatherers in a state of mourning," wrote Michael Paul Williams of the *Richmond Times-Dispatch*. "Wilder's headline-seeking antics were the gift that kept on giving. Wilder's scraps with the City Council and the School Board made for great theater. All that was missing was the popcorn."[314]

Wilder seemed relaxed and content in the days following his announcement. Though he had hinted all along he might run again, he had not assembled a re-election committee or undertaken other campaign requisites. His May 16 announcement also left little time for anyone seeking to replace him. Candidates faced a June 10 filing deadline for the general election in November.

Some council members openly welcomed his departure, but for others, a sense of shock and bewilderment had overwhelmed. Councilwoman Reva Trammell seemed particularly alarmed by the one-two punch of the Monroe-Wilder announcements. She emailed me after hearing the news. "What a hell of a day!!!!! God be with all of us!!!!"

Two months later, Hill-Christian abruptly resigned. She chose to give her notice with a one-word handwritten note left on the desk of Wilder's assistant, Ruth Jones. It read simply: "Bye!" She served just over eight months. To the end, her office remained sparsely decorated with only a few personal effects. ". . . No more than could fit in a cardboard box," observed *Style Weekly*.[315]

Her unexpected resignation in July shocked people throughout City Hall, including the mayor. She officially gave two days' notice. His term would end soon so she may have had limited time remaining anyway, as she had no assurance the next mayor would keep her. She explained in a cryptic email sent to the media that "in every position I have accepted, I have given my all" and "when my ability to do so is compromised, I believe it is in my personal best interest, and the interest of taxpayers to move on."[316] She did not say why she felt compromised and could not be reached by the media for further comment. By the time word got out, she had already left the building.

Her sudden departure prompted an immediate press release with a statement from the mayor. It read in part: "We well understand that, at the time she was hired in November 2007, I had not determined whether to seek re-election, and I greatly appreciate having her as part of our team. She did a fine job in a very challenging situation, and we wish her well with her future endeavors."[317]

Council members and other City Hall observers were buzzing with theories about her departure. Some cited her frustration with Wilder's interpretation of city ordinances and the way city business was conducted. Others surmised she worried that adhering to the mayor on the budget and other matters might expose her legally. Several City Hall observers, who spoke anonymously with the local press, said she had made thinly veiled references that she might be leaving her job soon. Two days before her announcement, she did not attend a meeting between city and council officials to discuss contentious budget issues. Some speculated that her star had dimmed over time.

Richmond Times-Dispatch columnist Michael Paul Williams put it this way:

> Eight months ago, Sheila Hill-Christian was hired as Richmond's chief administrative officer amid smiles and plaudits. If she wasn't a savior in a power suit and pumps, she loomed as the best hope to bring a cease-fire between the Richmond City Council and Mayor L. Douglas Wilder.
>
> But the gushing seemed over the top, the optimism forced. You could liken it to the wedding reception of a clearly incompatible couple. Imagine plastic champagne flutes held aloft in toast as everyone grins and thinks, "It'll never work."
>
> It didn't.[318]

CHAPTER FOURTEEN

SEEKING CLARITY OVER WHO CAN DO WHAT

MAYOR PUSHES TO REVISE CITY CHARTER

The dust had barely settled after the school board eviction when Wilder began pushing again for revisions to the city charter. Only two weeks earlier, City Hall had been on a military-like lockdown as the contents of school offices were packed up and moved out. The eviction was halted by a judge's midnight restraining order.

Wilder sent a letter to city council members and the city's General Assembly representatives reminding them of the need to revise the charter to clarify the balance of power between the mayor and council. The letter (excerpt below) was issued as a press release the next day:

> In the absence of clarity, we may well continue to bicker, to articulate our differences of opinion publicly, to avoid direct dialogue, and to engage in costly litigation.
>
> I think we can all agree that none of this is productive. What would be productive, however, would be to initiate a discussion of what aspects – if any – of the Charter need to be clarified through the legislative process. While I do not have a laundry list of such items, on more than one occasion I have indicated a desire for clarity on two fronts: one, the role of the City attorney; and two, the need for legislative staffing. Nevertheless, I would await the outcome of our discussion, before submitting anything for consideration.[319]

By this time, it was early October 2007. The clock was ticking.

They met at an annual legislative dinner in early November to agree on proposed charter revisions to send to the upcoming assembly session. "I want to follow the law. I know you want to follow the law," he told them. "What we need to do is find out what the law is."

Wilder passed out copies of a chart comparing Richmond's government with Washington, DC, Baltimore, and Atlanta, which also have strong mayors. While not making any specific proposals, he said the central issue was the mayor's inherent authority as the city's chief executive. "The city cannot be governed by ordinance," he said, adding it should not be left up to judges, either. "If we do nothing, I see where we will stay in court and have the city run by judges, people who were not elected to do that."

After the mayor spoke, no one commented or asked any questions about the city charter. "The response: Silence and a quick change of topic," is how the *Richmond Free Press* described the mayor's appeal. "Nobody picked up on it – it fell," Delegate Dwight C. Jones, D-Richmond, chuckled to a reporter.

While not disputing the need to clarify the charter, some legislators noted the lengthy process involved. "A whole bunch of things should be spelled out that are not spelled out," advised Delegate Franklin P. Hall, D-Richmond. A public hearing and council's approval would first be needed, he explained.[320]

State legislators typically require strong consensus among all parties before agreeing to sponsor a charter bill that they would have to shepherd through the assembly. Ongoing legal battles between the council and mayor, however, posed a definitive obstacle to making any changes to the charter. Council already had lawsuits pending against the mayor for his attempted school system eviction and his claim of hiring authority over council staff and city assessor employees. "Historically, the legislature has never taken up matters that are in litigation," Delegate Donald McEachin told a reporter after the dinner.[321]

Virginia, like most states, operates under "Dillon's Rule" which defines the power of local government. It stipulates that municipalities only have powers that are expressly granted to them by the state, so any proposed changes in Richmond's government would require approval from both the assembly and the governor. Council, however, decided not to propose any changes. "Absolutely not," Councilman Bruce Tyler commented. "Let's let the court finish the discussion. The judge is in charge."[322]

Several council members preferred that a commission review any suggested charter changes before making recommendations. Despite the lack of interest shown at the dinner, Wilder continued to push. He viewed the mayor's role as equivalent to that of the governor. "The legislature does not tell the governor what to do," he reminded reporters.[323]

Wilder described the existing charter language in his *Visions* newsletter:

> The City Charter states that "The mayor shall be the chief executive officer of the city and <u>shall</u> be <u>responsible</u> (emphasis added) for the proper administration of city government." "Shall" imposes a duty that cannot be shirked; it is not discretionary. "Responsible," by any definition, means accountable and the burden upon the Mayor rests thereon. No other entity under our Charter has been conferred with equal authority as that which the State Legislature granted to the position of Mayor.
>
> A strong mayor of any city, a governor of the state, and the president of the country are all chief executive officers and their responsibilities, for the most part, are the same. Because Richmond is the first city in Virginia to have a strong mayor, we must look elsewhere to other strong mayor forms of local government, as well as the state and federal government models, when addressing the unique issues that arise. And we must continue to be guided by our Charter.[324]

With little time remaining before the assembly session, Wilder asked Council President William Pantele to join him in inviting members of council and Richmond's state delegation to visit other cities with a strong-mayor form of government "to see how their charter stacks up against Richmond's charter."[325] A newly released Metro Richmond report by consultant James Crupi had recommended such a field trip. Despite the cool reception he received at the legislative dinner, Wilder used the report as an opportunity to make another pitch to revise the charter.

The following exchange between the mayor and Pantele, however, showed they were far apart on how to proceed. Wilder's November 20th letter (excerpted) to Pantele read:

Dr. Crupi states that it is critical that the Mayor and the Council President work together to ask the Virginia General Assembly to support adjustments to the Richmond City charter to which they have agreed. Therefore, our study should be undertaken quickly so that proposed charter adjustments for the City can be agreed upon and then presented to Richmond's legislative delegation, prior to the General Assembly session which convenes in early January.

At the meeting earlier this month with our state and local legislators, I distributed information comparing Richmond with the strong mayor forms of government in Atlanta, Baltimore, and the District of Columbia. We might choose to visit any of these or other cities to begin the necessary task at hand. Our collective review and consensus are the crucial factors at this time, in order for Richmond government to resolve the difficulties it has faced for the past three years. As Dr. Crupi stated in his report, "It is inconceivable that the State Assembly would turn down such a request knowing that there was political agreement as to its request."

Let me know when you and I can announce to the media our plans for accomplishing this important recommendation in Dr. Crupi's report.

The next day, Pantele replied to the mayor:

In light of recent communications regarding potential changes to the City Charter, as yet not defined, I wanted to make some recommendations to help move the conversation forward.

Recently when you and I met, I said I had heard some Charter change suggestions from various sources and understood that you might desire one or more. At that time, with your agreement, I observed that the logical next step would be to make several joint appointments to the existing Charter Review Commission and to convene it for the purposes of evaluating the Charter as it stands, considering this form of government as applied in Virginia, and receiving and considering any potential changes submitted by others and any changes the Commission deems appropriate.

That kind of considered and thoughtful analysis is important, and will help avoid inherent problems with rushed legislation that does not adequately consider impacts or inconsistencies with other parts of state and local law that might arise.

If you have any specific changes that you desire, it would seem appropriate for those to be communicated now, or to the Commission once initiated.

As you know, Council and I joined with you for a series of Charter changes when you took office, and the next year participated in a few more. Perhaps if a standing Charter Commission had been in place during those times, at least some greater clarity about the purpose and intent of certain changes would have been better understood and not left to self-serving arguments about them.

Your offer to visit some other jurisdictions is welcome. If a Commission is appointed promptly, there could be an additional opportunity of having some of those members participate, which would provide a broader and deeper understanding of many issues.

I look forward to meeting with you soon.

Later that same day, Wilder sent this response to Pantele:

Thank you for your letter of today. I was surprised that it offered no immediate action that we [the Mayor's Office and the City Council] could take to resolve our current and foreseeable disputes regarding Charter authority. Your suggestion that we wait to hear from a commission that has not only never been convened, but has never been staffed is perplexing. Your letter states the commission's purpose. From this broad grant of purpose, I see continued delay in eliminating the root of the disputes that have led to the pending litigation between us.

I have stated on more than one occasion, and I will repeat here, I am most interested in resolving who the City Attorney represents: is it the Mayor and the Administration or the Council? If the City Attorney "represents" both branches of government, there needs to be a separation in that office to reflect the same, and the appointment should be collective as between the branches of government – appointed by one with the consent of the other.

If you feel a visit to another locality will not be productive for this oncoming session of the legislature, let me know.

Wilder's conciliatory offer to co-host a field trip went nowhere.

Council Is in No Rush

Council established a City Charter Review Commission nine months earlier, in March, but no appointments had been made. It existed in name only, and with no staff support. The person designated to provide staff support to the commission, council's director of legislative services, had been fired months earlier after refusing Deputy CAO Harry Black's demand that she re-apply for her job, as other council staff members had been asked to do.

Continuing legal disputes became a painful reminder that any hope to reach consensus on revising the charter—with agreed-upon proposals in place—remained beyond reach. Still, Wilder continued to make his case. In his *Visions* newsletter he reminded council and the state delegation that they had a responsibility to make it happen. He wanted his authority as mayor to be defined by the state legislature instead of a judge.

"The governing of the City of Richmond is not a dispute to be mediated by a judge. That governance is a collective effort by the Mayor and the City Council – all of whom are elected by the people and are ultimately responsible to them. Likewise, the members of the General Assembly are responsible to the people. The General Assembly should have, then, a vested interest in making sure the rules that it has in place for the operation of the City are clear," he wrote.[326]

In December, with less than a month to go before the General Assembly convened, Wilder proposed the city attorney should become the chief legal advisor for the mayor's office, the CAO and city departments. The city attorney would be appointed by the mayor, but council would have to confirm the selection. It was how the city attorney was chosen in other strong-mayor cities such as Baltimore, Atlanta and Washington, DC, he indicated. The same process was also used to appoint Richmond's chief administrative officer (CAO).

The existing charter language called for the city attorney to serve as legal advisor to both the mayor and council. When the two sides disagreed on an issue, though, the city attorney was rendered unable to assist either side. "As currently stated in the City Charter, the City Attorney represents both the Mayor and the City Council," Wilder wrote. "Yet how can the City Attorney serve as the legal counsel for both the Mayor and the Council if they have a disagreement between them? Who's right and who's wrong?"

Wilder noted the city's cost for attorneys' fees. Revising the charter to clarify the city attorney's role "is the only way we can begin to cut the cord on the hefty and unnecessary legal expenses being placed upon the City of Richmond" which totaled about $415,000 from 2005 to 2007, he wrote.

Wilder again stressed it was not too late to reach an agreement. "There is still sufficient time for the Council and the Mayor to discuss this proposal and then have Richmond's delegation introduce the measure to the General Assembly in January. Doing so can result in saving additional hundreds of thousands of taxpayers' dollars now used to pay outside attorneys. It's simply a question now as to whether Council is willing to step up to the plate." [327]

Council wasn't willing. Soon, the mayor's overtures for revising the charter began to take a harsh turn.

No More Olive Branches

A week before Christmas, Wilder gave a defiant speech at a Richmond Crusade for Voters holiday dinner, saying he would not seek any changes to the city charter to expand his powers but also would no longer try to make peace with his political adversaries, either. "I've heard that I'm supposed to extend the olive branch," he gruffed. "I've extended all the olive branches I'm going to extend. I heard I was going to be more conciliatory – you've seen all you're going to see of me being conciliatory."

He pledged to maintain an aggressive stance in dealing with his opponents. Scattered applause and occasional shouts of support punctuated his fiery remarks. "I don't intend to do anything with the charter – leave it as it is," he told the 200-member audience that included members of the council, school board, and the city's General Assembly delegation.

Referring to the next mayoral election, he warned, "I've dealt with it for three years, I can deal with it for one more year or five more years." He accused council of "turning back the clock" on Black political representation, referring to the council's sole Black member, Martin Jewell, who sat on only one committee and chaired none. "The clock's been turned back. And it isn't the form of government that turned it back." He also scolded Governor Kaine and State Senator Henry Marsh for not appointing a single African American to the Virginia Court of Appeals. "I'm disappointed, Henry," he said to Marsh, who sat in the audience.[328]

The mayor told me earlier that day he had some firecracker remarks to deliver. Wanting his speech to make the late news, I convinced a television reporter to attend but the mayor's scolding remarks proved too complex to depict in a brief news spot. Still, the mayor's remarks later aired for several weeks on the city's public access cable channel.

Fast forward to 2008: Council planned to take up the charter issue and complete its study by mid-year. However, things did not move on schedule. The mayor and council did not make their appointments to the nine-member City Charter Review Commission until late in the year. The delay ended any chance for proposing changes to the charter during the 2009 assembly session. By then, the mayor would have already left office anyway.

Public Assessment of Wilder

During his remaining months in office, the mayor turned his attention to other matters such as two public opinion polls that assessed his performance in office.

A council-sponsored poll showed 81 percent of citizens said Richmond was headed in the right direction. "That's pretty high cotton," Wilder told the *Richmond Times-Dispatch*. City residents gave a 73 percent approval rating about the condition of their neighborhoods and 44 percent were satisfied with how their tax dollars were spent.

A *Richmond Times-Dispatch* poll, however, was largely critical of the mayor. Only 35 percent of voters gave him a rating of "excellent" or "good," while 61 percent rated him "fair" or "poor," with 4 percent undecided. When voters were asked how important it was for the next mayor to work cooperatively with the council and school board, 87 percent replied "very important."[329]

Despite his lukewarm survey ratings, Wilder focused on results rather than personality. "I've done everything I could do. The people didn't like my style, but they liked the direction the city was heading," he told the *Virginian-Pilot.* "I wouldn't expect people to emulate my style. You're not going to get things done by sitting around singing, 'Kumbaya.'"

While insisting he did not relish confrontation, he added, "I'm not afraid of it, either. I don't look for trouble but when it comes down, I'm in it."[330]

Richmond's first directly elected mayor in nearly sixty years also acknowledged the complaints about his confrontational style in a *Richmond Times-Dispatch* commentary in October 2008.

> I would have preferred to push for the changes we have brought without "bickering." It would have made me look better in the eyes of others and the city's progress even more evident.
>
> For example, many called the imbroglio over the "hole on Broad Street" bickering, but the project was dead in the water until the city took new action and provided the necessary leadership and funding, along with assistance from the business community.
>
> Look at the downtown today: the Hilton Hotel is scheduled to open in a few months, the National Theater is hosting shows each week, and the Arts Center will open in the fall of 2009. These and other successes are never the result of standing still.[331]

As the mayor's race heated up, Wilder chose not to endorse any of the five candidates running. Yet he kept his eye on all of them.

One morning the mayor and I took a ride to a rear alley in Shockoe Slip where candidate (and council president) William Pantele was speaking to a handful of reporters. The mayor's Grand Marquis bounced from side to side as we rolled along the cobblestone path, stopping about thirty yards from the gathering. The mayor stepped out and leaned against the car, looking down at the ground but obviously aware he could be seen by the group. I stood nearby, amused to see the mayor upstaging Pantele. Within minutes the reporters came over, leaving Pantele without the press.

Attorney Robert J. Grey Jr. was widely viewed as the mayor's likely choice for mayor. He had encouraged him to run but was unhappy with his somewhat lackluster campaign style. In Wilder's view, Grey made several missteps hindering his ability to gain broad support. The lack of opposition research was a major one. The location of his campaign office in the Cary Court Shopping Center offered little visibility to motorists traveling by. He would enjoy a quiet drink at the nearby CanCan Restaurant but hesitate to work the tables for votes.

With his own popularity sinking from the battle scars of office, Wilder may have thought he could be doing Grey a favor by not endorsing him. On the campaign trail, Grey also found that associating himself with Wilder could be counterproductive.

At a candidate forum sponsored by the local NAACP, Grey was showered with boos and moans when he said he would continue changes initiated by Wilder. He later admitted his campaign had shifted away from Wilder and explained why. "I think his leadership style hasn't gotten us where we need to go, and that's what I meant by that," Grey told the *Richmond Times-Dispatch*. "I think many of his priorities and goals are accurate, and I think where we ran into a problem was his style of leadership. I want to continue the progress that has been made by this administration, but I've been pretty clear that I want to do it in a different way. I have a different style."[332]

During his final months in office, Wilder accelerated his messaging by issuing his newsletter every week to remind the public of his accomplishments. The lowest crime rate in twenty-six years. A consolidated 311 phone system. A data-driven citizens service tracking program called RichmondWorks. Stepped-up building code enforcement. A streamlined building permit process.

Two weeks before leaving office, the mayor led a media tour around the city to show examples of downtown development projects totaling more than $1.2 billion. That included pending proposals to redevelop land along North Boulevard and in Shockoe Bottom. He encouraged the incoming mayor, Rev. Dwight Jones, to proceed with those projects and "if you've got something better, put it up," he told a reporter.[333]

In his final days, Wilder met with the *Richmond Times-Dispatch* editorial board to reflect on his four years as mayor. During an expansive interview, he said the General Assembly needed to more clearly define the authority between the mayor and council.

"You've got to make up your mind if you want a strong mayor or not," he said, adding he believed most citizens thought they were voting for a strong mayor. "The form of government we have, people have come to accept it and believe in it. But one of the mistakes we made – collectively – was not outlining the responsibilities of the council. There's a misconception out there. The budget starts and ends with the executive office. The council can amend it."[334]

Wilder also let it be known that he would not fade away. "I won't seek public office again, but I will not be quiet. I'm still concerned."[335]

Appeals to Virginia Supreme Court Dropped

Two months after leaving office, Wilder's appeals to the Virginia Supreme Court were dropped. Rev. Dwight Jones, the incoming mayor who had campaigned for improved working relations with council, ended those court appeals that arose from Wilder's attempted school board eviction and his claim of hiring authority over council staff and city assessor employees. Meanwhile, the City had spent more than $1.1 million in legal fees.[336]

The State Supreme Court should have been allowed to hear the cases, Wilder told an NBC12 reporter in early 2009. "Dropping those suits after spending all that money was not the right decision and the citizens deserve to know what the state's highest court would have decided. There are still problems with the City Charter that need to be worked out," he reminded everyone.[337]

Epilogue

Wilder tested the boundaries of his authority—considerably. His landslide victory gave him a huge mandate to improve local government, and he moved quickly to address the tasks before him. As Richmond's first "strong mayor," he obtained additional powers that strengthened his position and produced fundamental changes, many of which did not sit well with city council.

Having led the charge for Richmond's new form of government, Wilder had hoped for clarity in the roles and responsibilities between the mayor and the council. As mayor, he learned how difficult that would be. During his four years in office, he remained unapologetic for his purposefully bold actions that were designed to establish his realm of authority. Yet nearly two decades after Richmond became the first city in Virginia to adopt a strong mayor system (and as of 2024, still the only city to do so), considerable work remained to fully transition to this new model of government. The ambiguous language of the city charter largely contributed to the problem.

Wilder advocated for a clear separation of powers between the executive and legislative branches, similar to the distinctions at the state or federal level. Like the governor or president, the mayor would have chief executive officer (CEO) authority to oversee the City's administration and be directly accountable to all of the voters. Meanwhile, city council, similar to the state's General Assembly or the U.S. Congress, would act in a legislative role in setting policies.

Wilder achieved undeniable improvements in public safety, fiscal prudence, and government efficiency. At the same time, many criticized him for what they viewed as bullying and pettiness.

Wilder had hoped that his appeals to the Virginia Supreme Court would help clarify roles between the executive and legislative powers.

That did not happen. In many respects, questions as to who held the authority to do what would continue unanswered for years to come.

The outgoing strong mayor was not pleased with those who followed him. Wilder intentionally remained silent for seven years before making any public comment about his successor, Rev. Dwight Jones, who had strongly criticized the change to the strong mayor system—until he ran for mayor.

Leaving office at the year-end of 2008, Wilder remarked about Mayor Jones in 2015, ". . . I feel I have no choice but to now break that silence . . . I wish we were not at this point. Unfortunately, what we have almost seven years later is a near regression to the previous ceremonial-mayor form of government."[338]

Wilder later expressed a number of complaints about Richmond's next mayor, Levar Stoney, in 2022, but held that those issues were not due to the city's strong mayor form of government. "The strong mayor system should still work," Wilder said. "The problem is leadership."[339]

Nearly twenty years after the start of what some described as Richmond's "political experiment in progress" to establish a strong mayor form of government, the work remained unfinished.

Endnotes

PROLOGUE

1. *L. Douglas Wilder, Son of Virginia—A Life in America's Political Arena*, (Lyons Press, 2015), 13, 15.
2. Donald P. Baker, *Wilder—Hold Fast to Dreams* (Seven Locks Press, 1989), 6.
3. Baker, *Wilder—Hold Fast*, 5-6.
4. Margaret Edds, *Claiming the Dream—The Victorious Campaign of Douglas Wilder of Virginia* (Algonquin Books of Chapel Hill,1990), 26.
5. Baker, *Wilder—Hold Fast*, 8.
6. Wilder, *Son of Virginia*, 20, 22.
7. Wilder, *Son of Virginia*, 24.
8. Wilder, *Son of Virginia*, 91, 20.
9. The Community Weekly's City Edition, Vol. 2, No. 46, February 20, 2006, 14.
10. Wilder, *Son of Virginia*, 29.
11. Wilder, *Son of Virginia*, 30.
12. Wilder, *Son of Virginia*, 42-43.
13. Encyclopedia.com, U.S. History: Biographies, "L. Douglas Wilder," section titled "Became Known As the State Senate's Angry Young Man." https://www.encyclopedia.com/people/history/us-history-biographies/l-douglas-wilder#C.
14. Encyclopedia.com, U.S. History: Biographies, "L. Douglas Wilder," section titled "Became Known As the State Senate's Angry Young Man." The Community Weekly's City Edition, February 20, 2006.
15. Wilder, *Son of Virginia*, 9-10.
16. Laura Vozzella, "Doug Wilder: At 84, the Virginia Maverick Is Still Bucking," Washington Post, November 28, 2015.
17. Lawrence Cosentino, "He Never Gave Up," Lansing (Michigan) City Pulse, January 17, 2019.
18. Encyclopedia.com, "L. Douglas Wilder," section titled "Took on a More Conservative Bent." https://www.encyclopedia.com/people/history/us-history-biographies/l-douglas-wilder#C.
19. Encyclopedia.com, "L. Douglas Wilder," section titled "Won the Governorship by a Slim Margin." https://www.encyclopedia.com/people/history/us-history-biographies/l-douglas-wilder#C.
20. L. Douglas Wilder, Virginia Commonwealth University, faculty listing: https://wilder.vcu.edu/people/faculty/l-douglas-wilder.html.
21. J.L. Jeffries, *Virginia's Native Son—The Election and Administration of Governor L. Douglas Wilder* (Purdue University Press, 2000), 112.
22. Greg Schneider, "Wilder to Launch Career as Radio Show Host," Virginian-Pilot, January 10, 1995, A-2.

ENDNOTES

23. Ray McAllister, "Franklin Brings 'New Excitement,'" Richmond Times-Dispatch, June 4, 2000, B-1.
24. Jeff E. Schapiro, "Wilder Often Got, Even as He Gave," Richmond Times-Dispatch, January 4, 2009, B-1.
25. Lorne Manly, "Who Will Tell the Story of Slavery?", New York Times, June 29, 2016.
26. Rob Gurwitt, "Wilder's Last Crusade," Governing, June 2005, 24, 28.
27. Gurwitt, "Wilder's Last Crusade," 24.
28. "Bliley-Wilder," Style Weekly, February 12, 2003.
29. Garry Kranz, "The City Crusader," Virginia Business, April 2005, 16-17.
30. Virginia Public Access Project, VPAP.org.
31. Scott Bass, "Numero Uno—2005 Richmonder of the Year Mayor L. Douglas Wilder," Style Weekly, January 4, 2006, 17.

CHAPTER ONE

32. Chris L. Jenkins, "Ever the Gadfly in Richmond, This Time at City Hall," Washington Post, August 22, 2005.
33. Jeremy Redmon, "Mayor's Office May Gain Powers," Richmond Times-Dispatch, November 23, 2004.
34. Scott Bass, "Wilder Levels Richmond," Style Weekly, December 28, 2005.
35. L. Douglas Wilder, Mayoral Inaugural Address, January 2, 2005.
36. Kiran Krishnamurthy and David Ress, "Wilder Says Loss of Braves Hurt," Richmond Times-Dispatch, February 1, 2008, A-1.
37. Kranz, "City Crusader," Virginia Business, 13-14.
38. Sridhar Pappu, "Wilder's Odyssey," Richmond Magazine, August 2006, 146.
39. Greg Weatherford, "The Wilder Show," Richmond Magazine, September 2005, 24.
40. Pappu, Wilder's Odyssey, 146.
41. Weatherford, "Wilder Show," 24.
42. James A. Bacon, "The Wild One Bypasses the Mainstream Media," Bacon's Rebellion blog, February 4, 2008, https://www.baconsrebellion.com/wp/wild-one-bypasses-mainstream-media/.
43. City of Richmond, VA. "Announcing RichmondsMayor.com." Mayor's Office press release. May 5, 2008. Published on Richmondgov.com website (now RVA.gov) but no longer archived at time of publication.

CHAPTER TWO

44. David Ress, "Appointments Made to Wilder Transition Team," Richmond Times-Dispatch, November 9, 2004, A-1.

45. Jeremy Redmon, "Wilder Asks City to Pause Hiring, Raises," Richmond Times-Dispatch, November 19, 2004, B-1.
46. Tara Morgan, "Tense Moments Between Wilder and City Council During Meeting," NBC12.com, December 9, 2004.
47. Robb Crocker, "Jamison To Keep Severance," Richmond.com, December 22, 2004, https://richmond.com/jamison-to-keep-severance/article_0d57a963-6285-57eb-8005-db931ea9c10e.html.
48. "Wilder to Seek Injunction Today," NBC12.com, December 20, 2004.
49. Lindsay Kastner, "School Board Meets With Wilder," Richmond Times-Dispatch, November 30, 2004.
50. David Ress, "City Council Endorses New Powers for Mayor," Richmond Times-Dispatch, January 11, 2005, A-1.
51. David Ress, "Wilder Accepts Charter Change," Richmond Times-Dispatch, February 8, 2006, B-2.
52. Melissa Scott Sinclair, "Enter the Veto," Style Weekly, February 15, 2006.
53. Caine O'Rear, "A Middle Ground," Richmond.com, February 8, 2006, https://richmond.com/a-middle-ground/article_8ea241c6-9983-5810-ad22-021971b178f3.html.
54. Jeremy M. Lazarus, "Wilder Wipes Out 3 Offices," Richmond Free Press, March 10, 2005, A-1; David Ress and Jeremy Redmon, "Three Agencies Eliminated," Richmond Times-Dispatch, March 10, 2005, B-1.
55. Bass, "Numero Uno," 15, 18.
56. City of Richmond, VA. "Crime in Richmond Down in Almost All Categories." Mayor's Office press release. October 30, 2006. Published on Richmondgov.com website (now RVA.gov) but no longer archived at time of publication.
57. United States Conference of Mayors press release: "Under Richmond Mayor Wilder, Virginia's Capital Experiencing Lowest Crime Rate in 25 Years," October 8, 2007.
58. Melissa Scott Sinclair, "The Man Behind the Curtain," Style Weekly, March 1, 2006.
59. Olympia Meola, "Governor's Middle Daughter Marries Saturday," Richmond.com, June 1, 2011, https://richmond.com/news/governors-middle-daughter-marries-saturday/article_94110be3-fda4-5440-8b4e-3ae81c73298d.html.
60. Dwayne Yancey, *When Hell Froze Over—The Untold Story of Doug Wilder* (Taylor Publishing Company, 1988), 98-99.
61. Matthew Philips, "Money Where His Mouth Is," Richmond.com, April 11, 2005, https://richmond.com/money-where-his-mouth-is/article_d6d9ef3b-c3dc-5ec5-aa01-bbbf142e6e31.html.
62. Jason Zengerle, "Doug Wilder's Swan Song—Best for Last," The New Republic, August 8, 2005, 14.

ENDNOTES

63. David Ress and Jeremy Redmon, "The Budget Battle," Richmond Times-Dispatch, May 28, 2005.

64. L. Douglas Wilder, "Taxpayers' Dollars Wasted," Visions newsletter, August 6, 2007.

65. Jeremy Redmon and Will Jones, "Wilder Pushes Ahead on Budget," Richmond Times-Dispatch, June 2, 2005, A-1.

66. David Ress, "Smiles Abound Following Budget Deal," Richmond Times-Dispatch, July 2, 2005, B-1.

67. Anita Kumar, "Power Struggle Rattling Richmond," Washington Post, October 1, 2007, B-1.

68. City of Richmond, VA. "Downtown Booster Organizations to Merge." Mayor's Office press release. March 8, 2006. Published on Richmondgov.com website (now RVA.gov) but no longer archived at time of publication.

69. David Ress, "Mayor Vetoes Budget Actions," Richmond Times-Dispatch, June 14, 2006, B-7.

70. Jeremy M. Lazarus, "Wilder Goes Veto Happy," Richmond Free Press, June 15, 2006, A-1.

71. City of Richmond, VA. "Future Proposals Before City Council to Require Fiscal Impact Analysis." Mayor's Office press release. March 10, 2006. Published on Richmondgov.com website (now RVA.gov) but no longer archived at time of publication.

72. David Ress, "Mayor Vetoes Budget Actions," Richmond Times-Dispatch; Jeremy Lazarus, "Wilder Goes Veto Happy," Richmond Free Press.

73. Jeremy M. Lazarus, "Schools Chief: I Apologize," Richmond Free Press, June 15, 2006, A-1.

74. City of Richmond, VA. "Mayor Speaks to Council's Review of FY 2007 Budget." Mayor's Office press release. June 22, 2006. Published on Richmondgov.com website (now RVA.gov) but no longer archived at time of publication.

75. L. Douglas Wilder, "Cutbacks Mean Cutting Back," Visions newsletter, August 8, 2006.

76. David Ress, "Wilder's Trash Threat Draws Fire From Council," Richmond Times-Dispatch, August 10, 2006, B-3.

77. City of Richmond, VA. "Mayor Announces 100% Tax Relief for Elderly and Disabled Citizens." Mayor's Office press release. June 11, 2007. Published on Richmondgov.com website (now RVA.gov) but no longer archived at time of publication.

78. City of Richmond, VA. "Mayor Acts Decisively to Grant Tax Relief, Para-Transit Service, and Retiree and Public Safety Measures." Mayor's Office press release. June 24, 2007. Published on Richmondgov.com website (now RVA.gov) but no longer archived at time of publication.

79. Olympia Meola, "Tax Relief for Elderly at Hand, Wilder Says," Richmond Times-Dispatch, July 25, 2007, B-1.

80. Will Jones, "Wilder on the Job: Now Watch the Video," Richmond Times-Dispatch, May 4, 2008; A-15.
81. Dionne Waugh, "Pricing the Press Office," Richmond.com, March 25, 2008, https://Richmond.com/pricing-the-press-office/article_a858ecce-ded1-5c7d-9bdd-47c0e90afa9c.html.
82. City of Richmond, VA. "Council Proposal Will Mean $14 Million Cutback in City Services." Mayor's Office press release. February 22, 2008. Published on Richmondgov.com website (now RVA.gov) but no longer archived at time of publication.
83. City of Richmond, VA. "Mayor Speaks on Preventing Reductions in City Services." Mayor's Office press release. April 1, 2008. Published on Richmondgov.com website (now RVA.gov) but no longer archived at time of publication.
84. City of Richmond, VA. "Mayor Comments on Reversion to Original Proposed Budget." Mayor's Office press release. June 10, 2008. Published on Richmondgov.com website (now RVA.gov) but no longer archived at time of publication.
85. City of Richmond, VA. "Council Passed a Legal, Valid and Balanced City Budget on May 27, 2008." City Council press release. June 11, 2008. Published on Richmondgov.com website (now RVA.gov) but no longer archived at time of publication.
86. City of Richmond, VA. "City Administration Comments on City Attorney's Opinion." Mayor's Office press release. June 12, 2008. Published on Richmondgov.com website (now RVA.gov) but no longer archived at time of publication.
87. City of Richmond, VA. "Mayor Comments on FY2009 Budget." Mayor's Office press release. July 3, 2008. Published on Richmondgov.com website (now RVA.gov) but no longer archived at time of publication.
88. Will Jones, "Wilder, Pantele, McQuinn Meet," Richmond Times-Dispatch, July 26, 2008, B-2.

CHAPTER THREE

89. "Wilder's Blueprint," Richmond Times-Dispatch editorial, January 11, 2006.
90. L. Douglas Wilder, "City of the Future Address," January 9, 2006.
91. Lindsay Kastner, "Mayors and Schools: Who's in Charge?", Richmond Times-Dispatch, August 12, 2007, A-1.
92. L. Douglas Wilder, "State of the City Address," January 26, 2008.
93. Kastner, "Mayors and Schools."
94. Ress, "City Council Endorses New Powers."
95. Lindsay Kastner, "Schools Committee Sees Its Role as 'Insight' Panel Established by Wilder," Richmond Times-Dispatch, August 23, 2005, B-1.

96. Caine O'Rear, "Cleaning the Slate," Richmond.com, July 20, 2005, https://richmond.com/cleaning-the-slate/article_de3680d5-ce5c-5077-a8a4-1e7e0a686cd2.html.

97. L. Douglas Wilder, "Richmond's Schools," Richmond Times-Dispatch editorial, March 28, 2007.

98. City of Richmond, VA. "City Improves School System's Funding Schedule to More Clearly Track Operational Efficiencies." Mayor's Office press release. February 20, 2007. Published on Richmondgov.com website (now RVA.gov) but no longer archived at time of publication.

99. City of Richmond, VA. "Mayor Comments on State Supreme Court's Decision to Deny Appeal by Richmond Public Schools." Mayor's Office press release. May 31, 2007. Published on Richmondgov.com website (now RVA.gov) but no longer archived at time of publication.

100. Michael Martz, "Wilder Joins Council at Retreat," Richmond Times-Dispatch, February 18, 2007.

101. Michael Martz, "Wilder Sets New Audit of Schools," Richmond Times-Dispatch, March 9, 2007, B-8.

102. Richmond School Board Member Keith West, WRVA-AM, March 12, 2007.

103. City of Richmond, VA. "City Administration's Statement on the Performance of the City Auditor's Office." Mayor's Office press release. December 28, 2007. Published on Richmondgov. com website (now RVA.gov) but no longer archived at time of publication.

104. David Ress and Michael Martz, "Schools Audit Sparks Calls for Change," Richmond Times-Dispatch, April 4, 2008, A-1.

105. "Obscene," Richmond Times-Dispatch editorial, April 5, 2008, A-10.

106. City of Richmond, VA. "Mayor Issues Statement on School Superintendent." Mayor's Office press release. April 7, 2008. Published on Richmondgov.com website (now RVA.gov) but no longer archived at time of publication.

107. Zachary Reid, "Deborah Jewell-Sherman," Richmond Times-Dispatch, April 7, 2008.

108. City of Richmond, VA. "City Vindicated in Handicapped Access Lawsuit, Federal Court Rules." Mayor's Office press release. January 23, 2007. Published on Richmondgov.com website (now RVA.gov) but no longer archived at time of publication.

109. City of Richmond, VA. "Mayor Issues Statement Regarding Court's Refusal to Require City to Pay School Board Legal Fees." Mayor's Office press release. April 17, 2006. Published on Richmondgov.com website (now RVA.gov) but no longer archived at time of publication.

110. L. Douglas Wilder, "It Takes the Whole City," Visions newsletter, July 9, 2007.
111. Michael Martz, "Wilder Power Struggle Escalates," Richmond Times-Dispatch, March 27, 2007, B-1.
112. L. Douglas Wilder, "Taxpayers' Dollars Wasted."
113. Michael Martz, "Council Refuses to Budge on Black," Richmond Times-Dispatch, May 30, 2007, A-1.
114. L. Douglas Wilder, "Taxpayers' Dollars Wasted."
115. Michael Martz, "Court Rules Richmond Council Can Sue Wilder," Richmond Times-Dispatch, October 2, 2007.
116. City of Richmond VA. "City Awaits Truancy Data From School System." Mayor's Office press release. September 14, 2006. Published on Richmondgov.com website (now RVA.gov) but no longer archived at time of publication.
117. Jeremy Redmon and Lindsay Kastner, "Mom and Dad, Will You Make the Grade?" Richmond Times-Dispatch, March 4, 2005, A-1.
118. Ric Young, "Parents Protest Mayor Wilder," CBS6, WTVR.com, April 2, 2007.
119. Michael Paul Williams, "'Pimp' Barb Can't Mask Police Issue," Richmond Times-Dispatch, March 10, 2006.
120. L. Douglas Wilder, "In Inner Cities: With Rise of Pimps, Educating Black Males Grows Harder," Richmond Times-Dispatch, April 2, 2006.
121. Melissa Scott Sinclair and Scott Bass, "Taming Wilder," Style Weekly, June 21, 2006.
122. "Goldman's Exploits," Richmond Free Press editorial, December 15, 2005, A-10.
123. City of Richmond VA. "City Administration's Statement Regarding Mr. Paul Goldman." Mayor's Office press release. March 22, 2006. Published on Richmondgov.com website (now RVA.gov) but no longer archived at time of publication.
124. Lindsay Kastner, "Focus on Elementary Schools, Goldman Says," Richmond Times-Dispatch, March 23, 2006.

CHAPTER FOUR

125. Brandon Walters, "Arrested Development," Style Weekly, August 30, 2006; David Ress, "No Place for the Water to Go," Richmond Times-Dispatch, September 22, 2004, B-1.
126. City of Richmond VA. "Mayor Announces Declaration of Local Emergency in Aftermath of Shockoe Bottom Flooding." Mayor's Office press release. August 16, 2006. Published on Richmondgov.com website (now RVA.gov) but no longer archived at time of publication.

ENDNOTES

127. Kent Jennings Brockwell, "Tackling Shockoe's Problem," Richmond.com, August 24, 2006, https://richmond.com/tackling-shockoes-problem/article_2a06935a-1c32-51b1-8ef7-2144d3db04bf.html.

128. L. Douglas Wilder, "Many Ask Questions About Delay," Visions newsletter, October 16, 2006.

129. L. Douglas Wilder, "Residents, City Staff Deserve Kudos for Fast, Safe Evacuation of Battery Park," Visions newsletter, September 18, 2006.

130. Don Dale, "Help Is on the Way," Richmond Free Press, September 7, 2006, A-1.

131. Wilder, "Residents, City Staff Deserve Kudos."

132. Will Jones, "Battery Park Cleanup Effort Moves Forward," Richmond Times-Dispatch, September 8, 2006.

133. David Ress and Michael Martz, "State Will Appeal Storm-Aid Denial," Richmond Times-Dispatch, September 26, 2006, A-1; Caine O'Rear, "No Help for the Man," Richmond.com, September 26, 2006, http://www.richmond.com/printer.cfm?article=4427117.

134. Don Dale, "Battery Park Exodus," Richmond Free Press, October 12, 2006, A-1.

135. City of Richmond VA. "Legal Threats on Property Acquisitions in Battery Park Area Not to Be Tolerated." Mayor's Office press release. November 16, 2006. Published on Richmondgov.com website (now RVA.gov) but no longer archived at time of publication.

136. City of Richmond VA. "One Year After Ernesto, City's Responsive Actions Help Return Normalcy to Battery Park Area." Mayor's Office press release. August 31, 2007. Published on Richmondgov.com website (now RVA.gov) but no longer archived at time of publication.

137. L. Douglas Wilder, "City Wins FEMA's Financial Support," Visions newsletter, April 2, 2007.

138. L. Douglas Wilder, "Utility Rate Cuts and Drainage Solutions," Visions newsletter, October 15, 2007.

139. Will Jones and Jeremy Slayton, "Wilder Abandons Stormwater-Fee Plan," Richmond Times-Dispatch, May 9, 2008, B-3.

CHAPTER FIVE

140. David Ress, "A Stirring Year," Richmond Times-Dispatch, January 1, 2006, A-1.

141. City of Richmond VA. "Mayor Wilder Issues Statement Regarding Performing Arts Center Deadline." Mayor's Office press release. May 19, 2005. Published on Richmondgov.com website (now RVA.gov) but no longer archived at time of publication.

142. Jeremy Redmon, "Wilder Blasts Council, Ukrop," Richmond Times-Dispatch, May 25, 2005, A-1.

143. Jeremy M. Lazarus, "City Council Stands Its Ground," Richmond Free Press, May 26, 2005, A-6.
144. Virginia Public Access Project, VPAP.org.
145. Caine O'Rear, "Mexican Standoff," Richmond.com, August 12, 2005, https://richmond.com/mexican-standoff/article_0a7bbb3b-99ac-58a5-a687-a4554adc45bd.html.
146. Will Jones, "Billing for Arts Center Flagged," Richmond Times-Dispatch, September 28, 2005, B-1.
147. Scott Bass, "Numero Uno," Style Weekly, January 4, 2006.
148. Will Jones, "At Last, Showtime's Set," Richmond Times-Dispatch, January 14, 2007, A-1.
149. Christina Nuckols, "The Challenges of Unifying a City," Virginian-Pilot, July 5, 2005, A-1.
150. David Ress and Will Jones, "Inspection Says Carpenter Center Is a Fire Hazard," Richmond Times-Dispatch, November 10, 2005, B-1.
151. Scott Bass, "Point of No Return," Style Weekly, September 19, 2007.
152. Bass, "Numero Uno," Style Weekly.
153. Will Jones, "Wilder: No Debt for Arts Project," Richmond Times-Dispatch, September 12, 2006.
154. Associated Press, "Happy Elliott Goes 'Home' to Richmond," Today.com, May 12, 2006. https://www.today.com/popculture/happy-elliott-goes-home-richmond-wbna12760528.
155. Melissa Ruggieri, "The Rebirth of Richmond's National Theater," Richmond.com, December 19, 2007, https://richmond.com/entertainment/the-rebirth-of-Richmonds-national-theater/article_c7f3bd71-51b1-53e9-a279-8175c3bf61f3.html.
156. L. Douglas Wilder, "No Time to Waste in Renovating Carpenter Center," Visions newsletter, January 22, 2007.

CHAPTER SIX

157. Scott Bass, "Miller & Rhoads Hotel Delayed," Style Weekly, September 29, 2004.
158. Scott Bass, "Wilder Criticizes Downtown Deal," Style Weekly, May 4, 2005.
159. City of Richmond, VA. "Miller & Rhoads Joins Hilton Family of Hotels." Mayor's Office press release. April 26, 2006. Published on Richmondgov.com website (now RVA.gov) but no longer archived at time of publication.
160. Brandon Walters, "Arrested Development," Style Weekly, August 30, 2006.
161. David Ress, "Council Approves Bus Route Changes," Richmond Times-Dispatch, March 28, 2006, B-1.
162. Tom Campbell, "A Mini-Boom on Broad," Richmond Times-Dispatch, October 29, 2007, A-1.

163. Michael Martz, "Wilder's Legacy as Complex as the Man," Richmond Times-Dispatch, December 4, 2014.

164. David Ress, John Reid Blackwell and Jeremy Redmon, "Philip Morris Will Add Jobs Here," Richmond Times-Dispatch, April 5, 2005, A-1.

165. L. Douglas Wilder, "MeadWestvaco Chooses Downtown for Future Home," Visions newsletter, May 14, 2007.

166. John A. Luke Jr., "Mayor L. Douglas Wilder: A Review of Accomplishments" DVD, April 2008.

167. Thomas F. Farrell, "Mayor L. Douglas Wilder: A Review of Accomplishments" DVD, April 2008.

168. L. Douglas Wilder, "State of the City Address," January 26, 2008.

169. L. Douglas Wilder, "Cleaning Up Our Neighborhoods and Our City," Visions newsletter, August 11, 2008.

170. L. Douglas Wilder, "State of the City Address," January 26, 2008.

171. L. Douglas Wilder, "State of the City Address," January 20, 2007.

172. L. Douglas Wilder, "On the Table—All Politics May Be Local, But Local Issues Demand Attention," Richmond Times-Dispatch, December 4, 2005, E-5.

173. David Ress, "Wilder Housing Initiative Killed," Richmond Times-Dispatch, November 28, 2006, B-1.

174. L. Douglas Wilder, "RichmondWorks Is Working!", Visions newsletter, September 30, 2008.

175. L. Douglas Wilder, "State of the City Address," January 26, 2008.

CHAPTER SEVEN

176. Deborah Cox, Maymont Bears, CBS6, WTVR.com, March 4, 2006.

177. Rosalind S. Helderman, "Killing of 2 Captive Bears Ignites Va. Protest," Washington Post, March 5, 2006, A-7.

178. City of Richmond, VA. "Findings on Maymont Bears Incident: Full Report." March 28, 2006.

179. Christina Bellantoni, "Bears' Deaths Spark Uproar in Richmond," Washington Times, March 1, 2006.

180. Patrick K. Phillips, "Visitors Mourn Maymont Bears," February 25, 2006, https://www.patrickkphillips.com/life/visitors-mourn-maymont-bears/.

181. Mark Holmberg, "Why Do Bears' Deaths Elicit More Sorrow Than Humans?" Richmond Times-Dispatch, February 26, 2006, B-1.

182. "Why Bears Matter," Richmond Times-Dispatch editorial, March 7, 2006, A-10.

183. Melissa Scott Sinclair, "Goodnight Bears," Style Weekly, March 8, 2006.
184. Holmberg, "Why Do Bears' Deaths Elicit."
185. Helderman, "Killing"; Bellantoni, "Bears' Deaths Spark Uproar."
186. Bellantoni, "Bears' Deaths Spark Uproar."
187. City of Richmond, VA. "Memorial Service Scheduled for Maymont Bears." Mayor's Office press release. February 28, 2006. Published on Richmondgov.com website (now RVA.gov) but no longer archived at time of publication.
188. City of Richmond, VA. "Findings on Maymont Bears Incident."
189. "Why Bears Matter," Richmond Times-Dispatch.
190. Janice Carson, "Low Risk for Rabies," Richmond Times-Dispatch, March 14, 2006.
191. City of Richmond, VA. "Findings on Maymont Bears Incident."
192. Jim Nolan and David Ress, "Boy Unquestioned; City Replacing Bears," Richmond Times-Dispatch, March 30, 2006.
193. Bellantoni, "Bears' Deaths Spark Uproar."
194. "New Bear May Be Coming to Maymont," CBS6.com, April 30, 2006.
195. Janet Caggiano, "Phoenix, Spirits Rise," Richmond Times-Dispatch, June 18, 2006, B-1.
196. City of Richmond, VA. "Maymont's Newest Bear Named Midnight." Mayor's Office press release. January 10, 2007. Published on Richmondgov.com website (now RVA.gov) but no longer archived at time of publication.

CHAPTER EIGHT

197. "What Oliver Hill Told The Queen," Richmond Free Press, May 10, 2007, A-1.
198. "God Save the Queen ... From Virginia's 400th Celebration," Style Weekly, December 25, 2007.
199. "What Oliver Hill Told The Queen," Richmond Free Press.
200. Bob Lewis, "Queen Speaks in Richmond, Heads to Williamsburg," Virginian-Pilot, May 3, 2007.
201. Darren Samuelsohn, "When Tim Kaine Met the Queen," Politico, August 2, 2016.
202. Jim Nolan, "Word of the Day: Security – A Not-So-Thin Blue Line of Protection Envelops Queen During Her Richmond Visit," Richmond Times-Dispatch, May 4, 2007, A-9.

CHAPTER NINE

203. City of Richmond, VA. "Atlanta Braves Organization Reneges on Plan to Support New Ballpark in Richmond." Mayor's Office press release. March 15, 2006. Published on Richmondgov.com website (now RVA.gov) but no longer archived at time of publication.

ENDNOTES

204. David Ress, "Wilder: Braves Balking on Downtown Ballpark," Richmond Times-Dispatch, March 16, 2006.
205. City of Richmond, VA. "Mayor Supports The Diamond For Future of Baseball in Richmond." Mayor's Office press release. June 30, 2006. Published on Richmondgov.com website (now RVA.gov) but no longer archived at time of publication.
206. Michael Martz, "Plans Pitched for Stadium on Boulevard," Richmond Times-Dispatch, December 10, 2006.
207. David Ress and Michael Martz, "Braves Strike Out . . . For New Home in Ga.," Richmond Times-Dispatch, January 16, 2008.
208. Michael Martz and David Ress, "Braves: Going, Going, Gone?", Richmond Times-Dispatch, January 15, 2008.
209. City of Richmond, VA. "Richmond Braves Involved With New Ballpark Plan in Georgia for Past Two Years." Mayor's Office press release. January 15, 2008. Published on Richmondgov.com website (now RVA.gov) but no longer archived at time of publication.
210. Ress and Martz, "Braves Strike Out."
211. Sheila Hill-Christian, "Richmond Will Have a New Baseball Team," Visions newsletter, January 22, 2008.
212. Ress and Martz, "Braves Strike Out."
213. City of Richmond, VA. "Regarding Richmond Braves Leaving City." City Council press release. January 15, 2008. Published on Richmondgov.com website (now RVA.gov) but no longer archived at time of publication.
214. Tim Pearrell, "New Team May Have to Wait," Richmond Times-Dispatch, January 17, 2008.
215. Krishnamurthy and Ress, "Wilder Says Loss of Braves Hurt."

CHAPTER TEN

216. Michael Martz, "Richmond Seeks Nod For Public Marina," Richmond Times-Dispatch, October 5, 2007, A-1.
217. City of Richmond VA. "Developer of Controversial Waterfront Project to Address Planning Commission." Mayor's Office press release. December 28, 2006. Published on Richmondgov.com website (now RVA.gov) but no longer archived at time of publication.
218. Kiran Krishnamurthy, "Richmond Marina: $17.7 Million," Richmond Times-Dispatch, February 27, 2008, B-4.
219. Michael Martz, "Ukrop Backs Marina Plan," Richmond Times-Dispatch, December 25, 2007, A-1.
220. Michael Martz, "Doubts Flow Along River," Richmond Times-Dispatch, December 20, 2007, B-1.
221. Kiran Krishnamurthy, "Delay Likely on Richmond Land Buy," Richmond Times-Dispatch, January 13, 2008, B-1.
222. L. Douglas Wilder, "It's Your River, Richmond, But Not For Much Longer," Visions newsletter, June 2, 2008.

223. City of Richmond, VA. "Mayor Wilder to City Council: "Don't Sell Riverfront to Private Developers." Mayor's Office press release. June 6, 2008. Published on Richmondgov.com website (now RVA.gov) but no longer archived at time of publication.
224. L. Douglas Wilder, Visions newsletter, June 25, 2008.
225. L. Douglas Wilder, "Our Citizens Want a Vibrant Downtown," Richmond Times-Dispatch, April 27, 2008, E-6.
226. Will Jones, "Echo Harbour Faces More Obstacles to Approval," Richmond Times-Dispatch, August 16, 2009.
227. Mike Platania, "Conservancy to Buy Undeveloped Riverfront Real Estate and Give It to the City," Richmondbizsense.com, April 16, 2021, https://richmondbizsense.com/2021/04/16/conservancy-to-buy-undeveloped-riverfront-real-estate-and-give-it-to-city/.

CHAPTER ELEVEN

228. Anita Kumar, "Virginia Notebook: Wilder Again Plays His Hand Alone," Washington Post, October 1, 2009.
229. Bonnie V. Winston, "Ending Suspense, Wilder Endorses Webb: Mayor Gave Signal at Gold Bowl," Richmond Free Press, October 26, 2006, A-1.
230. "Senate Candidates Mine For Votes at Gold Bowl," NBC12. com, October 23, 2006, http://www.NBC12.com/news/state/4456242.html.
231. Associated Press, "Virginia Mayor Endorses Senator's Opponent," New York Times, October 26, 2006.
232. City of Richmond, VA. "Mayor Wilder Endorses Jim Webb for U.S. Senate." Mayor's Office press release. October 25, 2006. Published on Richmondgov.com website (now RVA.gov) but no longer archived at time of publication.
233. John F. Harris and Mike Allen, "Obama Supported by Wilder," Politico, August 28, 2007.
234. John King, "Racism, Personal Safety Factors in Obama's Deliberations," CNN, January 19, 2007.
235. King, "Racism."
236. Afi-Odelia E. Scruggs, "Beyond Race Baggage," New York Post, April 29, 2008.
237. Harris, Allen, "Obama Supported."
238. L. Douglas Wilder, "Trailblazing Fmr. Governor Gives Obama Advice," Michel Martin, Tell Me More, NPR, June 6, 2008, https://www.npr.org/templates/story/story.php?storyId=91236310.
239. Harris, Allen, "Obama Supported."
240. Mike Allen, "Douglas Wilder Cools on Obama," Politico, November 29, 2007.

ENDNOTES

241. Rosalind Helderman, "Wilder's Nod Remains Elusive," Washington Post, July 24, 2009.
242. City of Richmond, VA. "Mayor L. Douglas Wilder Indicates Position on Presidential Candidate Endorsement." Mayor's Office press release. November 29, 2007. Published on Richmondgov.com website (now RVA.gov) but no longer archived at time of publication.
243. City of Richmond, VA. "Wilder Endorses Obama for President." Mayor's Office press release. January 4, 2008. Published on Richmondgov.com website (now RVA.gov) but no longer archived at time of publication.
244. Heidi Przybyla, "Obama Gets Encouragement and Warning From Wilder," Bloomberg.com, April 24, 2008, http://www.bloomberg.com/apps/news?pid=20670001&refer=home&sid=aLE tPYAd_QRA.
245. Wolf Blitzer, Carol Costello, "The Situation Room," CNN, April 24, 2008.
246. King, "Racism."
247. Przybyla, "Obama Gets Encouragement."
248. Harris, Allen, "Obama Supported."
249. L. Douglas Wilder, "No Exit," New York Times, June 8, 2008.
250. Martin, interview.
251. L. Douglas Wilder, "The Potomac Primary," Wall Street Journal, February 9, 2008.
252. L. Douglas Wilder, "Being No. 1 Means Nothing Until There Is a No. 2," Richmond Times-Dispatch, June 22, 2008.
253. Kathy Kiely, "Obama Eyes Economy, Challenges," USA Today, August 23, 2008.
254. Jean-Robert Dantou, "Barack Obama, Campaign Rally, Chester, VA, 2008," San Francisco Art Exchange, August 21, 2008.
255. Kiely, "Obama."
256. "Road to the White House: Obama Rally in Richmond, Virginia," C-SPAN.org, October 22, 2008 (34:57) https://www.c-span.org/video/?281938-1/obama-rally-richmond-virginia.
257. Tyler Whitley and Olympia Meola, "Thousands Rally in Richmond—Obama: Hard Work Ahead," Richmond Times-Dispatch, October 23, 2008, A-1.
258. John F. Harris, "In Richmond, Romance Rumors Fly," Washington Post, June 30, 1990.
259. "Wilder on Obama: Dream Is Alive for All Americans," NPR Morning Edition, November 6, 2008.

CHAPTER TWELVE

260. Chris Dovi, "Lawlessness," Style Weekly, September 26, 2007.

261. Michael Martz, Olympia Meola and David Ress, "Chaos Erupts at City Hall—City Evicts School Officials But Judge Blocks Move; Police Ban Public From Meeting," Richmond Times-Dispatch, September 22, 2007, A-1.

262. Michael Martz, "L. Wilder's Style Is One of a Kind," Richmond. com, January 17, 2015, https://richmond.com/news/local/government-politics/l-wilders-style-is-one-of-a-kind/article_ce508faa-c15c-51a0-929b-928891011172.htm.

263. Martz, Meola, Ress, "Chaos Erupts at City Hall: City Evicts."

264. City of Richmond, VA. "City Begins to Move School Offices to New Location." Mayor's Office press release. September 21, 2007. Published on Richmondgov.com website (now RVA.gov) but no longer archived at time of publication.

265. Amy Biegelsen, "Wilder Defends Schools Assault at Press Luncheon," Style Weekly, September 25, 2007.

266. Lisa A. Bacon, "Famous Mayor Under Fire in Virginia," New York Times, October 21, 2007.

267. Michael Martz, Olympia Meola and David Ress, "Wilder Fulfills Threat to Evict School Offices," Richmond.com, September 22, 2007, https://richmond.com/news/wilder-fulfills-threat-to-evict-school-offices/article_8dd14c06-decb-555c-8c5f-c499e5f488d5.html.

268. David Ress, Olympia Meola and Michael Martz, "Uncertainty Pervades City Hill Amid Turmoil—Movers Put Back What They Took Out—Superintendent to Survey Disarray—City Schools Could Be Closed Tomorrow," Richmond Times-Dispatch, September 23, 2007, A-1.

269. Michael Martz and David Ress, "Council Joins Schools' Suit," Richmond Times-Dispatch, September 25, 2007, A-1.

270. City of Richmond, VA. "'Porn Site' Visits Discovered on Council President's Computer." Mayor's Office press release. September 21, 2007. Published on Richmondgov.com website (now RVA.gov) but no longer archived at time of publication.

271. Chris Dovi, "City Charter Crisis Looms as Judge Orders Movers Return," Style Weekly, September 25, 2007.

272. City of Richmond, VA. "Police Investigate Inappropriate Use of City Equipment." Police Department press release. September 21, 2007. Published on Richmondgov.com website (now RVA.gov) but no longer archived at time of publication.

273. Bill Wasson, "Richmond Police End Computer Porn Probe," Richmond Times-Dispatch, September 29, 2007.

274. Michael Martz and David Ress, "Chaos Erupts at City Hall—Wilder Alleges Porn Link to Pantele Computer; Council's Leader Denies It," Richmond Times-Dispatch, September 22, 2007, A-1.

275. Michael Martz, "Richmond Council Can Sue Wilder," Richmond Times-Dispatch, October 2, 2007, B-1.

ENDNOTES

276. Lindsay Kastner, "School Board Plans Spring Move," Richmond Times-Dispatch, November 8, 2005, B-3.
277. City of Richmond, VA. "Mayor Reiterates Call for School Administration to Vacate City Hall." Mayor's Office press release. June 29, 2007. Published on Richmondgov.com website (now RVA.gov) but no longer archived at time of publication.
278. David Ress, "Moving Offices Would Cost City Millions," Richmond Times-Dispatch, September 30, 2007, A-1.
279. Chris Dovi, "Barbarian at the Gate," Style Weekly, September 17, 2008.
280. "Recess Is Over," Richmond Times-Dispatch editorial, December 1, 2007.
281. Dionne Waugh, "Wilder, City Council Have Discussion for First Time Since Attempted School System Eviction," Richmond.com, October 2, 2007, https://richmond.com/printer.cfm?article=4850772.
282. Michael Martz and David Ress, "Wilder Wants Agreement With Richmond Council Over Who Holds Power," Richmond Times-Dispatch, September 30, 2007, A-1.
283. Michael Martz, "Support Drops for Wilder," Richmond Times-Dispatch, October 28, 2007, A-1.
284. L. Douglas Wilder, "The Charter Invests the Mayor with Administrative Authority," Richmond Times-Dispatch, October 21, 2007.
285. Bonnie V. Winston and Kim Thomas, "Mayor Booed on Second Street," Richmond Free Press, October 11, 2007, A-1.

CHAPTER THIRTEEN

286. "How Mayor Sees Sheila Hill-Christian and Her Response to Him," Richmond Free Press, November 15, 2007, A-7.
287. "More Tit for Tat," Richmond Times-Dispatch editorial, May 22, 2007, A-12.
288. Martz, Ress, "Wilder Wants Agreement."
289. Michael Martz, "Wilder Hires New Top Administrator," Richmond Times-Dispatch, October 6, 2007, B-1.
290. Osita Iroegbu, "Love Affair at City Hall, Hill-Christian Embraced by City Council," Richmond Free Press, November 15, 2007, A-1.
291. Martz, "Wilder Hires."
292. City of Richmond, VA. "Mayor Selects Sheila Hill-Christian as City of Richmond's Chief Administrative Officer." Mayor's Office press release. October 5, 2007. Published on Richmondgov.com website (now RVA.gov) but no longer archived at time of publication.
293. L. Douglas Wilder, "Schools Had Prepared to Leave City Hall By This Fall," Visions newsletter, October 29, 2007.

294. Chris Dovi, "Did Schools Help Plan Attempted Move?" Style Weekly, January 2, 2008.

295. L. Douglas Wilder, "Truth Crushed to Earth Shall Rise Again . . . Because No Lie Can Live Forever," Visions newsletter, January 7, 2008.

296. Michael Martz, "Eviction Attempt by Mayor Wilder Is Probed," Richmond.com, November 2, 2007, https://richmond.com/news/eviction-attempted-by-mayor-wilder-is-probed/article_a91844a3-854b-5c48-9879-1285bc37c814.html.

297. Michael Martz, "Funding of Eviction Attempt At Issue," Richmond Times-Dispatch, December 18, 2007.

298. Dionne Waugh, "Half-Million Dollar Debate," Richmond.com, December 17, 2007, https://richmond.com/half-million-dollar-debate/article_dfc55f41-2e6c-5172-88dc-f6f57f8476a0.html.

299. City of Richmond, VA. "Mayor Comments on Council Investigative Committee." Mayor's Office press release. January 4, 2008. Published on Richmondgov.com website (now RVA.gov) but no longer archived at time of publication.

300. Chris Dovi, "Update: Councilwoman Regrets Calling Hill-Christian a 'Criminal,'" Style Weekly, March 5, 2008.

301. Chris Dovi, "Mayor's Money Move: Budget Transfer or 'Money Laundering'?" Style Weekly, February 13, 2008.

302. Amy Biegelsen, "Threat of Criminal Investigation Looms Over City Administration," Style Weekly, March 13, 2008.

303. Will Jones, "Wilder Still at Odds With City Council Over Eviction Issue," Richmond Times-Dispatch, July 10, 2008, B-3.

304. Will Jones, "Eviction Report Stresses Waste," Richmond Times-Dispatch, May 6, 2008, B-1.

305. Jones, "Wilder Still at Odds."

306. David Ress and Michael Martz, "Official's Auto Allowance Questioned," Richmond Times-Dispatch, April 12, 2008, A-1.

307. City of Richmond, VA. "City CAO Speaks on Auto Allowance Situations." Mayor's Office press release. April 16, 2008. Published on Richmondgov.com website (now RVA.gov) but no longer archived at time of publication.

308. Will Jones, "Wilder Says He Was Unaware of Car Allowance," Richmond Times-Dispatch, April 17, 2008, B-1.

309. City of Richmond, VA. "Mayor to Council: Restore Chief Monroe's Funding." Mayor's Office press release. May 15, 2008. Published on Richmondgov.com website (now RVA.gov) but no longer archived at time of publication.

310. City of Richmond, VA. "Mayor Comments on Chief Monroe." Mayor's Office press release. May 15, 2008. Published on Richmondgov.com website (now RVA.gov) but no longer archived at time of publication.

ENDNOTES

311. "Still Mayor," Richmond Times-Dispatch editorial, February 1, 2008, A-12.
312. City of Richmond, VA. "Mayor Will Not Seek Re-election." Mayor's Office press release. May 16, 2008. Published on Richmondgov.com website (now RVA.gov) but no longer archived at time of publication.
313. "The Audacity of Mr. Wilder," Washington Post editorial, May 23, 2008.
314. Michael Paul Williams, "For Wilder and Media, Show Is Over," Richmond Times-Dispatch, January 1, 2009, B-1.
315. Chris Dovi, "Downhill," Style Weekly, August 6, 2008.
316. David Ress and Will Jones, "Richmond's Top Bureaucrat Quits," Richmond.com, July 31, 2008, https://richmond.com/news/richmonds-top-bureaucrat-quits/article_a0d4350d-a2f6-5ed0-b77d-c3597415424c.html.
317. City of Richmond, VA. "CAO Resigns Position With the City." Mayor's Office press release. July 30, 2008. Published on Richmondgov.com website (now RVA.gov) but no longer archived at time of publication.
318. Michael Paul Williams, "Deck Stacked Against Hill-Christian From Start," Richmond Times-Dispatch, August 2, 2008, B-1.

CHAPTER FOURTEEN

319. City of Richmond, VA. "Mayor Calls for Dialogue Among Richmond Officials on Whether to Refine the Richmond City Charter." Mayor's Office press release. October 4, 2007. Published on Richmondgov.com website (now RVA.gov) but no longer archived at time of publication.
320. Michael Martz, "Wilder Seeks Charter Changes," Richmond.com, November 9, 2007, https://richmond.com/news/wilder-seeks-charter-changes/article_b9d2d748-6982-5848-8f14-7dee12d5b82f.html.
321. Jeremy M. Lazarus, "After Trip Abroad, Wilder to Face Problems," Richmond Free Press, November 15, 2007, A-8.
322. Martz, "Wilder Seeks."
323. Lazarus, "After Trip Abroad."
324. L. Douglas Wilder, "What Is the Price of Progress?", Visions newsletter, July 23, 2007.
325. Amy Biegelsen, "Wilder Proposes Field Trip, Sparks Council Dispute," Style Weekly, December 5, 2007.
326. L. Douglas Wilder, "A Level Playing Field," Visions newsletter, November 12, 2007.
327. L. Douglas Wilder, "Why Not Save the Taxpayers' Dollars?" Visions newsletter, December 10, 2007.

328. Michael Martz, "Wilder: Leave Charter As It Is," Richmond Times-Dispatch, December 19, 2007; Kim S. Thomas, "Mayor: No Olive Branches Here," Richmond Free Press, December 20, 2007, A-1.

329. Will Jones, "Wilder Had Hits, Misses as Richmond Mayor," Richmond.com, December 28, 2008, https://richmond.com/news/wilder-had-hits-misses-as-richmond-mayor/article_71ce46bb-d4ef-5251-87ff-ee6016c68645.html; L. Douglas Wilder, "Detailing an 81% Approval Rating of a City Moving Forward," Visions newsletter, September 15, 2008; Will Jones, "Support for Wilder Declines," Richmond.com, October 27, 2008, https://Richmond.com/news/support-for-wilder-declines/article_4936ee06-667c-5a62-aaae-0b292cd58c4a.html.

330. Warren Fiske, "Mayor, Ex-Governor Says He Didn't Look to Fight But Didn't Flinch," Virginian-Pilot, December 31, 2008, A-1.

331. L. Douglas Wilder, "Would-Be Successors Just Don't Make the Grade," Richmond Times-Dispatch, October 19, 2008, E-1.

332. Will Jones, "Wilder Stays Mum on Endorsement," Richmond Times-Dispatch, October 18, 2008, B-6.

333. Will Jones, "Wilder Tours Downtown Sites," Richmond Times-Dispatch, December 18, 2008, B-1.

334. Bob Raynor, "When History Walks Through the Door," Richmond Times-Dispatch, December 28, 2008, E-1.

335. Fisk, "Mayor, Ex-Governor."

336. Will Jones, "Jones Ends Legal Fights of Council, Ex-Mayor Wilder," Richmond Times-Dispatch, February 27, 2009, A-1.

337. Rachel DePompa, "Wilder Says His Cases Should Have Been Heard," NBC12.com, March 12, 2009, https://www.nbc12.com/story/9995686/wilder-says-his-cases-should-have-been-heard/.

EPILOGUE

338. L. Douglas Wilder, "Richmond Needs a Strong Mayor, More Than Ever," Richmond Times-Dispatch, November 8, 2015, E-1.

339. David Ress, "Wilder: Governor Needs to Get Involved in Solving Richmond Crime Issues," Richmond.com, October 27, 2022, https://richmond.com/news/state-and-regional/govt-and-politics/wilder-governor-needs-to-get-involved-in-solving-richmond-crime-issues/article_63468317-8c0c-581b-ad5f-722bbd80af47.html.

Selected Bibliography

Baker, Donald P. *Wilder: Hold Fast to Dreams*. Cabin John, MD/ Washington, DC: Seven Locks Press, 1989.

Edds, Margaret. *Claiming the Dream: The Victorious Campaign of Douglas Wilder of Virginia*. Chapel Hill, NC: Algonquin Books of Chapel Hill, 1990.

Encyclopedia.com, "L. Douglas Wilder," sections titled "Became Known As the State Senate's Angry Young Man," "Took on a More Conservative Bent," and "Won the Governorship by a Slim Margin."

Jeffries, J.L. *Virginia's Native Son: The Election and Administration of Governor L. Douglas Wilder*. West Lafayette, IN: Purdue University Press, 2000.

Wilder, L. Douglas. *Son of Virginia: A Life in America's Political Arena*. Guilford, Connecticut: Lyons Press, 2015.

Yancey, Dwayne. *When Hell Froze Over, The Untold Story of Doug Wilder: A Black Politician's Rise to Power in the South*. Dallas, TX: Taylor Publishing Company, 1988.

Acknowledgements

Writing about a dynamic personality like L. Douglas Wilder is a nostalgic yet daunting task. I greatly appreciate the encouragement and support of the mayor, as well as those who offered substantive feedback as this book project progressed.

Former City of Richmond colleagues Jon Baliles, Chris Beschler, Harry Black, and the late Isaac Graves were sounding boards along the way. Members of my press office—Mariane Jorgenson, Shelby Crouch, and Alfonzo Mathis—also helped me retrace particular events during Mayor Wilder's term.

I am grateful to political cartoonist Gary Brookins for his generosity in granting permission to share several of his memorable works that appeared in the *Richmond Times-Dispatch*. Thanks also to Michelle Gullett of Lee Enterprises who helped me unearth the newspaper photos that are featured in this book.

I would like to thank Virginia governors George Allen and Bob McDonnell, and state senator John Watkins, for their strong support. I also appreciate the contributions made by others who have written about the mayor—Jonathan Eig, Dr. Stephen J. Farnsworth, Dr. Judson L. Jeffries, and Dwayne Yancey—and the support I received from Tommie Binga, John Gerner, Eva Teig Hardy, Loralyn Mears, and Kelly Hess Temple. Last but far from least, a big shout-out goes to Jenny DeBell, Ceci Hughes, and Robert Pruett at Brandylane Publishers for guiding this project to fruition.

(Courtesy: Mishal Alharbi)

About the Author

A Richmond native with a master's degree in journalism from Virginia Commonwealth University, Linwood Norman served as the city's director of communications during Wilder's "Strong Mayor" administration. As Mayor Wilder's press secretary, Norman obtained an insider's view on what compelled Wilder to take actions that were deemed courageous by some and abominable by others. Linwood Norman's career has spanned the public, corporate, and nonprofit sectors and includes posts as senior communications advisor for the U.S. Department of Health and Human Services; communications manager for Anthem Blue Cross Blue Shield; and communications director for ZERO—The End of Prostate Cancer. Earlier in his career, Norman was a reporter for the *Newport News Daily Press*; the *Petersburg Progress-Index*, where he received a Virginia Press Association First-Place Award for Investigative Journalism; and a contributing writer for *Richmond Magazine* and *Virginia Town & City Magazine*.

Now retired, Norman divides his time between Washington, DC, and Fort Lauderdale, Florida, as he ponders the topic of his next book.

LinwoodNormanBooks.com

Printed in the USA
CPSIA information can be obtained
at www.ICGtesting.com
CBHW021920300724
12438CB00001B/1/J